# Surveying
# Historic
# Buildings

# Surveying

# Historic

# Buildings

DAVID WATT
*Senior Research Fellow*
*Department of Building Surveying*
*De Montfort University, Leicester*

and

PETER SWALLOW
*Head of Department of Building Surveying*
*De Montfort University, Leicester*

DONHEAD

First published in the United Kingdom 1996 by
Donhead Publishing
Lower Coombe
Donhead St Mary
Shaftesbury
Dorset SP7 9LY
Tel: (01747) 828422

ISBN 1 873394 16 0

A CIP catalogue record is available for this book
from the British Library

Typeset by Carnegie Publishing, Preston
Printed in Great Britain by Redwood Books Ltd,
Trowbridge

# Contents

# PART THREE

# APPENDICES

# Preface

The last five years have seen many changes in the ways in which historic and traditional properties are perceived and treated by the public and their professional advisers. These changes have come about as a result of a growing awareness of the social and economic value attached to buildings, monuments and other structures deemed to be of architectural, archaeological or historic importance.

Changes have also come as a result of how we choose to make use of such properties. Requirements for greater comfort, safety and conformity have led to levels of intervention that are often at odds with how the buildings or structures were built or intended to be used.

As attitudes to our past develop and broaden so too do the needs for information on which to base decisions. Building surveys, requiring careful inspection, observation, analysis, understanding and communication, are crucial to decision-making, and it is therefore essential that the information they contain is accurate and appropriate.

The purpose of this book is therefore to consider the role of the building or condition survey in the management of historic and traditional buildings, monuments and structures; the information that is required; and how it is collected, presented and used.

Part One describes the reasons why buildings are surveyed, discusses the factors that make historic buildings different from more modern structures, and advises on how the surveyor prepares for, undertakes and reports on the condition of the building. Part Two considers the various elements and service installations of a building in terms of their history, development and typical faults, and gives specific advice on assessing industrial monuments and standing ruins. Although each chapter provides a summary of typical materials or methods of construction, it is not intended to provide a detailed study of architectural history or decorative style. The reader is therefore directed to the bibliography for additional sources of information. Part Three concludes with our own personal views on current architectural conservation practice, and speculates on changes in the future.

In explaining and questioning how the condition of a historic property is evaluated we have taken the opportunity to include practical examples that demonstrate a variety of symptoms and problems that practising surveyors may encounter. Many of these come from our work in the East Midlands and East Anglia. It is therefore hoped that readers, be they architects, builders, conservation officers, industrial archaeologists, planners, surveyors, or students of these disciplines will find the book of interest and value.

We are grateful to the many people who have provided invaluable help, advice and information on specific issues during the preparation of this book; and acknowledge the various owners, occupiers and other agencies who have allowed use of photographs, drawings or published material. In particular, thanks go to the Controller of Her Majesty's Stationery Office (Figure 2.2), the National Trust (Figure 2.3), the Royal Institution of Chartered Surveyors (Figure 2.5 and Appendix C), Arctic and Mountain Ventures (Figure 3.5), Mr and Mrs C. Cousins (Figure 4.2), Roger Gawn (Figures 5.2, 8.3, 8.4, 12.1 and 12.3), Ailwyn Best, Donald Insall and Associates (Figure 6.3), Peter de Sausmarez and the National Trust Textile Conservation Studio (Figure 12.5), Georgetown University (Figures 14.4, 14.5, 14.6 and 14.9), Steven Ashley (Figure 16.5), the Society for the Protection of Ancient Buildings (Figure 17.2), English Heritage (Appendix A), the Leicestershire Museums, Arts and Records Service (Figure 17.3), and Norwich City Council (Appendix D). Unless otherwise indicated, all photographs are by David Watt.

Finally, special thanks go to our respective wives, Julie and Lynne, for their continuing support and tolerance.

David S. Watt
*Reepham, Norfolk*

Peter G. Swallow
*Fleckney, Leicestershire*

June 1996

# PART
# ONE

*Chapter One*

# Surveying buildings

## SURVEYING BUILDINGS

The noun 'survey' has many different meanings and when used to describe a professional service undertaken in respect of a building needs to be qualified with a suitable adjective. The principal types of surveys are:

- *measured* surveys of buildings to provide drawings of their layout, construction and appearance;
- *valuation* surveys for acquisition, compensation, disposal, investment, insurance, mortgage or rating purposes;
- *building* surveys of the structure and fabric of properties to assess their condition and prepare reports, schedules of condition, schedules of dilapidations or specifications for programmes of maintenance and repair;
- *archaeological* surveys of the material remains of earlier societies including archaeological deposits below ground, ruins and standing structures.

This book deals with building surveys, which have been described as 'a comprehensive, critical, detailed and formal inspection of a building to determine its condition, and value, often resulting in the production of a report incorporating the results of such a survey'.[1]

A building survey of a property usually takes the form of an inspection and report, both confusingly referred to on occasions as 'the survey'. In this book the word 'survey' will be used to describe the actual inspection or investigation of the property, and 'survey report', the written document prepared for the client.

## THE NATURE OF BUILDING SURVEYS

A thorough survey to establish the condition of a building is essential if sound judgements are to be made about such issues as acquisition, or the formulation of policies or programmes in respect of alteration or repair. This is especially so if the building is old, and forms part of our architectural or historic heritage. Such a building will not only have suffered long exposure to the agencies of deterioration, but may also have been subjected to unsuitable uses, ill-considered structural alteration and negligent maintenance and repair.

An assessment of the condition of a building or structure can be based on a number of factors, the principal one being the data obtained from the survey. Others might include information gleaned from archive sources including record drawings, previous survey reports and maintenance records, together with information concerning past, present or future patterns of usage, client expectations and reports from commissioned specialists.

Surveys to establish accurately the physical condition of a property require the surveyor to develop a full understanding of how it was constructed, and how it has evolved over the years by a process of adaptation, including additions to and subtractions from the fabric and services installations. Moreover, the surveyor must appreciate how the building has been used in the past, what is expected of it in the future, as well as how it has responded to agencies of decay.

Once all the survey and other data have been collected they must be carefully evaluated and recorded in the form of a written report, giving a balanced assessment of the physical condition of the property. This report will usually be a most influential document as it will inform the decision-making process in respect of future repair, maintenance and adaptation of the subject property.

Building surveys need to be approached logically and methodically. The surveyor must have clear analytical thought; a comprehensive knowledge of construction (both current and obsolete); a knowledge of materials, their properties, behaviour and limitations; and a good appreciation of the causes of decay, damage and deterioration. Malcolm Hollis, in the foreword to his book *Surveying Buildings*,[2] makes the distinction between surveying as an art and verifying the causes of failure as a science, emphasizing the multidisciplinary nature of the work of a surveyor.

## PURPOSE OF BUILDING SURVEYS

A building survey is undertaken in order to provide information for a particular purpose. Such a purpose might be to:

- determine financial security against an intended loan or mortgage, or change of ownership;
- provide confidence for a potential purchaser or tenant undertaking repair liabilities, either by way of a report commissioned directly by the purchaser or by the vendor wishing to confirm or disclose material facts;
- determine stability and risk of failure following natural or man-made disasters;
- establish liability for disrepair (dilapidations);
- diagnose defects when symptoms appear to occupiers;
- determine the effectiveness of past repairs or maintenance;
- assess levels of disrepair in advance of legal proceedings;
- ensure compliance with legal requirements;
- understand and document factors affecting condition;
- provide a basis for planned works;
- provide a basis for physical change.

The building survey will often be an essential prerequisite to a programme of works and the potential scope of such works is outlined below.

## WORKS TO EXISTING BUILDINGS

The type and range of work carried out on existing buildings is very broad and the words used to describe the various elements are often misunderstood or imprecisely used. The following definitions illustrate the range of work and provide a concise explanation of their scope.

### Works carried out on the existing building fabric

*Conservation* – making a building fit for 'some socially useful purpose'.[3] '. . . the action taken to prevent decay. It embraces all acts that prolong the life of our cultural and natural heritage'.[4]
*Consolidation* – including protection and repair, to arrest the rate of deterioration suffered by the exposed ruins of buildings and monuments.
*Maintenance* – 'The combination of all technical and administrative actions, including supervision actions, intended to retain an item in, or restore it to, a state in which it can perform a required function'.[5]

*Preservation* – 'A method involving the retention of the building or monument in a sound static condition, without any material addition thereto or subtraction therefrom, so that it can be handed down to futurity with all the evidences of its character and age unimpaired'.[6]

*Repair* – necessary due to damage or decay that prevents further deterioration and reinstates structural integrity.

*Stabilization* – in response to an emergency in order to make safe and reduce further loss or damage.

## Works to provide for physical change

*Adaptation* – accommodating a change in the use of a building, which can include alterations and extensions.

*Alteration* – changing the structure of a building to meet new requirements.

*Conversion* – making a building of one particular type fit for the purposes of another type of usage.

*Extension* – increasing the floor area of a building, whether vertically by increasing height or horizontally by increasing plan area.

*Improvement* – bringing a building and/or its facilities up to an acceptable standard, possibly including alterations, extensions or some degree of adaptation.

*Modernization* – bringing a building up to a standard laid down by society and/or statutory requirements.

*Reconstruction* – reassembling a building using 'extant materials and components supplemented by new materials of a similar type, using techniques approximating to those believed to have been used originally, based on existing foundations and residual structure, historical or archaeological evidence'.[7]

*Refurbishment* – overhauling a building and bringing it up to the requirements of a client.

*Rehabilitation* – work beyond the scope of planned maintenance, to extend the life of a building, which is socially desirable and economically viable.

*Relocation* – dismantling and re-erecting a building at a different site.

*Renovation* – restoring a building to an acceptable condition, which may include works of conversion.

*Restoration* – restoring the physical and/or decorative condition of a building to that of a particular date or event.

*Revitalization* – extending the life of a building by providing or improving facilities, which may include works of repair.

## SURVEYING HISTORIC BUILDINGS

Each building survey is undertaken according to predetermined standards and conventions, set either by the surveyor or the client, or established by law. Often a standard assessment form is used, concentrating on those aspects of the construction, services and immediate site that relate to a typical property.

In the case of historic buildings, however, such a standardized approach is generally unacceptable, and unless the form being prescribed has a degree of flexibility, serious omissions may be made.

It is also important for the surveyor to be aware that the concepts of condition and quality have been, and to an extent still are, interrelated; and that for an accurate assessment of one to be made, it is first necessary to acknowledge the relative importance of the other. The ways in which we occupy and use our buildings may have changed, but it still remains important to understand what prompted the initial decision to build, and what influenced the choice of design and location.

*Chapter Two*

# Forms of building survey

## BASIS OF BUILDING SURVEYS

As noted in Chapter One, the purpose of a building survey can vary from building to building, and also for the same building over time as circumstances change. Whatever the purpose of the survey, certain features, both of the inspection and presentation of the facts, will be common. There will, however, be some issues on which the specific methods and standards will need to be set.

### Scope of assessment

In some cases the scope of a building survey may be limited to a particular defect, or element of construction, rather than the whole building. For many properties, particularly those constructed recently, well-established standard survey procedures and assessment criteria are usually employed. Standard assessment procedures may, however, prove inappropriate for historic properties, either because of their age, construction (which may be unusual or even unique) or size. In these cases it is necessary to devise an appropriate framework within which to operate, establish assessment criteria and prepare specific survey checklists.

Whatever the scope of the survey, the findings from the inspection will usually form the subject of a report, in which they are presented and analysed in a clear and concise manner, addressing both general and individual issues, and provide a reliable source of information.

## Levels of expertise

The quality of an assessment produced by a surveyor depends on that individual's skill and judgement, which requires knowledge gained from initial and mid-career training, refined by practical experience and continuing professional development.

Surveying and assessing the condition of historic properties is not simply an extension of general surveying work. An accurate and appropriate assessment of older building fabric can only be made by someone who has developed the necessary knowledge, skills, experience and understanding to appreciate the particular problems that these buildings may present.

Certain forms of assessment require the person undertaking the survey to have an appropriate level of training or experience for the particular task. Government quadrennial inspections are usually undertaken by Specialist Conservation Consultants,[1] and since the 1991 amendment to the Inspection of Churches Measure 1955 quinquennial inspections must be carried out by 'a qualified person or persons'.[2]

Where the assessment is non-specific, that is one which is based on a standard form, the surveyor should recognize the need for special care where historic buildings are involved and refer back to the client for further instruction.

The increase in cases of alleged negligence reaching the courts, and the subsequent rise in the premiums paid for professional indemnity insurance, has forced many surveyors to consider carefully the nature of the work they undertake and for some the potential risks attached to undertaking building surveys has made them wary of such work.

## Client expectations

It is important that the needs of the client are fully discussed at the outset and that their expectations are clarified so that the assessment criteria and level of service can be identified. The scope of the service, the level of detail and the terms of engagement must be made perfectly clear before a contract is entered into so that the client is left in no doubt as to what is being provided and the costs involved. Many practices produce useful brochures that clearly set out for their clients the various standard levels of service offered, together with information about any additional optional services that are available.

Where the client is a corporate body or institution there is a greater presumption that the client has clear views on the scope of the survey and the assessment criteria to be used, and will often require the work to be undertaken according to a prescribed format.

Where a client is unfamiliar with historic properties, but wishes to buy or obtain an interest in one, the surveyor must be able to help define the scope of the survey and also advise on the practicalities and costs of repair and maintenance. What a client might expect from such a property could require degrees of alteration or adaptation that are unacceptable with regard to the importance of the building or its site. In these cases the client must be advised appropriately and either helped to temper their expectations or encouraged to find a more suitable building.

In order to assist in offering a useful service to the client the Royal Institute of British Architects (RIBA) published a guide to architectural services relating to historic buildings in April 1990.[3] This document, and more recent advice,[4] details preliminary, basic and other services, together with conditions of appointment, and recommended fees and expenses. A similar document is, at the time of writing, being prepared by the Royal Institution of Chartered Surveyors (RICS).[5]

## SPECIFIC BUILDING SURVEY FORMATS

Standard forms for structuring information both during the inspection and report writing have been developed by various organizations. These range from detailed pro formas to simple checklists; some have been developed for specific purposes or types of property, while others have come about simply to suit a particular set of circumstances.

In order to understand how these various approaches are used, and the type and levels of information required by each, details of those most likely to be relevant to historic properties are detailed below.

### Church of England quinquennial inspection

Although regular inspections were originally introduced for parsonages in the middle of the last century, it was not until the Inspection of Churches Measure 1955 that a procedure was established for ensuring the inspection of churches at least once every five years. The purpose of this inspection and the resulting report, is to provide a general summary of the condition of the building, indicate necessary repairs and priorities for action, and make recommendations for further detailed inspection (Figure 2.1).[6]

The Care of Churches and Ecclesiastical Jurisdiction Measure 1991 (schedule 3) has amended section 1(2) of the 1955 Measure to allow 'a qualified person or persons' to perform quinquennial inspections, this having previously been restricted solely to architects. Thus, for the first time, other suitably qualified and experienced professionals are able to undertake this work.

**PRELIMINARY INFORMATION**
**Main report**

**Limitations**
Schedule of works completed since the previous quinquennial report
General condition

**External**
• Roof coverings
• Rainwater goods and disposal systems
• Parapets and upstand walls
• Walling
• Timber porches, doors and canopies
• Windows

**Internal**
• Towers, spires
• Clocks and their enclosures
• Roof and ceiling voids
• Roof structures, ceilures
• Upper floors, balconies, access stairways
• Partitions, screens, panelling, doors and door furniture
• Ground-floor structure, timber platforms
• Fittings, fixtures, furniture and movable articles
• Toilets, kitchens, vestries, etc.
• Organs and other musical instruments

• Monuments, tombs, plaques, etc.
• Service installations generally
• Heating installation
• Electrical installation
• Sound system
• Lightning conductor
• Fire precautions
• Disabled access provision
• Safety
• Bats

**Curtilage**
• Churchyard
• Ruins
• Monuments, tombs and vaults
• Boundary walls, lychgates and fencing
• Trees and shrubs
• Hardstanding areas
• Miscellaneous
• Logbook

**Recommendations**

*Figure 2.1* Outline form for the quinquennial inspection of churches.

## Government quadrennial inspection

All Government civil estate buildings that are listed in its Historic Buildings Register and for which there is a significant maintenance responsibility, are inspected and reported on at four-yearly intervals. The purpose of such quadrennial inspections is to establish priorities and costings, long-term objectives and a means by which these can be regularly reviewed (Figure 2.2).[7] Initial reports also contain a historical assessment.

**Introduction**
- Status and occupancy
- Building history and significance

**Conduct of the inspection**
- Scope of the inspection
- Other specialist reports
- Additional information
- Drawings and other documents
- Fire officers' reports
- Personnel
- Weather conditions

**Work done since previous inspection**

**General state of the building, installations and its setting**
- General soundness and importance of setting
- Degree of deterioration in relation to age
- Appropriateness of use
- Adequacy of maintenance and general care
- Major problems and defects
- Major recommendations for maintenance, repair and improvement

**Findings of the inspection**
- General structure
- Chimney stacks
- Roof coverings
- Rainwater disposal
- External wall surfaces
- External doors and windows
- External fittings
- Roof structure and roof spaces
- Floors, ceilings and staircases
- Internal partitions
- Internal doors
- Internal finishes
- Fittings and furnishings
- Schedules of fittings and articles
- Service installations
- Security and fire precautions
- Hard landscaping
- Soft landscaping
- Other features relevant to the building

**Recommendations and classifications of priorities**
- Further investigations
- Works services and priority classifications

*Figure 2.2* Requirements for quadrennial inspections of historic buildings on the Government Civil Estate.

## National Trust quinquennial survey

All buildings or structures held for preservation are inspected and reported on by nominated architects or other suitably qualified persons every five years, the purpose being to provide a detailed appraisal of condition, and identify present and future needs in order to maintain the structure and services in perpetuity (Figure 2.3).[8]

Intermediate surveys may, at the discretion of the Regional Buildings Manager, be undertaken in a reduced form where a full report is deemed unnecessary. This approach is also used for estate buildings, such as cottages and farm buildings, with the surveys undertaken by in-house staff.

**Introduction**
- Schedule of buildings included in survey
- Brief description of the building(s)
- Description of construction and materials
- Reference to inaccessible parts of building
- Recommendations for further opening up
- Brief recommendations for improving energy efficiency of structure and services
- Recommendations for further specialist advice
- Record of work undertaken since last survey
- Record of outstanding work from last survey
- Summary of general structural condition

**Description of defects**

**Exterior**
- Chimneys and high-level features
- Roof structures and roof coverings
- Gutters and above-ground rainwater disposal systems
- Walls
- Doors, windows and external joinery
- Metalwork
- External paintwork
- Pavings

**Interior**
- Roof spaces
- Ceilings
- Walls and partitions
- Floors and floor structures
- Lintels
- Internal joinery
- Staircases

- Glazing
- Fittings
- Metalwork
- Decorations
- Asbestos installations

**Services**
- Water supply
- Hot and cold water installations
- Heating installations
- Environmental/humidity control
- Electricity supply
- Electrical installation
- Lightning conductor installation
- Gas supply
- Gas installation
- Above-ground foul drainage
- Below-ground rainwater disposal system
- Below-ground foul drainage and disposal system, including effluence sampling facilities

**Fire precautions**

**Security precautions**

**Site features**

**Summary of recommendations with estimated costs**
- For immediate action
- For completion within two years
- For completion within five years
- For completion within ten years

**Observations**
- Suggested improvements
- Improvements in routine maintenance
- Monitoring of defects
- Likely major repairs beyond ten years

**Drawings and photographs**

*Figure 2.3* Requirements for quinquennial surveys of National Trust properties.

## Historic structure report

This American initiative is based on a detailed survey carried out on an individual historic building prior to its reuse or refurbishment, and includes the production of full measured drawings, structural analysis, archival research, analysis of the materials employed in the construction and often recommendations for repair.[9, 10] A full understanding of the history, fabric and needs of a building may be drawn from such a report prior to works being implemented and, despite the high initial cost, savings may follow from the information provided (Figure 2.4).[11]

## Sample surveys

Assessing the condition of a particular sample of buildings as a tool for providing a specific set of data can take many forms. For example, during 1990–91 a survey of some 43,000 listed buildings was undertaken in different parts of England in order to establish an overall picture of the general condition of listed buildings and the extent to which repairs were urgently required.[12]

The survey form used for the resulting computer-based English Heritage Buildings at Risk Register (Appendix A) makes use of four categories of condition assessment. This, together with the nature of occupancy at the time of inspection, is used to indicate the category of risk for each particular building.

GENERAL BUILDING SURVEY FORMATS

Certain general forms of building survey may also be employed in connection with a historic building. The most common of these are given below.

## Mortgage valuation

This gives a brief description of the property, together with an indication of the current open market value and the security of the property for bank or building society mortgage purposes. The valuation is based on a limited and superficial inspection of the property, and is not intended to give a full assessment of the condition.

Many mortgagees provide standard pro forma reports to be completed following an inspection of a property. These are, by their nature, brief and inappropriate for older properties, and surveyors using such a report may find themselves negligent through omissions necessitated by the format.

## Home Buyers' Survey and Valuation (HBSV)

This provides a concise report on the general condition of a property given using a standard form issued jointly by the RICS and Incorporated

---

**Methodology**
- Procedures followed in executing study and report

**History**
- Narrative history of the site, building or structure
- Identification of significant individuals associated with the property

**Site and landscape evaluation**
- Archival and physical research of the site and landscape
- Evolution and condition of site and landscape

**Archaeological evaluation**
- Identification and condition of archaeological features
- Contribution to understanding of site history and architecture

**Architectural evaluation**
- Archival and physical research of the structure
- Chronology of construction
- Documentation of missing features
- Identification of original fabric
- Condition of existing features and components
- Room by room description

**Structural evaluation**
- Archival and physical research of structural systems
- Evolution and condition of structural systems

**Building systems evaluation**
- Archival and physical research of mechanical, electrical, plumbing, fire and security systems
- Evolution and condition of building systems

**Construction chronology**
- Evolution of structure
- Physical and documentry evidence

**Materials conservation analysis**
- Primary building materials
- Characteristics and composition
- Interpretation of field and laboratory analysis
- Identification of material failures

**Identification of significant features**
- Identification of features of note for historical significance, architectural and engineering design, materials or craftsmanship

**Recommendations**
- Cost estimates
- Outline scope of work
- Recommendations and alternatives

**Bibliography and reference sources**

**Appendices**
- Drawings
- Photographs
- Copies of reference documents

---

*Figure 2.4* Typical contents of a historic structure report.

Society of Valuers and Auctioneers (ISVA).[13] The purpose and provision of the report are as set out in the standard conditions of engagement. Prior to its release in August 1993 separate report forms had been used for houses and flats since their introduction in 1980.

Such a report is intended to identify major defects and provide information on the general condition of the fabric (Figure 2.5). The published form clearly points out that the inspection is not a building or structural survey, and the report is not intended to detail minor defects that do not materially affect value.

In this respect the standard form of assessment is considered to be inappropriate for very large properties, houses exceeding three storeys in height, properties of non-standard construction and new buildings in the course of construction.

## Building survey

This is a detailed technical examination of a property, often termed a 'structural survey', resulting in a comprehensive report explaining the construction and condition of those parts readily accessible to the surveyor. Recommendations for repair and a valuation may be provided if required.

The basis of this form of assessment will usually follow in outline the headings noted for the Home Buyers' Survey and Valuation noted above, but with greater emphasis being placed on defect diagnosis and the detailed assessment of condition. It is therefore more appropriate for complicated, older and larger properties.

After many years of usage it is now generally felt within the property professions that the term 'structural survey' should be replaced with one that reflects more closely the nature and extent of the task. A draft paper[14] giving the findings of a multidisciplinary panel that has been working on common definitions for building inspections and surveys suggests that two generic terms be adopted: 'building survey' for those not normally including advice of value and 'property purchase survey and valuation' for those that do. Copies of the paper have been circulated to solicitors, banks, building societies and members of the professions for comment.

## Schedule of condition

The purpose of such a schedule is to state the condition of a property at a specific point in time. This can take the form of a schedule prepared at the commencement of a lease to provide a benchmark from which to assess the performance of covenants when a schedule of dilapidations is

**Information**
- Name and address of clients
- Property address
- Council tax band or rating assessment
- Date of inspection
- Weather
- Limits to inspection
- Tenure
- Apparent tenancies

**General description**
- Description of property
- Accommodation
- Outbuildings and parking
- Approximate age
- Orientation
- Location and amenities
- Summary of construction

**External condition**
- Chimney stacks and boiler flues
- Roofs
- Rainwater goods
- Main walls and damp-proof course
- Windows, doors and joinery
- External decoration
- Garage(s) and outbuildings
- Site
- Drainage

**Internal condition**
- Roof spaces
- Ceilings
- Walls and partitions
- Fireplaces, flues and chimney breasts
- Floors
- Dampness
- Woodworm, dry rot and other timber defects
- Internal joinery
- Internal decorations
- Cellars and vaults
- Thermal insulation
- Services

**Common parts and services**
- Extent of inspection
- Condition of common parts
- Common services

**Further advice and valuation**
- Roads and footpaths
- Matters to be checked by legal advisers
- Matters that might materially affect value
- Conditions/hazards requiring immediate attention
- Building insurance
- Open market value

*Figure 2.5* Format of a Home Buyer's Survey and Valuation.

prepared at its termination, or as a record of the condition of a building likely to be affected by demolition or works to adjacent property on which to base negotiations for compensation at completion.

## Schedule of dilapidations

The basis for such an assessment of condition comes from the legal liability of a person who has entered into a lease to repair and maintain a property to a certain standard, both during the course of the lease and at its end. An Interim Schedule served with a Notice to Repair during the currency of the lease, or a Final or Terminal Schedule served with a Schedule of Claim at the termination of the lease, are based on inspections of the property and assessments of the standards of condition with regard to the law of dilapidations and the specific covenants in force.


## APPROPRIATENESS OF THE SURVEY FORMAT

The forms of building survey that are used specifically for historic buildings have been developed in order to fulfil a requirement that is common to all, namely the continued protection of a structure and its fabric through the implementation of informed repair and maintenance policies. These are formulated by having a detailed understanding of how the building is constructed, how it is used, and how it has reacted or is expected to react to physical and environmental changes and the agencies of decay.

The general forms of building survey that have been considered all have differing aims, whether for legal, financial, academic or technical reasons and their appropriateness to historic buildings depends on the skills of the surveyor and the flexibility of their format.

In the residential mortgage valuation guidance notes provided by the RICS and ISVA it is clearly stated that for properties of architectural or historic interest, those in a conservation area, or of unusual construction, valuers should seek the advice of appropriate specialists unless they themselves are competent to give advice that would not be detrimental to the architectural or historic integrity of the property, its future structural condition or conservation of the fabric.[15] This has been similarly endorsed in the revised *RICS Appraisal and Valuation Manual* or 'Red Book', which came into effect on 1 January 1996.[16]

Assessments made for the purposes of preparing schedules of dilapidations may not, for instance, relate directly to the historic nature of the building, while those made in providing a detailed survey report do. The surveyor must therefore acknowledge and address these differences in undertaking the work, whether it be in undertaking general or specific assessments, if a valuable service is to be provided for the client.

*Chapter Three*

# Historic buildings

Before describing how to conduct building surveys on historic buildings it is necessary to establish what makes a building or structure historic, and to consider what effect this will have on the inspection, assessment and report preparation.

The RIBA in its *Architect's Appointment* for repairs and conservation work defines a historic building as 'a building, monument or structure of architectural, historic or archaeological interest'.[1] The definition goes on to state that 'Others may warrant the same special care and attention because of their inherent artistic character or age.' It is these considerations, and others, that are so important in working with historic buildings.

## AGE

Age is just one of the factors that makes a building 'historic', along with architectural and historic interest, and historical association with important people and events. The older a building is, however, the fewer the surviving examples of its kind there are likely to be, and so older properties acquire a rarity value.

### Recent past

In recent years there has been a growing interest in protecting buildings not only from the distant past, but also from the immediate past. Buildings of the inter- and postwar years, many built within living memory, have now become eligible for listing as being of special architectural or historic interest. The adoption of the 'thirty year rule' by the Department of the Environment in 1987 has allowed many buildings of the recent past to be acknowledged and, ultimately, protected by legislation. Buildings that are less than 30 years old are only listed if they are considered to be of an outstanding quality, with those less than ten deemed too close to our own time to be objectively chosen.

## Period and purpose

The contemporary architecture of a particular period has often been viewed by its supporters as being infinitely superior to that of the previous period. While successive generations in turn scorn the architecture of the previous generation, they appear, however, to nurture a desire to preserve and protect objects and images of preceding years.

The Society for the Protection of Ancient Buildings (SPAB), founded in 1877, was the first body established to defend old buildings. Since then many others have followed. The architecture of the eighteenth century is championed by the Georgian Group (founded in 1937), that of the nineteenth century by the Victorian Society (founded in 1958), and the work of the present century by the Twentieth Century Society (formerly the Thirties Society founded in 1979), and more recently the work of the Modern Movement by DOCOMOMO-UK (Documentation and Conservation of the Modern Movement, founded in 1990).

Interest and concern has also been shown for certain classes or types of building or site, often as a response to contemporary misunderstanding or neglect. The SPAB Windmill Section was established in 1929, changing to the Wind and Watermill Section in 1948; the Vernacular Architecture Group in 1952; the Friends of Friendless Churches in 1957; the Garden History Society in 1965; the Association for Industrial Archaeology in 1973; the Theatres Trust in 1976; the Construction History Society in 1982; the Historic Farm Buildings Group in 1985; and the Folly Fellowship in 1988, to name but a few.

## Protection

Legislation has responded to the desire to keep our history safe. The present framework for historic properties in England and Wales is based on the Town and Country Planning Act 1990 and the Planning (Listed Buildings and Conservation Areas) Act 1990. Ancient monuments are legislated for with the Ancient Monuments and Archaeological Areas Act 1979.

Governmental guidance on the historic environment is offered within its *Planning Policy Guidance: Planning and the Historic Environment*,[2] which has replaced Circular 8/87 *Historic Buildings and Conservation Areas – Policy and Procedures*.[3] Guidance for ancient monuments is offered within *Planning Policy Guidance: Archaeology and Planning*.[4]

Exemption from controls relating to listed buildings and conservation areas for the Church of England is detailed in the *Ecclesiastical Exemption (Listed Buildings and Conservation Areas) Order 1994*.

## Attitudes

Although legislation, and the protection that it affords, offers a presumption against demolition or damaging change, it can itself be the cause of further distress or blight. Restrictions on alternative usage, location and the affluence of the owner or occupier are seen, in this respect, as strong determinants of condition. Figures from the English Heritage Buildings at Risk survey (1992) show that over 36,000 listed buildings (7.3 per cent of England's 500,000 listed buildings) are at risk from neglect, with a further 14.6 per cent considered vulnerable.[5]

The reasons for this neglect were shown to relate, in varying degrees, to occupancy, listing grade, location, economic factors and original building type, with a strong association proved between the condition of a property and the level of occupancy. Such a relationship was also found in the English House Condition Survey of 1991,[6] although it appears, in comparison, that listed buildings are in no worse condition than the average domestic dwelling. The English House Condition Survey did, however, establish a relationship between the state of repair and household income.

Owner-occupiers appear, from recent research carried out on behalf of Upkeep (formerly the Building Conservation Trust),[7] to consider the repair and maintenance of their homes on an *ad hoc* basis, reacting to damage and decay rather than proactively planning work in anticipation of failure. A reluctance to spend money on repairs was found to be a major factor, with improvements seen as being more worthwhile than non-essential repairs. Professional advice was shunned in favour of assistance from friends, with changes of ownership playing an important part in the long-term future of a property.

## Awareness

The public's perception of, and interest in, historic property has altered over the past decade. It is now more familiar with, and to an extent more knowledgeable about, our nation's past than before, with the National Trust, Historic Houses Association and similar bodies placing a greater emphasis on interpretation and education.

Opportunities for staying in historic properties, including those offered by the Landmark Trust, National Trust and Vivat Trust for short-term holiday accommodation, and for longer periods during retirement through the Country House Association, are becoming increasingly popular, and satisfy a demand for comfortable and solid surroundings.

## Education and training

With these changes has come a need to educate those who are responsible for the tangible reminders of our distant and immediate past. Training for professional advisers lies with the Conference on Training in Architectural Conservation (COTAC), while opportunities now exist for craftspersons under the SPAB Craft Fellowship, established in 1987, and the English Heritage training centre at Fort Brockhurst (Hampshire), which opened in 1993. Training is also available at the European Centre for Training Craftsmen in the Conservation of the Architectural Heritage, Isola di San Servolo, Italy, and at a small number of other continental centres.

Advice for property owners and the public is available from their local authority conservation officers, the Conservation Unit of the Museums and Galleries Commission, local exhibitions and centres such as the Building of Bath Museum, and through the permanent exhibition and work of Upkeep based at Hampton Court Palace.

## BUILDING TYPES

Much has been written about the origins and developments of certain building types, including farm buildings, terraced housing, railway structures and, on a wider scale, vernacular architecture, with each being the subject for study in its own right. Through such typological studies it is also possible to consider related subjects, such as materials, techniques of construction, performance, and the influence of contemporary standards and regulations.

## Classification

Classifying building types can assist in ordering information obtained from primary research or secondary sources, and provide useful overviews of a particular area or settlement. Local studies and related publications also assist in providing an understanding of the history of a place and its people.

In considering a particular building type it is important to appreciate the potential range of the subject, and how one particular facet can

Chemical industries (e.g. agricultural chemicals)

Engineering and iron founding (e.g. furnaces, steel-yards)

Extractive industries and associated processes (e.g. clay pits, limekilns)

Food processing (e.g. maltings, slaughterhouses)

Power (e.g. pumping stations, tide mills)

Public services and service industries (e.g. civic buildings, theatres)

Rural industries (e.g. saw mills, smithies)

Textile and leather trades (e.g. dye works, tanneries)

Transport (e.g. bridges, inland waterways)

Miscellaneous (e.g. gunpowder mills, warehouses)

*Figure 3.1* Classifications of industrial monuments.

influence another. The study of industrial monuments, for instance, may be considered under a number of different headings (Figure 3.1), each of which can be further subdivided to give a full spectrum of the subject.

## Distinctiveness

When inspecting and assessing the condition of a particular building, or structure, it is easy to consider it in isolation from its immediate neighbours, and other properties of a similar age and type in the locality. To do so, however, may deny the surveyor the opportunity of fully understanding the purpose of the property within its local context, and thus to gauge its true historic and current significance.

A surveyor who is asked to assess the condition of a historic property should appreciate and respect the history of the building type, as well as the materials and methods of construction employed (Figure 3.2).

Certain building types may suffer from particular problems associated with either the manner in which they were built or used. Experience will guide the surveyor to anticipate and identify the conditions necessary for such problems to arise. For example, church towers are susceptible to vertical 'ringing cracks' caused by the stresses induced by bell ringing, while further cracks could normally be expected at the corners due to the spreading of the roof; between tower and nave as a result of differential movement; and at structural openings.

## Special building types

There are, within the study of buildings and their uses, a number that, by their construction or original purpose, are of such complexity or

*Figure 3.2* Old and new: Old Queen's Head public house, Sheffield (c. 1500) in the foreground, with Hyde Park flats (c. 1962) beyond. Between them is part of the recent city bus station (c. 1992).

individuality that standard procedures for inspection and assessment would be wholly inappropriate.

In 1987 Norfolk County Council adopted a policy of identifying, recording and assisting with the preservation of such 'special building types'.[8] These were types of building or structure that were not adequately

| | |
|---|---|
| Ancient monuments | Windpumps (drainage mills) |
| Churches in use | Industrial monuments |
| Redundant farm buildings | Country houses and estate buildings |
| Ruined churches | Cast-iron architecture |
| Watermills | Transport architecture |
| Cornmills | World War buildings |

*Figure 3.3* Classifications of 'special buildings types'.

protected by current legislation or grant policies (Figure 3.3). Each category forms a subject for detailed research to provide a topic paper for discussion and debate. At present, funded programmes are in operation for both cornmills and ruined churches, with papers on farm buildings and ancient monuments drafted for consultation.

From work undertaken so far, it is known that each category of 'special building type' faces problems that are peculiar to its location, use or form of construction. In most cases the original purpose for which the building or structure was erected has ceased to exist, leaving it subject to unsympathetic adaptation to a new use, or neglect and gradual decay.

By their very nature these special building types require an expert knowledge in order to understand their often unique forms of construction and associated problems (Figure 3.4).

## CHARACTER AND IDENTITY

Property speculation and mass production have reduced the character and appearance of a large proportion of modern buildings to a level of banality. Even the promise of new architecture is often watered down by compromise, with creativity stifled by imposed standards and regulations. The challenge of design appears more to do with problem solving than with what the twentieth-century architect Philip Johnson has described as 'building for glory, pleasure and eternity'.

The beauty and value of historic buildings is as subjective as design itself. In part, appreciation comes from an understanding of the physical character of the building – how it was built and what made it function. There is also an aesthetic appreciation – an awareness and understanding of the design, and a respect for the patina of age. Buildings can thus be the vehicle for expressing fashion, wealth and personal beliefs, whether as fine architecture or humble dwellings.

In order to appreciate a building fully it is essential to understand both its purpose and meaning. The first comes from the function for which it was designed or since come to fulfil; the second from the language of the architecture employed.

Architecture and the arts are obvious examples of a nation's cultural heritage, but there are also other expressions of creativity and natural beauty that are equally respected. The well-being of such monuments may be beyond the scope of most surveyors, but there are nevertheless implications that have to be addressed.

*Figure 3.4* Church of St Mary, Houghton-on-the Hill, Norfolk. In a ruinous state since the early 1950s, the church demonstrates the typical problems of isolated location, vegetation growth, loss of roof covering and collapsing flintwork.

*Figure 3.5* Ofaerufoss waterfall, Iceland. Courtesy of Arctic and Mountain Ventures, Aylsham, Norfolk.

The Ofaerufoss waterfall in Iceland has, for example, been revered as a national monument for many years, with countless tourists visiting and crossing the natural rock arch that spans the water (Figure 3.5). During the spring of 1993 erosion led to the collapse of this arch. Whether this loss could have been predicted, and ultimately prevented, is not known, but suffice it to say that part of Iceland's history and unique heritage has now gone.

HISTORY

Buildings and monuments have a meaning and purpose connected to a historical time and place. This history can explain and illustrate events in the past, such as the dissolution of the monasteries or the industrial revolution. Buildings can be considered as historical documents and it is therefore important to record and attempt to interpret and explain features disclosed during inspections and surveys.

## Education

Buildings are part of our cultural heritage and are seen as the subject, in varying degrees, of education, preservation and commerce. Organizations such as the National Trust, English Heritage, Cadw (Welsh Historic Monuments) and Historic Scotland provide a means by which this heritage is interpreted and presented to a public that is becoming more conscious of its surroundings.

Furthermore, owners and occupiers of historic buildings are becoming aware of how much importance is attached to their properties through the action of local authority planning and conservation officers, amenity societies and national bodies.

## Understanding

Attitudes are also changing to reflect the increased awareness of the importance attached to more recent buildings, and those previously thought unimportant. The accelerated resurvey of listed buildings undertaken during the 1980s took account of these changes, while the present Monuments Protection Programme (MPP), administered by English Heritage, is considering the scheduling of ancient monuments.

Increasingly our below-ground heritage is being respected. The Department of the Environment's *Planning Policy Guidance: Archaeology and Planning* (PPG 16, November 1990) sets out the Secretary of State's policy for archaeological remains on land, and gives guidance for planning authorities, property owners, developers, archaeologists, amenity societies and the general public.

The challenge now is to keep an open mind as to why and how our heritage should be conserved, to make careful use of it in our education and leisure, and to develop adequate legal safeguards and funding arrangements to secure long-term protection.

## ASSOCIATIONS

The value of a historic building or structure may not come solely from its importance as an architectural composition. The associations of the property with persons, events or innovations may be sufficient to warrant its study and protection. Evidence for this social dimension can often be found on plaques commemorating the life or work of a former occupant.

The associations and particular identity of a building may, in themselves, be responsible for its survival. Those buildings that are picturesque, or contribute to the character of an area, often engender interest and assistance. Public enthusiasm for cornmills, railway buildings, schools and other distinctive building types has often been the cause of their survival.

## Conflict

Other building types, which often harbour distasteful images from the past, have suffered through disinterest and neglect, and survive only through the work of museums and charitable trusts (Figure 3.6). Often this apathy has gone further to include vandalism and arson. Former workhouses, prisons, asylums and factories have typically suffered in this way, and their architectural and social importance is only now being acknowledged. In this respect the work of the Royal Commission on Historical Monuments of England, and the Royal Commissions on the Ancient and Historical Monuments of Scotland and Wales, in recording such buildings is engendering a new interest and perhaps new hope for their survival.

Certain materials and forms of construction may be thought by some, through a lack of appreciation and understanding, to be inferior and not worthy of conservation. Timber-framed construction was, at one time, viewed in this way and as such was demolished or altered at will. Unburnt clay construction, such as cob, clay lump, and wattle and daub, is still perceived as inferior by the uninformed, and is vulnerable to

*Figure 3.6* Preserved late 19th-century bottle kilns at Gladstone Pottery Museum in Longton, Stoke-on-Trent. Notice the amount of vegetation growth to the open brick joints.

damage, neglect or inappropriate action in the belief that such construction is no longer practised.

Clay lump is often replaced with modern blockwork, and cement used for mortars and renders instead of lime, simply because the relevant knowledge or material supplies are hard to come by. Education for building owners, their advisers and builders is essential to overcome such prejudices and can be achieved by giving accurate and appropriate advice, producing information sheets or organising practical demonstrations (Figure 3.7).

*Figure 3.7* Experience being gained at an organized 'clay-lump day'.

TRADITIONAL BUILDING MATERIALS

The selection and use of building materials within a particular geographic area or for a specific purpose reflects a practical awareness of both economics and material science.

The term 'traditional material' is one that reflects an understanding of a local product or raw material in continued use for a certain purpose. Such materials are usually of natural origin, porous and flexible in nature, of textures and colours that complement the landscape, and ultimately are susceptible to decay. Studies of such materials include A. Clifton-Taylor's *The Pattern of English Building*,[9] R. Brunskill's *Illustrated Handbook of Vernacular Architecture*,[10] and G. Torraca's *Porous Building Materials: Materials Science for Architectural Conservation*.[11]

## Craft skills

Many traditional materials are no longer available either through a lack of demand or exhaustion of the source. The necessary skills of manufacture or use can easily become lost if not passed on to successive generations. The recent revival of interest in, and use of, such materials has led to supplies being re-established and training being instigated.

Gault clay peg tiles are again, for instance, being produced by the Cambridgeshire Tile and Brick Company at Burwell, to the south-east of Cambridge. With grant aid from English Heritage, King's Lynn and West Norfolk Borough Council and other local authorities, this newly established works hopes to be producing 5,000 tiles per week when full production is reached.

Traditional craft skills, such as thatching and flint knapping, are still practised, but only by a small number of craftspersons qualified by apprenticeships or experience (Figure 3.8). In other trades, such as mill-wrighting, numbers are dwindling.

## Character

In assessing the condition of a particular material it is essential to appreciate its qualities and characteristics in use in order to understand inherent defects and possible mechanisms of decay. Inappropriate usage, incorrect detailing and incompatibility with other materials can account for as many problems as natural deterioration itself, and the surveyor must be able to assess how and when a failure will occur if forward planning and appropriate intervention are to be considered.

*Figure 3.8* Long-straw thatching to 15th-century timber-framed barn at Newton Flotman, Norfolk. Courtesy of the Norfolk Historic Buildings Trust.

## Limitations

As an instance of inappropriate selection of materials, the First Lord Leverhulme is recorded as having constructed a house of peat in Leverburh on the Isle of Harris in the early twentieth century. The material subsequently dried out and was used piece by piece as fuel by its occupants.

Practical advice on the nature and use of specific traditional materials is, however, available through a number of organizations and individuals, including the Building Limes Forum, the Lime Centre, the Traditional Paint Forum, and the various professional and craft training courses.

The selection of traditional materials for replacement or repair itself requires an understanding beyond simple technical and financial matters. The Norfolk pantile, for instance, can be seen in three forms: plain, smut and black glazed. Each was used for a particular purpose, so that the visible front roof slope of a house might be covered with glazed tiles, while smuts or plain tiles might be used for the rear slopes, or those facing into a valley.

## TRADITIONAL FORMS OF CONSTRUCTION

The use of traditional materials imposes natural limitations and influences the form of construction, and until recent times techniques of building have remained constant and generally understood. An appreciation of traditional methods of building, including selection of materials, material handling, specific user requirements, limitations in use and design considerations, is thus necessary if a building or structure is to be understood and correctly assessed.

### Experience

The flintwork seen in many Norfolk churches, particularly those in ruins, gives evidence, for example, of a form of construction largely unconsidered with this material. The regularity of the face, together with acknowledged limitations of building with flint and characteristics of early lime mortars, have led to the view that much of this work was undertaken with shuttering. Additional support for this thesis has come from the archaeological evidence of post holes considered to be for the supports to such shuttering found at Hadstock St Botolph (Essex) during the excavations in the 1970s (Figure 3.10).[12]

### Knowledge

The surveyor can learn much about traditional forms of building by studying early construction texts, particularly those of the eighteenth, nineteenth and early twentieth centuries. Original volumes as well as facsimile reprints, can be purchased directly from second-hand bookshops and fairs, or through specialized mail order businesses.

*Figure 3.9* Traditional stone and thatch construction on Isle of Skye. Notice the use of ropes and stone anchors to hold the thatch in place.

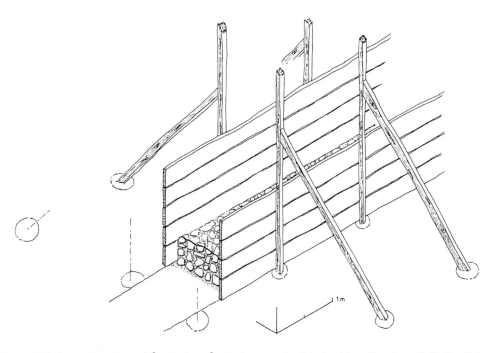

*Figure 3.10* Reconstruction of the timber shuttering required to build walls of small flint rubble. Reproduced from *Anglo-Saxon Church Building: Aspects of Design and Construction*, credited to Warwick Rodwell.

Modern texts covering specific aspects of conservation tend to appear under a small number of publishers (publishers and specialist bookshops are listed in Appendix E). Excellent introductions to building types, materials and forms of construction are also available from Shire Publications.

Information on specific aspects of construction or related matters may also be produced by manufacturers, producers and governing bodies. The Central Council of Church Bell Ringers has, for example, produced useful guidance on the maintenance of towers, bells and associated equipment, while the Council for the Care of Churches, through Church House Publishing, produce a number of useful booklets for those responsible for the repair and maintenance of churches.

When dealing with more modern forms of construction, particularly those buildings erected since World War II, it is now necessary to consider why particular materials were chosen and how they were used.

The historian, Robert Thorne, argues that these later buildings must be considered in a different light from more traditional forms of construction, as they have been executed in a fundamentally different manner.[13] Where once materials and construction formed part of the overall design, now the execution has become divorced from it, leaving building forms that, in Thorne's words, are designed as 'complete and flawless objects, fine-tuned to a particular purpose'.

Furthermore, the introduction of modern materials and technologies has offered new challenges and possibilities, particularly in relation to the repair and maintenance of historic fabric. These, it is felt, should be judged on individual merits, and not adopted as a panacea for all ills.

## BUILDINGS IN USE

An understanding of the materials and forms of construction employed in a particular building is only part of the story. It is equally important to appreciate why the building came about and how it was put to use.

### Purpose

The location, form and planning of a particular building, or part, is a product of how it was originally intended to be used. When this use ceases or changes it leaves evidence that has to be identified and understood. For this reason an awareness of social, cultural and domestic arrangements, both basic and pretentious, will assist in interpreting the evidence.

Often buildings or structures were built to perform a specific role within the context of an estate or as part of a complex. Examples of such buildings could include dovecotes, ice-houses and gas-making plant for country houses; and production, administration and retail facilities on an industrial site.

## Usage

The condition of a property in use, and its decline into disuse and disrepair, may be related to a number of separate and interrelated issues. These must be understood if appropriate action is to be taken.

The processes of obsolescence that might affect a building can be related to either changes in the use of the building or changes in the building user. Within the first category may be considered functional, economic, locational, community, statutory and physical obsolescence. The building user will also have objectives and perceptions on which to base decisions relating directly to the condition of the fabric. These might include status, tastes and fashions, and personal beliefs.

### THE FUTURE

If the buildings of the past are to survive they must possess either a cultural or financial value that is identified, understood and respected. Much of what has been said above reflects a growing concern and appreciation for our built heritage, but often the costs of repair and maintenance are greater than the funds of the owners or responsible parties. In such cases expenditure on historic properties must be seen to be economically and socially rewarding in order to ensure that the work is done.

Recent research has begun to show a growing acceptance among developers and investors that older and listed properties can perform as well as new office premises, attracting tenants and so achieving rates of rental value growth that are as good as other categories of property.[14] Restrictions and uncertainty may, however, continue to discourage long-term investment and enhancement of value.[15]

For those building types that can be satisfactorily brought back into viable commercial usage, whether in their intended role or adapted for another, their value can be readily assessed. For those building types for which conversion or reuse offer no solution it must be argued that their retention offers a valuable resource to be used in education, recreation and leisure. The future of many such buildings rests with charitable trusts, supported by public money, and reliant on the skills and energies of their advisers, local volunteer groups or individuals (Figure 3.11).

*Figure 3.11* A pair of redundant lodges (c. 1784) designed by Sir John Soane at Thurton, Norfolk. Purchased and repaired by the Norfolk Historic Buildings Trust during the 1980s. Courtesy of the Norfolk Historic Buildings Trust.

Central to any involvement with existing buildings and structures is an understanding and respect for their presence and continued survival. Inspection, assessment and reporting on the condition of the fabric will inform and influence decisions as to their future. It is therefore crucial that those undertaking such work are fully informed and competent to deal with historic properties.

*Chapter Four*

# Building
# surveys I:
# Basis of inspection

## COMMISSIONING A BUILDING SURVEY

### Surveyor selection

Before commissioning a building survey, the client must clearly define
what is required and be satisfied that the surveyor is capable of carrying
out the work competently for a reasonable fee. Clients are usually
unfamiliar with building matters, particularly where historic building
fabric is involved, and consultants are often now appointed – especially
by corporate clients – to act as an intermediary on their behalf with the
surveyor. The alternative is to require the surveyor to develop and work
to his or her own brief.

In either case it is essential that the surveyor has the appropriate
experience. A consultant who both understands the wishes of the client
and who is familiar with the locality will be able to advise on the selection
of the surveyor by reference to past performance. The uninformed client
may also use the same selection criteria, and will, in addition, be
responsible for agreeing the terms of appointment.

Both consultants and clients will find the lists of professional services
(such as the RICS accreditation scheme or *The Building Conservation
Directory*) useful, though caution should be exercised as firms' entries can
be misleading.

A carefully drafted brief, covering fully the nature and extent of the
services required, and emphasizing appropriate initial selection, will
benefit all parties. Such circumstances, however, are rarely achieved.

Fee tendering is increasingly used to achieve competitive commercial rates. Consequently fees are being cut to unrealistically low levels, and the client risks having to accept substandard work in an ever competitive market.

The services of a surveyor should be judged on quality, rather than cost alone, and in this respect 'quality-weighted' fee bidding, as put forward by the Arts Council for commissioning new work, could be adopted to take account of a surveyor's experience and track record.

Such an arrangement (also known as the 'two envelope system') has been accepted by the Construction Industry Council as a method of introducing competitive tendering for the benefit of the client.[1] Tenderers submit two envelopes, one marked 'Technical Proposals for Services in Connection with (project name)' and the other 'Fee Tender for Services in Connection with (project name)'. The client opens the technical proposals first, and ranks them in order of preference. The fee tender for the first choice is then opened, and if acceptable the commission offered to that tenderer. If not acceptable, the fee tender for the second choice is opened. Remaining fee tenders are returned unopened.

## Basis of agreement

Once the surveyor has been selected, it is important to establish the basis on which the service will be offered. This can take many forms, but should include a formal agreement of appointment, conditions of appointment or engagement, a schedule of the service(s) to be provided, and, where appropriate, a project brief.

Using standard appointment agreements and conditions of engagement (published by the various property professional bodies) ensures that both parties are aware of their duties and responsibilities. Similarly, the extent of the services offered by the surveyor may be set out in standard formats or by individual agreement; in either case the scope of the service must be unambiguously defined.

## Project brief

Where the scope of the service required is not covered by a standard form of assessment, it is necessary to agree a brief for the service with the client. The brief should be a unique document detailing the requirements of the client and the nature of the task. This may be limited to a general assessment of condition or require investigation and diagnosis of a specific defect. Advice may also be needed on subjects such as fire safety, security precautions and energy conservation.

## Contract

The relationship between surveyor and client is a contractual one in which the surveyor owes a duty of care to his client. In addition, duties of care are owed to the owner(s) of the property and to other third parties who may place direct or indirect reliance on the actions of the surveyor.[2]

The conditions or warranties of a contract define the rights and obligations of the surveyor and client, and may be expressly set by the parties or implied by the law. In order to discover the unexpressed intentions of the parties, the courts may take notice of professional standards, the conduct of the parties and the need to give business efficacy to the contract under the Supply of Goods and Services Act 1982. Exemption clauses, intended to limit or exclude the liability of one of the parties to the contract, must satisfy the common law rules of contract and the Unfair Contract Terms Act 1977.

Misrepresentations made to a client before a contract has been entered into, on which reliance is subsequently placed and loss sustained, will lead to the contract being voidable and the surveyor liable for damages.

## INSTRUCTIONS

In accepting an instruction from a client, the surveyor must establish certain basic facts before providing the service. A standard instruction sheet setting out the following essential details and conditions is helpful.

## Address and general description of the property

Where a full postal address is not available, such as with a standing ruin, clear directions and an Ordnance Survey map grid reference are essential, together with instructions for gaining access to the site. A brief description of the property will establish the likely nature and scale of the task, and ensure correct identification on arrival.

An initial reconnaissance may be prudent to locate the property and to ensure that the necessary resources are available. The client should be advised at this stage if the services of other consultants or specialists will be needed.

## Precise and firm instructions

Where an instruction comes from a consultant or informed client it should be possible to establish the precise nature of the task and the requirements of the client, either from direct discussion or a prepared brief. When dealing with uninformed clients, however, it is necessary to discuss in detail their needs, and explain and agree the scope of the service to be provided.

In all cases the surveyor should confirm the client's instructions and any subsequent variations in writing, and if aspects are unclear the inspection should be postponed until these are resolved. The client should also confirm the terms of the instruction by countersigning and returning a copy of the surveyor's letter to this effect. If the surveyor has to act before letters can be prepared, a standard draft can be read to the client for approval, and letters prepared as soon as is practicable.

## Purpose and extent of the survey

The nature and extent of a survey may be determined by a standard form of assessment (such as the RICS/ISVA *Home Buyers' Survey and Valuation*) or as a list of requirements such as provided in certain dioceses for use when undertaking quinquennial inspections. Alternatively, as with detailed inspections or surveys, the surveyor may be required to provide guidance for the client on the basis of the service being offered.

It is essential that the client is always fully aware of the proposed level of inspection, specific omissions and limitations on the scope of the service. Common areas of confusion occur over domestic services, boundaries, grounds and outbuildings.

## Fees

An estimate of the fees should be given when the instruction is received. Specific costs cannot be given until the property has been seen, but a schedule of rates may be appropriate.

## Timescale

It is important that the surveyor is aware of when the client expects to receive the findings of the survey. In certain cases the report, together with the findings of specialist(s), test results and costings, may be required by a specific date. Despite pressure from a client the surveyor should avoid giving summaries and opinions over the telephone which can sometimes become confused.

The surveyor should be aware that by giving a date for delivering the report to the client he runs the risk of this being seen as part of a contract in law.

## Specific requirements

Clients may sometimes need advice or information on particular aspects of the property, such as specific defects or the condition of service installations, and frequently, specialized advice is sought with the agreement of the client. Usually the basis of the professional indemnity insurance held by the surveyor restricts work to that for which he has appropriate qualifications and experience.

The client may require or expect the survey and report to be undertaken by a particular person, whether because of particular skills or personal preference. Their details should be given to the client as a matter of course.

Requirements may also be made on the number and distribution of survey reports and their layout.

## Matters of particular concern

Separate to, or in connection with, instructions on specific requirements are concerns of the client for which advice is being sought, such as properties listed as of special architectural or historic interest, scheduled as nationally important monuments, or located within designated conservation areas, or the implications of altering, extending or changing the use of the property. Specific requirements may, for instance, require consideration under the Building Regulations (or London Building Acts); Fire Precautions Act 1971; Offices, Shops and Railway Premises Act 1963; or Health and Safety at Work, etc. Act 1974.

## PRELIMINARIES

Once instructions have been received and confirmed it is important to collect as much information as possible before carrying out the survey.

## Date and time for survey

These are arranged to suit the vendor, client, surveyor and other parties who are either required or wish to be in attendance, and should be confirmed to all in writing. Problems of limited access and restricted visibility during bad weather should be taken into account.

## Access arrangements

Access to the site and into the property may require keys to be collected and returned, third parties to be informed, and equipment such as ladders and hoists to be provided. Site security, including disarming and re-arming alarm systems, and arrangements for keys to doors and windows, may need to be discussed.

To avoid trespassing, the surveyor must have the express or implied consent of the owner or occupier before entering the building. Once consent is given a licence is created. If such consent is given only for a certain period or relates to a particular purpose, anything done beyond this will constitute a trespass. Tortious liability will arise where there is direct injury resulting from the trespass.

Where access is required onto the land of a third party for the purposes of inspection, and for which consent cannot be gained due to absence or unreasonable obstruction, there is provision under the Access to Neighbouring Land Act 1992 for an application to be made to the court for an access order. The order should be served on anyone who has an interest in the land or buildings over which the access is to be taken. Compensation and consideration may be payable.[3]

## Reconnaissance

Where the location is unknown or the scope of the work uncertain it is prudent to visit the site before the main inspection in order to confirm access arrangements and establish the need for preliminary research and specialized advice or equipment.

## Permission to open up

Certain parts of the property may be either obscured by fixtures or fittings, or form inaccessible voids. Where the agreed scope of the service requires a full explanation of the facts, without reliance on exclusion clauses, it may be necessary to move furniture, lift carpets and floorboards, cut access ways and open up to scrutinize the construction of the property.

Such action requires the consent of the vendor or client, whether as owner or occupier, and that of any interested third parties. Arrangements for reinstatement and temporary works should be made clear in writing, including who is responsible for payment, and the implications for users of, and visitors to, the building considered. In addition, notice of the risk of damage to the fabric of the property caused by the taking of samples or drain testing should be provided to all parties.

Where the property is listed it is an offence to remove internal or external fixtures without the formal consent of the local planning authority. If in doubt it is wise to discuss the works on-site with the local conservation or planning officer before arrangements for attendance are made.

## Empty buildings

The surveyor should be aware of the particular problems with empty buildings. Aside from deliberate damage caused by acts of vandalism and arson, the theft of building materials and fittings can cause secondary problems to develop such as damp penetration and instability following removal of structural members.

Empty buildings are also subject to extremes of temperature, risking frost damage and the failure of undrained pipes or tanks.

Where a surveyor is asked to assess the condition of an empty property he should confirm with the client whether the survey report is to include comment on existing precautions and suggestions for further measures. Emergency repairs and temporary works undertaken to mothball a building are themselves subject to failure and decay, and require a different set of criteria to those for occupied premises.

It is important for the surveyor to note, and for the client to be made aware, that insurance cover under most household policies lapses after 30 days consecutive absence.

## Specialists and/or specialized equipment

Based on experience and an early reconnaissance of the property it should be possible to establish the need for third-party advice and non-standard equipment. This advice may come from specialist contractors, related professional disciplines or particular individuals, and take the form of site meetings, reports or simple confirmation of anecdotal information. In certain situations monitoring of a defect may be required, either by measurement or observation.

Where a surveyor is required to comment on aspects of a building or structure that lie outside his area of experience, he should seek such specialized advice and reach an agreement as to the responsibilities and duties of all parties concerned. The surveyor should be aware that in approaching commercial firms or organizations there is a risk that advice may be biased towards a particular product or aspects of the work may be omitted in order to keep the cost down in an attempt to secure the work.

On the other hand, surveyors should not exploit specialist craftspersons whose opinions and advice are sought, but for which no payment or credit is given.

## Local enquiries

The need for preliminary research may arise when the surveyor is working outside his usual locality or on a type of property about which he has little direct experience. Sources of such general information include a local studies library, neighbours and members of the parish or parochial church councils. Anecdotal information should always be treated with extreme care.

## Background and historical information

Where specific information is required, either to answer selected questions or to form the basis of detailed investigation, it may be necessary to consult local authority conservation, planning and building control officers; repositories of information such as museums and the county Sites and Monuments Record (SMR); or specific persons, such as the church incumbent.

The present or previous occupants of a building may be able to provide useful information, particularly concerning apparently mundane matters such as past incidences of damage or repair, the vagaries of the plumbing and drainage systems, or the occasional incidence of flooding. Current disputes, such as with boundaries or trees, may also come to light. The accuracy of such information should be checked.

Where bat roosts are suspected inside the property, confirmation with the Government's Statutory Nature Conservation Organization (SNCO) is needed for the purposes of the Wildlife and Countryside Act 1981, be it English Nature, Scottish Natural Heritage or the Countryside Council for Wales.

Historical information from the volumes of the *Victoria County History*, local trade directories, topographical studies and collections of early postcards or photographs may prove useful. Extracts from early editions of Ordnance Survey sheets or other local cartographic sources may help identify earlier features and land uses (Figure 4.1), while the *Legend* database (operated by Landmark Information Group Ltd) provides an account of land use during the last 150 years from the integration of 800,000 Ordnance Survey sheets. Other sources of information includes tithe maps, deed plans, rate books, census returns and local estate archives.

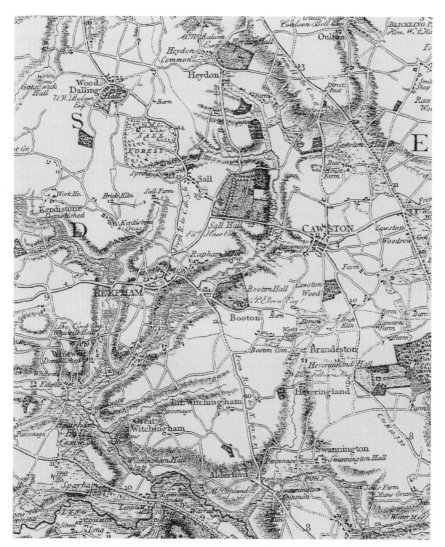

*Figure 4.1* Extract from Faden's 1797 map of Norfolk.

Similarly, aerial photographs can often help in identifying temporary uses and boundaries. A collection of early aerial photographs is housed at Cambridge University, while the Luftwaffe reconnaissance photographs of World War II, captured by the Americans, are now in the National Archive in Washington.

Material of an artistic nature should, however, be treated with caution. Paintings and engravings were often commissioned as works of art, rather than accurate records, and as such may be subject to artistic licence or flattery that can cause confusion.

Documentation of historical events, such as the postcard of the damage caused by a lightning strike to a barn in 1913 (Figure 4.2), can provide useful information to the surveyor commissioned to report on the condition of the buildings as they now appear. Local museums and antique fairs are good sources for such material.

Again, anecdotal information should also be treated with a degree of caution, and be duly investigated. It might appear from conversations with locals that, for instance, almost all medieval buildings had tunnels leading to or from the parish church, regardless of the relative periods of the properties.

Lastly, the name of the village, road, lane or property may give a clue as to the past activities of the occupants or use of the land. Names such as Brick Kiln Farm or Gaswork Hill give direct information, while others related to historic events may give indirect clues as to the date of construction, alteration or change in ownership.

## Documentation

A great deal of information may be derived from earlier inspections and reports. The local authority planning and building control officers will have records of previous submissions and proposals, and survey reports, drawings and specifications may be held either by the client or his

*Figure 4.2* Postcard showing lightning damage to barn at Grove Farm, Terrington St John, Norfolk. Courtesy of Mr and Mrs C. Cousins.

previous adviser(s). For older buildings useful documents may have found their way into local archives such as the County Record Office.

Guarantees for works such as damp-proofing, timber treatments and underpinning; maintenance and service charge agreements; lease or licence documents; maintenance and operating manuals; health and safety files prepared under Construction (Design and Management) Regulations 1994; details of covenants and easements; and recent utility service bills will all provide useful information on which to base an inspection.


BASIC EQUIPMENT

The principal tools the surveyor uses when inspecting a property are the natural senses, and for many inspections these, and professional experience, is enough. Useful qualitative judgements cannot, however, be made without comparative measurement. For this the surveyor uses the increasing number of calibrated instruments or specialized services available.

Some of the more sophisticated instruments and techniques are discussed in Chapter Five, but first it is necessary to establish the basic items of equipment the surveyor will need. These essential 'tools of the trade' have been shown in case law to be the minimum the courts expect a competent surveyor to carry, and use, when undertaking a building survey.


## Survey sheets and other forms of data capture

- Clipboards with blank sheets of paper or pre-printed pro forma sheets.
- Personal checklists (see Appendix B), or *aides-mémoire*, such as the 'pink panther' prepared by the Institute of Structural Engineers[4] or the RICS Building Conservation Group checklist for timber-framed buildings.[5]
- Standard text entries, such as the proposed RICS Home Buyers' Survey and Valuation (HBSV) *Report Writer Manual*,[6] made up of a site form and a set of model paragraphs.
- Annotated drawings showing doors, windows, fireplaces and chimney stacks.
- Enlarged photocopies of recent photographs can also be used as the basis for site notes. Certain photocopiers can produce an image to an approximate scale based on simple site control measurements. A further refinement is to produce a rectified photograph for direct or screened printing from which dimensional information of an often acceptable accuracy can be abstracted.[7]
- Stone-by-stone drawings where accurate identification is needed (Figure 4.3). Stereo photogrammetry or computer-aided mono-photogrammetry

*Figure 4.3* Stone-by-stone drawing of principal façade to Bagshaw Hall in Bakewell, Derbyshire (dated 1684), prepared using computer-aided mono-photogrammetry. Drawing by David Watt, courtesy of Oulsnam Design Associates.

may be employed to produce such drawings, but such techniques are relatively expensive.[8]

- Hand-held data loggers with a series of prompts and menus of standard responses.[9] The surveyor is able to input information about a property on-site and download this into the office computer system for analysis and presentation either on returning or via a telephone modem link.
- Specific forms for use with optical mark readers.

## Dictaphone

Surveyors may find that dictaphones are more convenient to use on-site than making handwritten notes, although high levels of background noise may prove problematic.

## Photography

Photography is an important tool in recording the condition of the fabric, whether to illustrate a later report or form a record at a particular point in time.

Video coverage, and the availability of video-still cameras for direct or delayed transmission of a digital image to a printer, may be useful tools in certain instances.

## Moisture meters

The increased need for comparative measurement when considering levels of free moisture in materials and elements of construction has forced the use of moisture meters as standard tools.

When using a moisture meter it is important to know that most instruments are calibrated to give percentage readings of free moisture in timber only, and for other materials readings are given as percentage wood moisture equivalent. Different timber species, particularly between hard and soft woods, may also give different readings, and calibration tables are provided by some manufacturers for this reason.

False readings can occur when the probes come into contact with hygroscopic salts, aluminium foil used as a vapour barrier, foil-backed plasterboard or carbon in certain types of breeze-block or black wallpapers.

## Additional equipment

A powerful armoured torch; a lamp secured to a headband; various screwdrivers; claw hammer and bolster for lifting floorboards; a knife or other tool for probing; manhole cover lifting keys; spirit level; plumb bob and line; measuring rules, tapes and rods; hand mirror; a pair of binoculars; magnetic compass; a sectional or articulated ladder; and containers for samples.

A complete first-aid kit should always be carried for self-treatment or to assist others.

## PERSONAL SAFETY AND COMFORT

Assessing the condition of a property that is derelict, unoccupied, or in use for hazardous or disagreeable purposes can pose particular problems, but often no less real danger can arise when inspecting a typical building in use (Appendix C).

It is essential that surveyors, and others, working in conditions where they are exposed to irritants and toxins, such as chemical treatments, asbestos and other fibrous materials, should be informed and adequate training given to minimize the level of risk.

Standard equipment to ensure safety and comfort during inspections should include overalls, gloves, face masks, safety helmets, ear protection, safety goggles, shoes with strengthened toecaps, waterproof and warm clothing, soap, towel and bottled water (if mains supply cannot be relied upon). Food and drink may be necessary.

Mobile telephones and two-way radios are important in certain remote situations, but a preliminary check should be made on the working range, levels of interference and power supply.

Additional lighting may be required when inspecting unoccupied properties or areas such as roof spaces and cellars, and in certain circumstances background heating may be necessary. In all cases electrical equipment should be protected by appropriate circuit breakers (30 mA or less) and be connected using correctly-fused plugs, sockets and extension leads.

The surveyor should be aware of the hazards that might be found when inspecting a property, and a preliminary reconnaissance with another surveyor or the client should alert him to such situations. Decay and deterioration of floorboards, joists, ceilings, stairways, balustrading and guarding, windows and doors should be investigated, and a check made for protruding nails, spikes and wires, and broken glass. Prolonged access within a roof space, or in areas where floorboarding has been removed, may necessitate the use of crawler boards to ensure safety and reduce the risk of damage to ceilings.

An assessment of the risk from falling masonry and roof coverings may prohibit direct inspection or necessitate temporary works. Access to specific areas or whole floors may have to be prohibited, and notice to this effect secured to the property and issued to the local authority, owner and users of the building.

The dangers associated with vermin (including Weil's disease or Leptospirosis), wasps and bees should be considered, as well as the possibility of respiratory problems caused by dead pigeons. Appropriate protective clothing should be worn and inoculation against tetanus considered.

Unlawful users of a derelict or otherwise unoccupied property can pose a risk through direct assault, acts of vandalism and arson. The contraction of Hepatitis B or C, Human Immunodeficiency Viruses (HIV) and other communicable diseases from discarded bottles, needles and faeces is also possible. Lice and fleas can be expected in certain situations.

In carrying out inspections of certain properties it is often desirable to be accompanied by a colleague or trusted individual. In this respect greater care must be given to safeguarding female surveyors in their work.

Where the surveyor has not been adequately warned of defects or hazards present within the building to be surveyed, the owner, occupier or other party may be liable for any injury suffered by the surveyor in carrying out his work through the common law duty of care defined in the Defective Premises Act 1972 and the Occupier's Liability Acts 1957 and 1984.

# Chapter Five

# Building surveys II: The inspection

During the inspection phase of a building survey observations are made and samples may be taken for analysis. From these data inferences may be drawn, defects diagnosed and conclusions reached. It is an intensive and time-consuming activity that requires keen senses, patience and sound common sense as well as a working knowledge of the building type and its construction.

## SAFETY

The first responsibility of the surveyor is to make sure that colleagues know where the property is and are given estimated times of arrival and return to the office. Female surveyors should not be expected to meet with strangers on-site unless accompanied by a colleague.

If working alone or outside the usual locality, especially if the property is in a remote area, it is suggested that those involved with access arrangements should be similarly informed. A simple notice left on display in the surveyor's vehicle should allow contact to be made in the case of an emergency. Total reliance on mobile telephones or two-way radios is not recommended.

## ESTABLISHING A BASE

Once inside the property the surveyor should establish a secure base from which to work, where equipment can be stored. The base should preferably be close to toilet and messing facilities, and provide access to power and lighting. In occupied properties a spare bedroom or other little-used space will suffice.

## ORDER OF INSPECTION

Whether a complete building is being inspected or the survey is restricted to a particular element of construction or defect, it will be useful to work in a logical order, whether from 'the top to the bottom' or 'the whole to the part'.

A number of the standard building survey formats referred to in Chapter Two suggest that an inspection is undertaken in a sequence from the roof to the ground, externally and then internally. This enables the earlier observation of roof covering or external wall surfaces to inform the later internal inspection.

Some practical points to note: the sequence of the inspection must take into account the movements of the occupants and the weather conditions; time spent in the roof space at the start of the inspection is likely to deter all but the most inquisitive of occupants; an early start will prove to be cooler than having to work under a roof covering at midday; inspecting the site and drains at the end of the day will avoid the problem of having to wash and change before entering a potentially spotless interior.

A suggested order for an inspection is laid out below, although it should be noted that with historic properties, where each building is potentially different, this is only an indication of the scope of the inspection and not a definitive checklist.

**Reconnaissance**
- personal introductions
- locked doors and security alarms
- familiarization with building layout
- dead areas (e.g. ducts, flues)
- items to be moved
- information from occupants
- manner of occupation
- internal and external hazards

**Exterior**
- roof covering
- parapet walls
- roofscape features (e.g. cupolas, dormers, balustrading)
- chimney stacks
- flashings and weatherings
- plant rooms and external service installations
- gutters and rainwater pipes
- foundations
- main walls
- structural frames
- balconies
- external escape stairways
- damp-proof courses
- subfloor ventilation
- doors and windows
- foundations

**Interior**
- roof structure and void
- ceilings
- walls and partitions

- beams and columns
- floors
- cellars and vaults
- doors and windows
- stairways
- internal joinery
- finishes and decorations
- fixtures and fittings

**Building services**
- water supply
- foul-water disposal (e.g. septic tanks, cesspits)
- rainwater disposal (e.g. soakaways)
- utility services
- service fittings (e.g. sanitary fittings)
- heating installations (e.g. fuel storage tanks)
- mechanical services
- telecommunications, computer networks and data links

- cable and satellite television
- fire protection systems
- security systems
- lightning protection

**Site and environment**
- aspect
- prospect
- access and circulation (e.g. drives, paths, steps)
- flora and fauna
- water courses
- boundaries (e.g. walls, hedges, fences, ditches)
- retaining walls
- hard and soft landscaping
- garden buildings and structures
- statuary and ornamentation
- security

In archaeology the sum of the parts, however humble, is deemed as important as any one individual part. This theory of the disassembled site can be usefully employed in surveying buildings to ensure that relationships and interrelationships are acknowledged and understood, both in terms of the construction itself and any failures that have occurred.

SITE RECORDS

The surveyor should decide how descriptions and statements of fact are to be recorded, though routines may need to be revised in response to specific site conditions. For example, the use of a dictaphone may have to be suspended in noisy areas or where confidentiality needs to be maintained.

Written records may take the form of site notes prepared for later reference or complete text forming the basis for a first draft of the report. This latter technique, or the direct reproduction from audio tapes, should not, however, be used without the opportunity to reflect upon or modify the report.

Annotated drawings are particularly helpful, especially in connection with the diagnosis of defects. By recording observations and survey data onto plans, sections and elevations, and relating them to the construction of the building, the surveyor is able to consider the problems in three dimensions, relating the presence of internal symptoms to external defects, and vice versa.

Making site sketches can also help in the understanding of structural behaviour and associated defects. Sections and metric projections can be used to record load paths, faults and deformations and assist a basic appraisal (Figure 5.1).

Once the report has been prepared it is important to retain the original site records on file, whether they be written notes, completed text, dictaphone drafts or drawings. Such information may be relevant with later commissions, but more importantly can be used as evidence of site observations in the case of litigation.


## OBSERVATION

Looking, touching, smelling, listening are all used in attempting to understand the relative or absolute condition of an element or component of construction. Responses to these will be governed both by personal experience and knowledge of the building so far gained.

The responses that might apply to the examination of a particular element or component would, to a degree, be based on the assessment criteria established for the particular building or type of property (see Chapter Six). In assessing a window, for example, the following questions might be asked:

**Performance against agreed or accepted standards**
- Does the casement or sash open and close properly?
- Does the latch operate?
- Are there security locks fitted?
- Is there double or secondary glazing fitted?
- Does the window conform to current fire regulations?
- Are ultraviolet filters fitted?
- Does the glass have solar control or low emissivity coatings?
- Does the glass have safety or security films?
- Is the glass toughened, laminated or wired?
- Do shutters open and close properly?
- Are there curtains or blinds for privacy?
- Are security bars fitted to the window opening?
- Are mothballing or boarding-up measures adequate?
- Is the window draughty?
- Does the opening light(s) admit sufficient air?
- Does the window admit sufficient light?
- Are acoustic measures satisfactory or required?
- Can the window be safely cleaned, internally and externally?

**Levels of decay, deterioration or disrepair**
- Is there any broken or cracked glass?
- Are the window fittings complete and in working order?
- Is the window wind and watertight?
- Is there any evidence for fungal attack?
- Is there evidence for beetle infestation?
- Is there evidence for physical damage?
- Are the putties or beads satisfactory?
- Are traditional repair techniques appropriate?

**Social values**
- Is the appearance of the window fashionable?

- Does the window conform to current ideals?
- Is the building listed or does it lie within a conservation area?
- Is the glass clean or dirty?
- Does the window display stickers or notices?

**Economic considerations**
- Will the window perform to current and future expectations?
- Is it cheaper to keep or replace the window?

- Are traditional repair techniques cost-effective?

**Aesthetic judgements**
- Is the window contemporary with the property?
- Does the window indicate a later building phase or alteration?
- Is the glass of a historical pattern or type?
- Does the window blend with the present appearance of the building?

The basis of an overall assessment and appraisal of an element or component is usually reached by observation against a set of established criteria and by gauging levels of condition in relation to the age and type of property. Where positive evidence is not available, the suspected condition can often be inferred from what facts and reliable evidence are known.

When dealing with a building type for which set criteria would be inappropriate the surveyor must establish a suitable order of inspection and level of response. Criteria for assessing the condition of industrial monuments and standing ruins are provided in Chapters Fifteen and Sixteen respectively.

## DEFECT DIAGNOSIS

The diagnosis of defects may either be the main purpose for undertaking the survey or form only part of a building survey. In both cases it is crucial that the surveyor is in possession of all material facts and is able to make a full inspection of the property in order to pose and answer questions.

### Diagnosis and prognosis

In order for building defects to be correctly identified two factors are essential: good observation to discover symptoms and establish the nature of the construction; and a thorough understanding of the mechanisms of decay, damage and deterioration. Once a defect has been detected, further investigation may be necessary before final diagnosis is reached. At each stage during an inspection the surveyor should be mindful that the absence of evidence is not evidence of absence.

Where evidence of a potential defect is available to a surveyor by

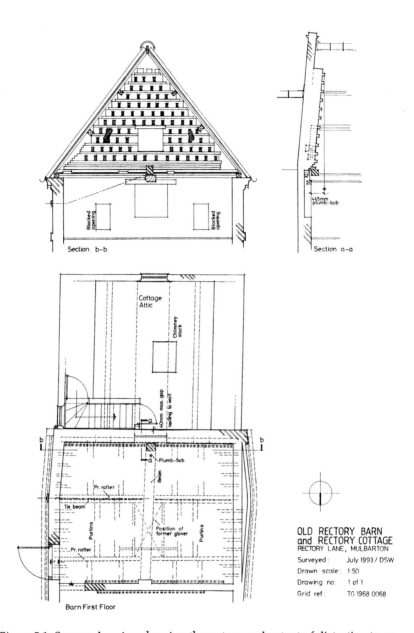

*Figure 5.1* Survey drawing showing the nature and extent of distortion to an early 18th-century barn. The additional, eccentric loading from the inserted nesting boxes had caused the gable wall to pivot about an embedded timber member (section a–a), while movement in the flank wall had caused separation of the brick facing to the west.

way of symptom or assumption, the probability of the defect being actually present must be assessed by considering all available information. The time spent in raising this probability, often through a process of elimination, will be reflected in time, resources and cost, and should be carefully considered with regard to the purpose of the survey and agreed brief.

*Figure 5.2* Localized settlement is obvious, but when it did take place, is it progressive and how has it affected the performance of other parts of the building? The bottom rail of the later first-floor window had been cut to accept the angle of the cill.

The surveyor may find that many initial concerns are unfounded, as when a number of symptoms are traced back to a single cause. Attention must, however, be given to all indications, as the sum of these may well prove to be of more importance than the single obvious defect. In this respect, the inspection of previous works of maintenance and repair, as a potential source of problems, is often overlooked.

During diagnosis the surveyor should be able to refer to a mental or actual 'library' of good and bad construction, and related defects, drawn from previous dealings with similar properties, on which to base comparisons and opinions. Knowledge gained about historic buildings solely from books is not sufficient.

Diagnosis of a defect on its own is informative, but not particularly useful unless accompanied by a prognosis or forecast of how the problem will develop.

The skills of diagnosis and prognosis required when dealing with historic property are in no way different to those relating to more modern buildings. What sets older buildings apart, however, is that each is different, there is little or no standardization, and an understanding can only come from experience.

Advice for the surveyor faced with an unusual problem or particular set of circumstances can come from many sources. County or district conservation officers will have knowledge of local materials and traditional forms of construction, and should be able to direct the surveyor to similar properties or comparable sites.

Nationally, many of the amenity societies are able to give advice or suggest suitable contacts. The Society for the Protection of Ancient Buildings, in particular, can offer specialized advice to its members and public alike. Advice to the public is also available from local authority conservation officers, and Upkeep (formerly the Building Conservation Trust).

The Building Research Establishment (BRE) has undertaken extensive research into the causes and effects of defects in historic buildings. The Heritage Support Service offers advice and a consultancy service to building owners and professional advisers on a wide range of matters, including materials technology, timber conservation, fire protection, structural and geotechnical monitoring, and security.

## Mechanisms of failure and decay

The most common defects affecting traditionally constructed buildings are those resulting from excess moisture, fungal attack, beetle infestation and structural failure. Inappropriate intervention and poor site practices may cause or contribute to current problems, and the way in which the building is used or managed will also affect its performance. These mechanisms of failure and decay are:

**Excess moisture**
- rising damp
- penetrating damp
- condensation
- leakage
- spillage

**Fungal attack**
- dry rot
- wet rots
- moulds

**Beetle infestation**
- Common furniture beetle
- Death watch beetle
- Lyctus powderpost beetle
- House longhorn beetle

**Structural failure**
- loss of strength through material decay
- loss of stability caused by excess loading
- failure of framing members or joints and loss of rigidity
- changes to load paths and loss of equilibrium
- inadequate bracing and stiffness
- inadequate robustness for purpose

**Inappropriate intervention**
- incompatible materials
- alterations and adaptations
- poor material selection

- changes or intensification of use
- changes in environmental conditions

**Poor site practice**
- inadequate supervision
- inadequate preparation
- inadequate protection against sun and rain
- failure to understand and appreciate traditional building materials and their limitations
- failure to understand and appreciate traditional building practices
- failure to understand basic structural principles
- failure to understand purpose of design decisions
- poor site storage facilities
- inappropriate material storage and handling
- failure in communications between adviser, contractor and subcontractor

**Performance in use**
- lack of maintenance
- lack of repair
- changes of use
- abuse
- inappropriate interventions
- old age
- obsolescence

## NON-DESTRUCTIVE SURVEYING

When a building is inspected visually, less than ten per cent of the fabric may be available for direct observation and assessment, the rest being hidden below ground, lying within the construction or is covered by finishes and decorations. In certain cases, however, it is necessary to investigate beneath the surface in order to understand the construction and identify actual or potential defects.

Aside from physically opening up the structure, it is possible to employ non-destructive techniques to provide a level of information, which is based either on direct penetration into the fabric or indirect/remote imaging techniques. These techniques, it should be noted, are used to aid diagnosis of a defect, not to locate it in the first place.

The term non-destructive surveying or testing covers a collection of techniques that may be used to inspect or observe materials or elements of construction in place without causing alteration, damage or destruction to the fabric of the building. Each technique is able to provide a specific set of measurements or data in response to known or suspected conditions. This may be for the analysis of material properties, detection of hidden aspects of construction or subsurface anomalies, or the evaluation of performance in use.

Each technique must be selected appropriately and their application, and most importantly the interpretation of the results, is usually best left to specialist firms, although equipment lease or hire is possible for certain types of inspection.

The most common forms of non-destructive survey, together with their usual applications, are briefly described below. Further information, including lists of equipment suppliers, are given by Fidler[1] and Hollis.[2]

## Radiography

Penetrating X-rays or gamma rays are used to see inside a wide range of materials and elements of construction to detect discontinuities, cracks, voids, density variations, hidden details, foreign objects or changes caused by deterioration. Materials such as plaster and wood are easily penetrated to show embedded fixings and structural members, but with denser materials, such as masonry and concrete, a more powerful radiation source is usually required.

## Thermography

The measurement of infrared energy, in the form of waves radiated from the surface of building elements, is commonly used to detect and quantify heat losses and temperature variations through roofs and walls. It can also be used to detect subsurface details, such as the presence of embedded timber-frame members, voids, inconsistencies, and deterioration in timber members.

## Infrared photography

Based on the same technology as thermography, photography using infrared film, together with appropriate filters, can indicate subtle variations in surface colour that might result from an increased moisture content or subsurface deterioration.

## Ultrasonic testing

High-frequency sound waves directed through, or into a material, can be used to detect and locate hidden details, voids, faults, cracks and cavities, and measure thickness and density. This technique is particularly useful in dealing with homogeneous materials, such as ceramics, metals and masonry, rather than with less uniform forms of construction.

## Microwave analysis

The strength and direction of projected energy that is reflected back from surfaces and changes within a material can record inconsistencies, discontinuities, faults and hidden details. This technique has been used successfully on mass constructions, such as ramparts and redoubts found in military architecture.

## Magnetometer

The measurement of an induced magnetic field can, through distribution patterns, identify and locate magnetic features buried within non-magnetic materials such as wood, concrete, brick and stone. Cover meters are commonly used to locate and identify reinforcement within concrete constructions, but can also be used to detect metal cramps, armatures and fixings within masonry or timber, and buried pipes, conduits, flues and ducts. Certain non-magnetic materials and subsurface anomalies can also be detected due to changes in magnetic fields induced by stimuli such as heat. Simple metal detectors are also widely available for use in the home to locate hidden cables, pipes and fixings.

## Fibre-optic surveying

Direct penetration into cavities or voids within the fabric of a building using a fibre-optic probe can provide useful information on aspects of construction, or the condition of specific elements or components. The probes may be either endoscopes, which are flexible tubes filled with bundles of optical fibres that can illuminate and view remote objects, or boroscopes, which are rigid tubes, again with fibre bundles, that deliver illumination to the subject and carry the image back to the eyepiece. Both systems can be used to inspect and photograph hidden or obstructed details through existing cracks or openings, or small drilled holes.

## 'Rothounds'

The detection, and subsequent monitoring, of dry rot (*Serpula lacrymans*) has, in the past, been undertaken by periodic opening up and direct inspection of suspect timbers. Recently, a new approach has been developed by Hutton + Rostron Environmental Investigations Limited that relies upon indirect detection without the need for costly physical intervention. Trained dogs, or 'rothounds', are able to detect the scent of the metabolites produced by living dry rot, thus discriminating between living and dead outbreaks, and indicating the extent of an infestation.

## Geotechnical surveying

The term geotechnics describes an array of techniques and procedures used in investigating ground conditions, either in response to a defect or in advance of new development. These include destructive techniques such as sampling and testing using trial pits and boreholes, penetration testing, plate testing, as well as site and laboratory testing and monitoring of soils, rocks and contaminated landfill. Non-destructive techniques are also used, such as impulse radar for detecting cavities and obstructions below ground level.

## Geophysical surveying

Archaeological prospection using non-destructive geophysical techniques can be used to detect subsurface features that may have an importance in understanding a building or relevance to any planned works.

Resistivity surveying is based on the resistance of an electric current passing through the ground relative to its moisture content. Subsurface variations in this resistance can be interpreted to indicate features such as ditches, walls and built-up surfaces.

Magnetic surveying, or magnetometry, is used to detect changes in the magnetized iron oxides in the earth caused by the fires and cultivation associated with occupation of a site. Magnetic anomalies can assist in the identification of industrial sites, hearths, kilns and filled pits.

Ground-penetrating radar is also being used to detect subsurface features, often at depths of several metres, and is likely to become a more familiar technique as interpretation improves.

Detection of subsurface features can also come from direct probing, percussion variations known as bosing, by using metal detectors and dowsing.

## Remote sensing

Remote sensing is the general name given to the acquisition and use of data about the earth from sources such as aircraft, balloons, rockets and satellites.

Many of the techniques used in this field are applicable to the non-destructive surveying of buildings, and indeed a number of photographic techniques have been employed in ground-based remote sensing to identify and record surface and subsurface anomalies. The work of Dr Chris Brooke, Principal Historic Buildings Officer with Leicestershire County Council, in this field is of particular note.[3]

## Dowsing

Dowsing can be used to discover buried features as well as its more common role in discovering underground water.

## Full-scale load testing

Applying load to an individual member or assembly allows its behaviour to be assessed. The technique is useful in assessing damage following a fire or explosion, or establishing the efficacy of a repair. With this technique it is important to consider carefully the safety of the personnel undertaking the tests and the effects the tests might have on the building.

## Close-circuit television surveying

Remote CCTV or video inspection and tracking of drain runs, flues, ducts and other concealed voids can provide direct information on condition, blockages and defects, and allow record drawings to be prepared for later use.

## Sampling

Small samples of materials, or foreign matter, removed from site for laboratory analysis and testing, should be taken and stored in such a way as to avoid contamination from other samples or its surroundings. Drill sampling should, for instance, be carried out using cleaned or new bits for each sample. Containers should be chosen to avoid contamination, with liquid samples stored in screw-top glass jars.

The minimum size of sample taken for off-site testing should be 20 grammes for mortar analysis and 10 grammes for carbide moisture measurement. Duplicate sampling may be appropriate if the material can be easily spoilt, and is of particular importance if part is to be retained as a reference.

Detailed notes and sketches should be made on-site to indicate the position where each sample has been taken – including drill-bit depths, height above floor, proximity of differing materials or possible contaminants, present and past uses of the building – and the samples themselves should be clearly identified.

## MONITORING DEFECTS

Most defects are progressive in nature and as such can be monitored over a period of time. In order to provide evidence as to the nature and timing of the defect, monitoring usually includes a level of absolute or relative measurement.

Early techniques of monitoring were simple, limited by the available resources and relatively undemanding user requirements. Increased sophistication has stemmed, in part, from a growing need to understand the underlying cause of a building defect rather than just the effects it will have on the fabric.

The holistic approach to defect diagnosis, and the wider study of total building performance, has arisen in part as a response to an increase in concern for the quality of the environment in which we live and work. This approach has prompted the adoption of techniques and working practices from other disciplines as diverse as archaeology, medicine and remote sensing.

In addition to monitoring current defects, it is important to appreciate the opportunities for comparing present defects with the state of the property in the past. In this respect the use of earlier photographs and other visual material may assist in confirming and quantifying levels of decay, deterioration or disrepair. Evidence provided by photographs taken in the 1940s, for instance, indicated that the leaning angle of the medieval wayside cross at Northwold (Figure 5.3) had not become appreciably worse. Simple remedial works proceeded in favour of the mini-piling and partial dismantling that had been suggested on the basis of earlier anecdotal expressions of concern.

How monitoring is performed depends on the difficulties of access, the overall condition of the fabric, the need to obtain a standard and continual sequence of information, and available finance. Accuracy will typically increase with complexity and cost. The reasons for monitoring must also be considered, whether it be to record progressive conditions, or detect certain changes or conditions before damage is sustained.

## MONITORING STRUCTURAL MOVEMENT

Monitoring of structural movement can take many forms, depending on the underlying cause and how it has manifested itself in the fabric of the

*Figure 5.3*  Archive photograph of Northwold Cross, Norfolk (c. 1947).
© RCHME Crown copyright.

building. BRE Digest 343[4] considers the measurement and monitoring of cracks in low-rise buildings; Digest 344[5] settlement, heave and out-of-plumb distortion, and Digest 386[6] building and ground movement by precise levelling.

## Cracking

Cracking in masonry was, and no doubt still is, monitored either by forming a mortar dab or securing a piece of glass across the crack; a break denoting continuing movement. This technique does not provide evidence for the direction and magnitude of the movement, nor whether it is related to the time of the day, season or weather conditions.

In order to obtain a more accurate measurement of in-plane deformation, together with an awareness of how it responds to variable conditions and external factors, one of a number of different approaches should be adopted.

### Crack width gauges and rules

For basic internal monitoring it is possible to use a graduated plastic gauge or rule with discrete marks on the wall surface to either side of a crack.

### Calibrated tell-tales

Tell-tales, such as those produced by Avongard™, usually take the form of two thin graduated plastic sections secured to either side of a crack, one on top of the other. The upper section moves relative to the lower one, and the movement measured by reference to a crosshair on the upper section in relation to a gridded origin on the section below.

Different models are available to allow measurement of movement across single-plane, two-plane or stepped cracks, and external and internal angles.

In all cases it is important to secure the tell-tales to a suitable stable surface, and in a location that is free from extremes of temperature, unwanted tampering, and yet is accessible for regular inspection.

Such tell-tales rely to a large extent on being securely and accurately placed using either mechanical fixings or adhesive. This, together with their vulnerability to damage and vandalism, limits their suitability to only carefully chosen locations.

### Demountable strain gauges

In order to increase the accuracy and reduce the risk of unwanted disturbance, metal discs or studs may be fixed to either side of a crack and measurements made between these using a mechanical strain or Demec™ gauge. By using three locating points to a crack, two to one side and one to the other forming a right angle, it is possible to measure movement in both axes.

## Vernier gauges

An accurate, but less costly, technique of measuring movement is to use a digital vernier gauge or calliper in conjunction with screws or studs in a similar manner as noted for the strain gauge above.

## Data loggers

The increase in computer processing power has opened up the possibility of monitoring movement by the use of site-located or remote data loggers that pick up signals from sensors, such as linear variable differential transducers (LVDT), positioned across the crack. Digital information is converted for analysis and increasing use is now being made of computer enhancement and visualization.

The cost of such an approach is high, but for long-term monitoring of inaccessible fabric there is little else that will provide a ready supply of information in a form that, for complex structures, will allow for easy usage.

## Stereo photogrammetry

It is possible to make use of the high dimensional accuracy of stereo-photogrammetry to give a graphical record of a section of fabric, and so relate the digital information derived at intervals over time in order to establish the direction and magnitude of movement.

The dimensional recording of crack propagation by such means has been explained in detail by Uren et al.[7, 8]

## Horizontal planes

Deflection of a structural member implies either a flexing under increased load or movement as a result of material deterioration. It is important in both cases to establish whether loadings have been altered, as for example, with changes of use, intensity of occupation or furniture re-distribution.

*Levelling*

Deflection in the horizontal plane, such as with a floor, can be monitored by taking spot levels related to an Ordnance Survey benchmark (OSBM) or a carefully chosen temporary benchmark (TBM) on-site. Levels should be taken at regular recorded positions in each room or space in order to allow for later comparison. Presentation of this information can be by drawn section using an exaggerated Y-axis scale or histogram.

Where a building exhibits a tilt this can be quantified using basic levelling techniques. For more accurate assessments of settlement and verticality precise levelling using an Invar staff or a rotating laser may be employed.

*Inclinometers*

Measurement of the amount to which a horizontal, or vertical, member is out of line can be made using a specialized instrument based on a micrometer and level bubble.[9]

*Level gauges*

For long-term monitoring, particularly of parts of a building difficult to reach, electro-level gauges can be employed to give data over a period of time. This technique is in use by the Building Research Establishment for monitoring the leaning tower in Pisa, Italy.

## Vertical planes

*Plumb-bobs*

Out-of-plumb measurements can readily be made by suspending a weighted line from the top of a wall and measuring the gap between the plumb-bob and the wall surface or datum at a lower level. Exposed and windy conditions, as often experienced close to the corners of buildings, can cause problems, but a heavier weight, finer line or bucket of water in which to suspend the plumb bob may help to reduce such oscillations.

An alternative to a plumb-bob and string is to use a 1200 mm bricklayer's spirit level with a reliable straight edge that can be placed against the wall and plumbed in using the appropriate vial. This method is, however, limited by the length of the straight edge that is available on-site.

*Plumbed offsets*

Vertical-plane deflection requires measurements to be taken at intervals in the full height of the member relative to a vertical datum. This usually takes the form of measured offsets related to a graduated plumb line, but this requires access to the full height of the fabric, both to set up the line and measure the offsets at regular intervals.

It is possible, instead, to use a remote device to raise a weighted line up the wall in a series of regular lifts, and at a known distance from the surface of the wall. The distance from the line to the base of the wall or other datum will allow the profile of the wall to be recorded and plotted.

## Optical plummets

For greater accuracy optical instrumentation, such as an Autoplumb™, may be used in conjunction with a suitable target(s) secured to the wall to measure the amount to which it is out of plumb.

## Three-dimensional distortion

Distorted or bulging masonry is essentially a three-dimensional problem that requires techniques of monitoring in both the horizontal and vertical planes. Internally, it is often possible to record movement using the techniques noted above, but such an approach depends on gaining unobstructed access to the spaces in which to operate. For this reason it is often more appropriate to consider external monitoring.

### Theodolite intersection

Survey markers, or identified features of the construction, located around the area of distortion, are used in conjunction with a theodolite to record at regular intervals the horizontal and vertical angles from two related survey stations. The intersection of these readings places the points in three-dimensional space, from which movement can be readily quantified.

This technique obviously benefits from the use of an electronic theodolite, that is one which can digitally record data for storage on a field computer for later CAD restitution and plotting. It is nevertheless possible to use an optical theodolite with manual plotting to record similar information.

The use of a total-station theodolite, which combines electro-magnetic distance measurement (EDM) with conventional angular measurement, will allow more accurate monitoring, but at present typically requires the positioning of reflective targets on the face of the building.

For regular monitoring over time it is important to establish survey stations that are dimensionally stable and free from obstruction. Monitoring of movement in the thirty-metre high crooked spire of St Mary and

All Saints' Church in Chesterfield has been undertaken by means of theodolite intersection since 1973 (Figure 5.4).

Survey stations located in the churchyard relate the degree of annual movement to a stable internal control point set up at floor level beneath the tower. The survey work takes place early in the year while sight lines

*Figure 5.4* Crooked spire of St Mary and All Saints' Church in Chesterfield, Derbyshire.

are unobscured by trees in leaf and during stable weather conditions. Measurements taken to the top of the spire in October 1973 showed a distortion of 2.612 m to the south and 1.135 m to the west with reference to the centre point of an assumed symmetrical spire. By December 1980 this had increased by a further 22 mm to the south, but with a 5 mm move to the east. In October 1993 distortion had increased in relation to the 1973 figures by 25 mm to the south and 5 mm to the west.[10]

Movement in the Round Tower at Windsor Castle has, similarly, been monitored using theodolite intersection on to survey markers from three stations on other towers, fixing points in three-dimensional space with an accuracy of ±2 mm. Monitoring was initiated once slippage of the tower on its man-made mound had been noted, and importantly continued during excavation and underpinning, and later to assess the performance of the repairs. Only by such long-term monitoring can an understanding of the dynamics of the structure be gained.

## Basic calculation

Where a wall or part of a structure is considered unstable it is possible to prepare simple calculations to determine the risk of distortion or failure. These can only give a basic prognosis, and advice should usually be sought from a structural engineer experienced in working with historic structures.

### Slenderness ratio

In order for a wall to avoid failure by crushing or buckling it must be built of sufficiently strong materials, and be of adequate thickness and stiffness. The relationship between thickness and height, or the slenderness ratio, provides a means of identifying likely excesses with regard to current approved practice[11] (Figure 5.5).

Slenderness ratio = effective height/effective thickness

As stiffness can be increased by providing lateral restraint to a wall by means of floor and roof bearings, the effective height is that determined by the effectiveness of the connections.

For walls taking the bearings of floors or roofs the effective height may be taken as three-quarters of the clear distance between lateral supports that provide enhanced resistance to lateral movement, or the clear span between lateral supports that provide simple resistance to lateral movement. Where there is no such restraint the effective height is increased to that of one and a half times the actual height. Eccentricity of load will also need to be taken into account.

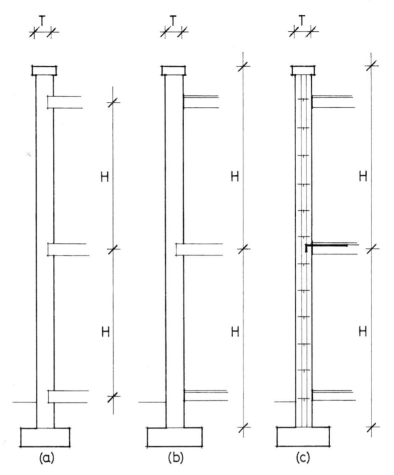

*Figure 5.5* Practical implications of slenderness ratio. In (a) the effective height for both floors is taken as ¾ × H, and the effective thickness as 1 × T. In (b) the effective height for the ground floor is ¾ × H and for the first floor is 1½ × H. The effective thickness is 1 × T. In (c) the effective height for the ground floor is ¾ × H and for the first floor is 1½ × H. The effective thickness is ⅔ × the combined thickness of the two leaves.

The effective thickness of a solid wall is taken as its full thickness. For an adequately tied cavity wall the effective thickness is two-thirds of the combined thicknesses of the two leaves. For walls stiffened by piers stiffness co-efficients are applied.

The maximum slenderness ratio for unreinforced masonry is set by British Standard 5628 as 27, except for walls less than 90 mm thick in buildings of more than two storeys. An earlier Code of Practice[12] was more specific, giving maximum ratios of 13 for buildings of more than two storeys and 20 for buildings of not more than two storeys, built of unreinforced brickwork set in hydraulic lime mortar; and 27 for buildings constructed of brickwork set in other than hydraulic lime mortar, except for those of more than two storeys with walls less than 90 mm thick where the ratio should not exceed 20.

## Middle third rule

When an unrestrained wall moves out of vertical alignment, compressive and tensile forces will develop in the fabric at its base or at the point from which the movement has taken place. While these forces are less than the ultimate strength of the materials, the wall will remain standing; further movement will cause instability.

As a guide to this degree of stability a section should be drawn through the leaning wall, with a line running vertically down from its centre of gravity. The base of the wall should be divided into equal thirds. Where the resultant line passes through the middle third the wall can be considered to be stable. Where it passes outside of the middle third the stability of the wall must be brought into question (Figure 5.6).

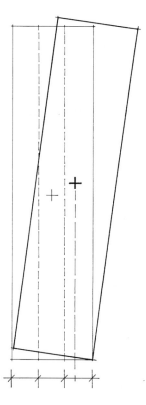

*Figure 5.6* Practical implications of middle third rule. In this freestanding wall with no lateral restraint the centre of gravity has moved outside the middle third, and is thus considered unstable.

A similar guide to assessing the stability of a bulging wall is to measure the extent of the bulge in relation to the thickness of the wall. Where the bulge exceeds one-third of the thickness, further, more detailed, examination is required.


## MONITORING MATERIAL DEGRADATION

The degradation and deterioration of building materials through various agencies and mechanisms can be complex. A detailed understanding of how materials respond to their environment and to each other is required in order that appropriate solutions may be specified and implemented. Monitoring of the degradation and the performance of remedial treatments is essential.

Basic tests can be carried out by the surveyor using equipment available either for hire or purchase. Many such tests are, however, applicable only to more modern materials, such as concrete and steel, and require an understanding of the underlying science. Where required, the surveyor is advised to consult a suitable laboratory for tests on material composition and decay.

The Building Research Establishment has conducted such work into various subjects relevant to historic fabric, including the decay phenomena of natural stones, the effects of acid deposition and particulate matter on building materials, footwear on historic surfaces, the durability of stones and mortars, and the behaviour of structures and materials in fire.


## MONITORING ENVIRONMENTAL CONDITIONS

The three environmental conditions that have the greatest effect on built fabric are temperature, humidity and sunlight. Each can be measured and monitored to provide the necessary information for corrective measures or suitable protection.

While immediate readings of environmental conditions can be obtained on-site by using various calibrated instruments it is usually more important to establish a pattern of readings over a period of time. Monitoring in this way should take account of such variables as seasonal, diurnal and nocturnal differences; times and levels of occupancy; movement of caretaking, security and cleaning staff; and use of service installations.

The simple diagnostic sets used by surveyors, such as the Protimeter 'Complete' Dampness Kit™, may include moisture meters, thermo-hygrometers, wall surface thermometers and salt detectors, and are suitable for establishing moisture levels in wood and other building materials, dew-point temperatures, the risk of surface condensation and the presence of hygroscopic salts. Whirling hygrometers, digital probes and dew-point indicators may also be used to measure conditions for psychrometric evaluation.

For continual recording of temperature and humidity, battery-operated thermohygrographs can be used to give graphical information, typically for one-day, seven-day or thirty-day periods. Such an instrument was used to establish the nature of the environment within specific parts of the basement housing the Norman House in Norwich as a preliminary to specifying repairs (Figure 5.7).

Continual remote monitoring of environmental conditions, allowing for the analysis of building behaviour, is possible using a system of sensors, data loggers, alarms and remote or hard-wired communication networks. The Hutton + Rostron Curator™ family of building and timber moisture monitoring systems can be used to detect and diagnose failures and defects as part of the maintenance and management of a building.[13]

For environmental monitoring in museum and gallery situations computer-based instrumentation and control systems are also available, which can operate to various parameters including temperature, humidity, air movement, lux and ultraviolet.

The damage caused to internal finishes and contents by daylight, and to an extent artificial light, means that curators and custodians must

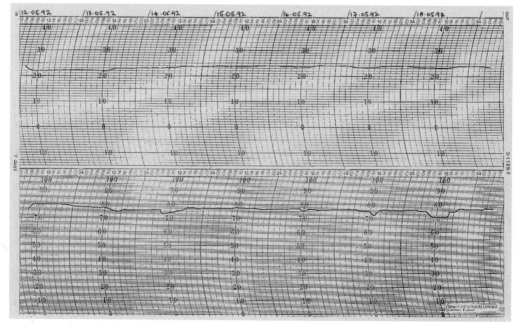

*Figure 5.7* Thermohygrograph chart showing temperature and humidity over a seven-day period within the basement housing the remains of an 11th-century undercroft known as the Norman House in Norwich.

monitor light levels and respond accordingly. Light and ultraviolet meters can be used to give immediate readings.

Traps and other devices are available for the monitoring and control of insect populations, again typically for museum and gallery usage. These can be used to establish the presence and species of insects, the location and extent of infestations, and the effects of treatment.

Air quality sampling may be required to assess levels of pollutants, including spores and fibres. Home monitoring of radon levels may be undertaken using detectors available from the National Radiological Protection Board (NRPB).

Noise pollution may be measured and monitored either to provide evidence for enforcement action or to assist with the design of acoustic treatments.

Finally, a recent development within the Building Research Establishment for measuring and monitoring vibration has been the laser interferometer, with the potential for remote monitoring of vibration in inaccessible architectural features, such as pinnacles and other fragile elements.

*Chapter Six*

# Building surveys III: Assessment and report

## ASSESSMENT CRITERIA

The inspection of building fabric is usually undertaken by looking, smelling, touching, feeling and, on occasions, listening and tasting. These natural senses may be enhanced by the use of simple or complex equipment, but ultimately it is the surveyor who will assess and record the condition of an element or component against specified criteria. The criteria used will vary according to the nature of the inspection so that the levels of decay, deterioration or disrepair expected and ultimately tolerated when considering an existing property will differ from those set for a building that is new.

When inspecting a building, a surveyor will make a judgement on the overall state of the property, together with any secondary buildings or structures, in the context of the site and its location. This judgement will be made on what is seen or reasonably inferred, but will invariably include a level of subjectivity based on personal standards and beliefs.

Templewood in Northrepps (Norfolk) was, for instance, built in the Palladian manner to designs by John Seely, 2nd Baron Mottistone, and Paul Paget for the politician Sir Samuel Hoare, 1st Viscount Templewood (Figure 6.1). The principal façade has a pedimented portico supported on Ionic columns, with a flight of stone steps flanked by two sphinxes rising to the main entrance. The verandah and terrace are surmounted by wrought-iron balustrading by Robert Bakewell of Derbyshire. Inside, the ceiling of the central saloon is painted in a Classical Renaissance manner.

This building was, in fact, built in 1938 as a single-storey shooting box, and described by Pevsner as looking like a stage-set for an Italian eighteenth-century opera, performed in England in the twentieth century. The columns were rescued from the Bank of England in the 1930s, and the stone steps, sphinxes and iron balustrading brought from the demolition of Nuthall Temple (1754–7) in Nottinghamshire in 1929. The painted ceiling was commissioned in 1964 by Paget, who had inherited the property from his uncle, and shows aspects of his life treated in a Classical make-believe manner, including school races, climbing and St Paul's Cathedral, with which Seeley and Paget were involved for a number of years.

In order to gain an objective view of a property and its various parts it is necessary to establish assessment criteria based on either relative or absolute values. Although this sounds far removed from the rigours of site and building surveys it is the principle that underlies successful decision making and surveying.

The question of whether the assessment of a property as a whole or in part should be based on relative or absolute values is one that depends on the nature of the task and the skills of the surveyor. The condition of a window taken in isolation might be considered poor, but by comparison with others in the building it may be thought acceptable and so left while

Figure 6.1 Templewood, Northrepps, Norfolk.

other more pressing needs are tended to. The criteria below will facilitate such decision-making:

+ Performance against agreed standards (e.g. thermal insulation);
+ Levels of decay, deterioration or disrepair (e.g. condition);
+ Social values (e.g. fashion);
+ Economic considerations (e.g. costs in use);
+ Aesthetic judgements (e.g. appearance).

Finally, the surveyor must always be aware of the reasons for undertaking the survey and how the survey report will be used to guide future action. Reasons will vary according to the type of client, from one who wants to find out how little will have to be spent to bring a property up to an acceptable standard prior to disposal, to one more interested in establishing how much work needs to be done in order to return a property to a correct historical state for personal enjoyment or show.

Public and institutional clients may have a range of concerns to be addressed by a surveyor. Those of a charitable trust occupying an industrial site as a museum, for instance, may include interpretation of the repairing covenants in their lease, establishing the standards of repair expected of an industrial site scheduled as an ancient monument, setting environmental requirements for the buildings and museum exhibits, and making recommendations for restoration based on limited factual information.

## Intensive and extensive assessments

While such criteria are used to assess the condition of a single building or element of its construction, they can also be employed to gain an understanding in a wider extensive context.

The survey of some 1,430 listed and historic buildings in the central conservation areas of Norwich, undertaken by the City Planning Department and a local firm of architects during 1986/7, provided information on which to base future conservation policies set against available grant aid.[1] Rapid external assessments using a simple survey form (Appendix D), and selective follow-up surveys, provided information on condition and costs of repair related to street, area and levels of occupancy.

The condition survey of over 50 defensible farmhouses (bastles) and fortified towers (pele towers) in the Northumberland National Park, carried out by an independent consultant in 1990, was undertaken in order to evaluate the physical condition of surviving structures, assess future threats, outline and prioritize conservation works required, and assess suitability for interpretation.[2] A scoring system based on the importance of the structure, relative to how much of the fabric had survived and its current condition, provided the necessary information for a programme of works to be prepared.

## Indirect assessment

Where direct observation is not possible, or the adopted criteria require specific qualitative or quantitative data, it will be necessary to employ indirect means of observation or assessment. The use of such non-standard equipment and techniques is covered in Chapter Five, but it is important at this point to stress that limitations in use must be reconciled with the relative importance of the specific data.

Many of the non-destructive techniques in use for building inspections today have come from other sciences, and the skill lies as much with the interpretation of the results as with the actual site work. It is important therefore to be fully aware of what a particular technique is capable of providing so that expectations are not unrealistically set.

## MEASURES OF CONDITION

Whatever the size or nature of the property to be inspected there will be perceived or prescribed standards of condition on which the assessment will be based. Without direct instruction, the measure against which judgements will be based will come solely from the experience and knowledge of the surveyor. The presence of cracks in the walls of a house will, for instance, probably cause more immediate concern than if found in those of a standing ruin.

The actual measurement of condition is, in most forms of assessment, made with reference to the severity of the particular defect. This will usually be based on observation of comparable defects. Experience will inform the surveyor of the likely prognosis, and what secondary effects need to be considered.

Certain factors, particularly appearance, may colour the judgements of a misinformed surveyor. Impressive levels of distortion may prompt unnecessary intervention (Figure 6.2), while soft lime-based mortars and renders may be condemned without understanding their nature or purpose.

Where prescribed standards (such as the Approved Documents of the Building Regulations, requirements of the National House Building Council or those described in technical publications) are not available, relevant or heeded, subjectivity can cause unnecessary intervention or destruction of historic fabric. The identification of dampness in a historic building during a mortgage valuation may, for instance, result in the

*Figure 6.2* Seemingly precarious masonry at the late Roman fort of Burgh Castle, Norfolk. Notice the construction of the wall with flint facing, regular brick courses and rubble core.

needless and damaging installation of a damp-proof course without consideration being given to the implications of such action.

In certain cases it may be more appropriate to measure the condition by reference to the ease by which the defect could be rectified. Although this requires the surveyor to be familiar with appropriate techniques of repair, owners and managers are often more impressed when presented initially with an indication of potential future repair and corrective maintenance costs arising out of neglect, than with the present cost of repair itself.

In the quadrennial system of assessment in use for Government civil estate buildings,[3] four priority classifications are employed to indicate the measure of condition with regard to the implications of doing nothing. It is easy then to appreciate the relative importance of each item of work with regard to separate managerial, financial and operational criteria. The priority classifications are:

*Unavoidable*
- Cannot be deferred without breaching statutory obligations;
- Cannot be deferred for health and safety reasons;
- If not undertaken will seriously affect operations and function;
- Needed to meet lease or covenant obligations.

*Essential*
- Cannot be deferred without risk of serious penalties in terms of dilapidation or increased cost.

*Urgent*
- Highly desirable to undertake to maintain value and utility.

*Desirable*
- Necessary to maintain proper standards;
- Would show a saving in running or operational costs.

## SURVEY REPORT

The observations and inferences derived from a survey are relayed to the client by a written report, often illustrated with photographs and drawings, and presented in a clear and concise manner according to the agreed instructions and brief.

The surveyor should give careful consideration to including the following additional information:

### Instructions

The instructions on which the survey was undertaken, together with any specific requirements and agreed variations, should be laid out.

### Limitations and exclusions

It is essential that limitations on access to parts of the building or certain elements of construction are made explicitly and that methods of inspection are explained. Similarly, where certain aspects of the property were instructed to be excluded from the inspection (such as service installations) this should be confirmed to the client. Limitations imposed by the client, either by denying access or not agreeing to additional costs, should also be stated.

The value of a report can be substantially reduced where undue reliance is placed on caveats. If the surveyor is unable to comment on particular aspects of the property, it should be clear to the client at the outset that the advice of specialists may be needed.

A clause stating that the survey report assumes 'that no deleterious or hazardous materials or techniques have been used' may satisfy the in-surers, but could leave the client worrying whether such materials are present and undetected. It would be better for the surveyor to undertake the survey with a view to discovering such problems, and responding accordingly.

The use of disclaimers or clauses seeking to exclude or limit liability for negligence must be 'reasonable' under the Unfair Contract Terms Act 1977 and with regard to the findings in recent cases.[4, 5, 6]

## Background information

A report should give sufficient background information to set the scene for the client and secondary readers, from which details may be drawn later in the report. This is particularly the case with historic, or multi-phase, buildings, where observations and comments on condition, repair, maintenance and costings may relate directly to the age, use and type of construction.

As well as historical information the surveyor should make reference to all material referred to before, during and after the survey; weather conditions during and preceding the day(s) of the survey; the names and job descriptions of persons met at the property; and details of any information given by such persons.

The surveyor should also explain the approach adopted in undertaking the survey and the criteria used in drafting the report. By the nature of the task a survey report frequently presents negative information in its discussion of faults and decay, and in this respect many clients can be given, or interpret, an unbalanced and gloomy picture of the property. The surveyor should therefore consider, and present, views on the quality expected of the type of property under consideration, reflect on how it has been used or abused, and provide a realistic statement as to the particular merits for its present or intended use.

## Structure of report

If a standard form of assessment is not being used, it will be necessary to consider carefully the structure of the report in order to present the findings of the survey in a clear, concise and logical manner – either room-by-room or element-by-element.

When reporting room-by-room, particularly to a client who is not familiar with the property, the report should be presented in a logical order so that the reader can easily relate to the various parts of the property. There is a risk of repetition when using this format and the surveyor must judge whether the client will derive more use from the information presented in such a manner than if it were given element-by-element.

The authors have found it particularly useful when reporting on complex sites, or to clients unfamiliar with the property, to use the room-by-room approach. Each room or space is handled under the three headings of description, condition and recommendations. A summary of the main defects and mechanisms of decay is provided, together with a programme of recommended works, prioritized and costed. This provides an initial overview and idea of costs, before considering each room in detail.

In either case floor plans should be provided, with each room numbered and referenced to the sections of the report. Reference numbers may also be useful when referring to doors, windows, fireplaces, chimneys and other elements on separate floors. With reports dealing with large or complex buildings, using coloured paper helps to identify individual floors and provides a structure for ordering text, plans and related material.

If cardinal compass points are used to identify certain elements or features within a room or part of a building it is essential that each plan is suitably marked with a north point to ensure correct orientation. Similarly, where reference is made to left and right, it will be necessary to explain in which direction the reader should be looking.

Finally, a survey report should include a summary of the main findings and firm conclusions as to the condition of the property. Where the final report is of a medium length (say up to 15 pages) then these may be provided in a final section. Where the report is lengthy it is suggested that the summary and conclusions, together with required recommendations as to action and cost, be presented at the front of the report, or perhaps as a separate accompanying document.

## Description of defects

When describing the nature and extent of defects found or reasonably inferred during the survey, the surveyor should give careful thought to how this information is presented, and how it will be used. Survey reports often contain little more than a list of findings on which the client has to make his or her own judgements.

Where defects have been found all relevant facts should be reported in a manner that allows the client to appreciate the severity of the findings. The client is likely to be a layperson and will require a description of the defect, brief details on how and why it has occurred, and guidance on what will happen if it is left unattended.

The client is entitled, and has usually paid for, the knowledge and experience of a surveyor in identifying and diagnosing defects, and offering a prognosis from which action can be planned and implemented.

## Third-party reports

Where reports have been requested from specialized third parties these should be included with the main report in full, perhaps as an appendix. The surveyor should not seek to summarize such reports, as by doing so a responsibility for errors or omissions will pass from the third party to the surveyor. If the report from a specialist is particularly long or technical in nature, the specialist should provide a summary for submission to the client as part of the main report.

## Priorities for recommended works

Where the surveyor suggests priorities for a programme of recommended works it is necessary to state clearly the criteria by which the judgements have been made.

Guidance for the preparation of Church of England quinquennial reports suggests the four headings: urgent works requiring immediate attention; works recommended to be carried out during the next 12 months; works recommended to be carried out in the quinquennial period; and works needing consideration beyond the quinquennial period.[7] For Government quadrennial reports priority classifications of: unavoidable, essential, urgent and desirable, together with details of further investigations, are specified.[8] The National Trust quinquennial surveys of buildings held for preservation require a summary of recommendations for immediate action, and for completion within two, five

and ten years, together with brief observations for suggested improvements, improvements in routine maintenance, monitoring of defects and
likely major repairs beyond ten years.[9]

## Standard text entries

The increasing use of word processors and desk-top publishing systems
in report preparation has increased the opportunity for standard descriptions and statements. It is possible to develop a library of such text entries,
which can be dropped into the document as required.

When dealing with historic buildings, aspects of the report, such as roof
construction or standard of finishes, are typically different for each
property. There is therefore little scope for prepared text beyond simple
descriptions of basic construction and defects.

## Illustrations

Sketches, detailed drawings and photographs can be used to illustrate
forms of construction, particular defects and the events leading to a
specific failure. In this manner they may take the place of lengthy and
complex text, and assist readers not familiar with the building to appreciate particular problems (Figure 6.3).

Where a surveyor has prepared a library of standard text entries it may
also be useful to include illustrations. These may be simply photocopied
from drawn masters and included with the report, or stored as a computer
graphics file. Scanning from original material can also provide a useful
way of storing and retrieving graphical information.

Illustrations are only worth providing in the body of a report when they
can explain or enhance what is being stated. Where there is a risk of
breaking up the text and flow for the reader, then such material may be
better placed in an appendix.

## Costings

When financial information about a recommended programme of works
is required, the surveyor must be confident that the costings accurately
reflect both the quality of work required and the time when it will be
carried out. The costs given by a local jobbing builder for reroofing a
property using close-matching second-hand tiles will bear no relation to
those presented by a competent tradesperson working to best practices
with a sympathy for the job in hand.

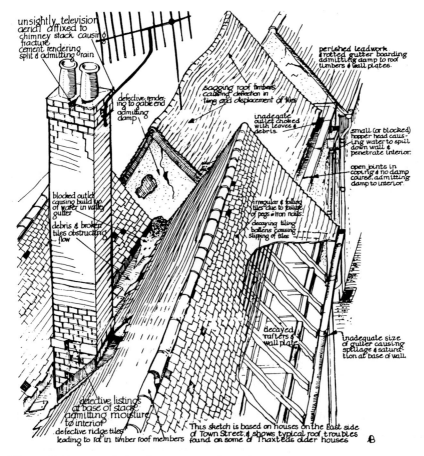

unsightly television aerial affixed to chimney stack causing fracture

cement rendering split & admitting rain

defective rendering to gable end admitting damp

sagging roof timbers causing deflection in tiling and displacement of tiles

perished leadwork & rotted gutter boarding admitting damp to roof timbers & wall plates.

inadequate outlet choked with leaves & debris

small (or blocked) hopper head causing water to spill down wall & penetrate interior.

open joints in coping & no damp course, admitting damp to interior.

blocked outlet causing build up of water in valley gutter

debris & broken tiles obstructing flow

irregular & falling tiles due to failure of pegs & iron nails.

decaying tiling battens causing slipping of tiles

decayed rafters & wall plate

inadequate size of gutter causing spillage & saturation at base of wall.

defective listings at base of stack admitting moisture to interior

defective ridge tiles leading to rot in timber roof members

This sketch is based on houses on the East side of Town Street & shows typical roof troubles found on some of Thaxted's older houses   B

*Figure 6.3* Annotated sketch giving simple explanation of defects. Courtesy of Ailwyn Best, Donald W. Insall and Associates.

Pricing books often give little detailed information for the sorts of work presented by historic buildings, and reliance must instead be given to experience gained with other similar projects. The surveyor should develop and maintain a personal price guide so that estimates of cost can be based on comparable evidence, adjusted for time, place and specific site conditions.

Where cost estimates are given in a report it should be made clear that they are provided without recourse to detailed price breakdowns, and that for more precise figures the client is advised to seek suitable professional guidance.

Where ascribing costs to prioritized works it will be necessary to state clearly whether the figures are based on present rates or projected for future action. It is also useful to indicate where works could be undertaken in an earlier phase in order to benefit from economies of scale.

Details relating to value added tax (VAT), particularly the opportunity to zero rate approved alterations to listed property, should be made. Details of appropriate sources of grant aid should also be given.

## Glossary

It is usual to restrict the use of technical terms in a report. There are, however, certain common terms that are used in order to avoid lengthy descriptions and it may be appropriate to include a glossary which gives standard descriptions of relevant construction or mechanisms of decay. Simple illustrations may prove particularly useful.

Once a working glossary has been established it can be appended to most reports though non-standard entries may have to be added.

## Appendices

Appendices should be restricted for material that is relevant to the report, but which is too long, detailed or in a form that would interrupt the flow of the text. It should not be used for irrelevant information that the surveyor feels should be on show to prove his earnest endeavours.

Examples include the reports and findings of specialists or subcontractors; basic test results; maps; a summary of documentary evidence; and essential illustrations.

Many surveyors include basic maintenance notes with their reports for use by the client. While this is a useful way in which to steer a client toward good husbandry, such notes must be relevant and not simply a copy of a standard office document. A short checklist, broken down into weekly, monthly and annual tasks, will be of more use than a full maintenance manual, which should carry its own fee.

## Oral presentation

The surveyor may be requested to personally present the findings of an inspection to the client or a representative committee, in addition to submitting a written survey report.

It is important to present only material that is covered in the report, and not to be drawn on unsubstantiated opinion or personal preference. An oral presentation provides the surveyor with a good opportunity to provide a clear summary of the findings, and address specific requirements or matters of particular concern raised in the instructions.

## Video presentation

A small number of surveyors present information by way of video coverage and commentary, particularly in connection with building society inspections. It is doubtful whether there is any advantage in using video presentations apart from coverage of particular aspects of the property. Video and editing courses are available or a professional video service can be employed.

## Archival value

Much of what is learnt about a property often comes from background and historical information. It is therefore incumbent on surveyors to make their own records available for storage and retrieval.

The county Sites and Monuments Record should be the first repository for survey reports, drawings, schedules of works and other documentation, which could give future generations a valuable source of information. Summaries of historical documents and other background information should be made available to owners, occupiers and others with an interest in the property as a means of increasing awareness and promoting a sense of pride in what they have. The consent of the client should be obtained as a matter of course before releasing any material.

## Confidentiality

A surveyor who prepares a survey report for a client is providing a service in return for payment. This service is personal and confidential. The client is at liberty to decide how the report is used notwithstanding the terms agreed in respect of the nature and purpose of the survey. Clients should be advised, however, against making the report available to third parties who may place reliance on its contents.

The surveyor holds the copyright to a survey report, but would be in likely breach of contract if the report was to be made available to other parties without the express consent of the client. This may also extend to the use of material for publication, exhibition and publicity. It should also be noted that security and privacy can easily become compromised when attention is drawn to valuable artefacts and personal effects.

The surveyor should be wary of giving verbal comments during the survey, either to the client or other parties present. Time is needed in order to reflect on what has been seen and follow up with any necessary research.

## RESPONSIBILITIES AND DUTIES OF CARE

The duty of care owed by a surveyor to a client arises not only from the conditions and warranties of the contract made between the two parties, but in addition from general liabilities imposed by the law in tort.[10] A duty of care is also owed to persons who may directly or indirectly suffer loss as a result of placing trust and reliance in the work of the surveyor.

These duties of care imply that the surveyor will undertake his or her work with the skill and care reasonably expected of a competent person exercising the particular calling and professing the particular skill in question. Where the surveyor professes to have special skills, for instance with regard to historic buildings, then those duties will be based on the reasonable standards of that speciality.

Failure to discharge a duty of care adequately, resulting in loss or damage, may lead the surveyor to be in breach of contract or be liable in tort.

The surveyor may be held to be in breach of contract for the following reasons:

- failure to carry out the client's instructions;[11]
- inadequate knowledge or experience for the work undertaken;[12]
- an inadequate inspection carried out;[13]
- suitable equipment not carried and used;[14]
- making inadequate field notes;[15]
- reliance on information provided by others;[16]
- presenting an inadequate report.[17]

Negligence as a tort is a breach of a legal duty to take care, owed by one person to another, which results in loss or damage. Where there is a special relationship, such as where a client places reasonable trust and reliance on the information or advice given by a surveyor, negligence on the part of the latter will result in liability. The loss or damage must, however, be to something other than the property itself.[18]

Where legal action is taken against a surveyor and damages awarded, the basis on which the compensatory sum is calculated is that established to return the plaintiff to the position he or she was in before the tort or breach of contract.[19] This may, as case law has shown, be based on the difference between the value of the property in the condition described in the report and its actual value,[20] or the cost of the repairs necessary to bring the property to its described condition.[21] Generally, damages are assessed as at the date when the cause of action arose.[22]

A duty of care has also been shown to exist with regard to third parties almost to the extent of that in contract. Where a third party places reasonable and foreseeable reliance on the work of a professional adviser, that adviser may be proved liable for reliance negligence.[23]

The period over which a report can be relied upon is governed by the Limitation Act 1980, as amended by the Latent Damages Act 1986. The starting date for this period has been taken as the cause of action which the plaintiff suffered,[24] although the period may be extended if there has been deliberate concealment of a cause of action.[25] Surveyors asked to comment on their findings at a later date should, therefore, be aware that the limitation period may start from this later reliance, and that they should seek to avoid re-establishing a contract. It should also be remembered that although an action in contract might be statute barred, there may, however, be liability in tort.[26]

## PROFESSIONAL INDEMNITY

It is a usual condition of a surveyor's membership of a professional society or institution that adequate professional indemnity insurance is held. Where such membership is absent the client must rely on the honesty and integrity of the adviser. In either case it is a foolish person who practises without such insurance.

Professional indemnity insurance is also required for surveyors who have ceased work, either through cessation of business, retirement or death. Indemnity insurance is based on a 'claims made' basis, which means that a policy must be in force when the claim is made and notified to the insurers. Run-off insurance is required to provide cover, usually at a reduced premium, for potential liabilities arising under contract during the period of six years in the case of loss of property or damage or 12 years for contracts made under seal, or longer in tort.

Employees should check that they are covered by the insurance of their employer or a written indemnity, particularly with regard to claims made by third parties, insurers and their own employers; advice given outside their usual area of work; and the period after they cease to be employed. Indemnity insurance may also require unqualified trainee surveyors to be accompanied by a suitably qualified supervisor.[27]

In response to the question of indemnity insurance and increasing premiums, the surveyor should give careful consideration to how and why building survey instructions are undertaken. In assessing the condition of buildings, whether of a historic nature or not, the surveyor has to perform to a certain standard in order to satisfy the client and, in the case of a claim, the courts. The key to continued success as a surveyor is establishing whether the expected standard can be achieved.

Assuming the answer to be 'yes', the surveyor should then give careful consideration to how the service is performed and the duties are discharged. Many claims are made on the basis of misunderstanding, rushed procedures and errors of performance, rather than fact.

Knowing this, the surveyor should check that procedures are in place for taking and recording instructions accurately and efficiently; ensuring that the client has agreed a workable brief and confirmed conditions of engagement; undertaking the survey in agreement with all parties in a careful and diligent manner; taking account of practice statements published by the professional bodies; using specialists and specialized equipment where appropriate; preparing the report carefully, checking it before delivery; inserting adequate caveat clauses that are reasonable and correct; and ensuring that all parts of the brief and instructions have been adequately addressed and completed. Investigation of complaints about incompetence is increasingly being undertaken by professional bodies, and it is therefore the surveyor's responsibility to be capable of carrying out the work with due skill and care, proper diligence and promptness.[28]

Formal quality management of professional services with regard to BS 5750/ISO 9000 is becoming more common, and specific guidance is now available for surveyors seeking to adopt such measures.[29]

# PART
## TWO

*Chapter Seven*

# Causes of deterioration and decay

## INTRODUCTION

In Chapter Five the principal causes of failure and decay were highlighted in the context of the diagnosis of defects. Before considering these causes in detail, it is necessary to understand how building elements are affected and to know what to look for during the inspection. Without this knowledge there is a risk of remedial work causing damage.

## EXCESS MOISTURE

### Typical causes of excess moisture

Excess moisture, caused by rising and penetrating damp, condensation, leakage or spillage, is the most widespread and damaging cause of deterioration and decay affecting historic buildings. The cause of the problem may be obvious – a leaking pipe or a slipped slate, concealed and undetected until decay is quite advanced.

The effects of high levels of moisture on the materials from which traditional buildings are constructed can be devastating, as the susceptibility of timber to fungal attack is increased, conditions for chemical and biological degradation are set up, and surface finishes are destroyed.

Changes in our lifestyles have also created higher levels of moisture. The drive for energy efficiency and personal comfort, with the increased use of insulation products, double glazing and draught-proofing, the move away from open fires, and the desire for higher levels of space heating, all have an effect on the internal climate.

## Symptoms and diagnosis

### Rising damp

Dampness will rise within a wall due to capillarity, natural osmosis causing water to move from solutions of lower to higher salt concentration, and differences in electrical potentiality. Movement of moisture is therefore dependent on the size and distribution of pores within the wall material, the presence and concentrations of soluble salts, and the potential of the wall in relation to the surrounding ground.

The presence of excess dampness will increase the risk of fungal attack to skirting boards, floorboards and embedded timbers; cause disruption to internal wall surfaces with staining and damage to finishes; and promote the risk of damage to external walling through salt crystallization and frost damage. It can also lead to the premature failure of clay- and earth-based constructions. Increased levels of associated moisture vapour within a building may also lead to surface or interstitial condensation.

Some of the more common reasons for the presence of rising damp to consider when inspecting a traditional building include:

- Absence or failure of a damp-proof course. It is important to remember that the absence of a damp-proof course does not always mean that the wall(s) will be affected by rising damp, and that such a problem cannot exist where there is an adequate damp-proof course in place. The surveyor should rely on experience and the correct use of a moisture meter to determine the nature and extent of any problem.
- Early damp-proof courses of slate may fracture as a result of ground movement, while lead or bitumen-based flexible courses may become compressed and extruded from the joint. Injected courses may be affected by ground-water contaminants, or fail to form a continuous band due to the construction of the wall or the rate of moisture movement.
- Damp-proof courses may become bridged externally by an increase in ground levels or pavings; accumulated soil or debris, such as ashes or vegetable matter; or by later deep pointing or render finishes. Internally they may be bridged by inserted solid floors.
- Absence or failure of a link between a damp-proof membrane and damp-proof course. This often occurs where the floor level is lower than the outside ground level, creating a band of unprotected masonry around the base of the wall.
- The installation or presence of a damp-proof course in a traditional solid wall construction will theoretically restrict the upward movement of moisture within the wall, but may cause moisture to evaporate out through adjacent solid floors, leading to the premature failure of sealed floor tiles.
- Impervious surface finishes (such as cement-based renders and paint systems with high vapour resistance) will deny evaporation of moisture from within a wall, causing it to seek alternative routes for dispersal.
- Hard surfaces around the outside base of a wall will deny evaporation of moisture from the ground, and may

cause surface water to run back towards the building. Rainwater will also splash up off hard surfaces causing localized saturation of masonry and an increased risk of frost and salt damage.

· Hygroscopic salts, often associated with past problems of rising damp, can give misleading indications of current problems unless contaminated plaster is removed or treated on the installation of a damp-proof course. Desalination of masonry by poulticing may be required.

## Penetrating damp

The movement of moisture absorbed into a porous material will relate directly to the severity of the conditions of exposure, the length of time it is subjected to these conditions and the internal pore structure of the material. Whether the moisture penetrates the thickness of a wall, and manifests itself on the internal surfaces, will depend on the rate at which it is lost through evaporation to the outside air.

Some of the more common reasons for the presence of penetrating damp to consider when inspecting a traditional building include:

· Damp patches on internal wall surfaces, particularly to exposed south or south-west elevations, where driving rain has saturated the wall or entered the construction through cracks and defective joints in the walling, or defects in external wall finishes. Cavity-wall constructions may be bridged by insulation material, debris or mortar droppings on the ties, or be without damp-proof courses at head, cill and jambs closures.

· Failure of render or other surface finishes to exposed faces of parapet walls, upstands and at copings. Saturation of the inside face of a parapet wall in exposed positions may provide a direct route for moisture into the accommodation below.

· Entry of moisture through open joints and fixing points behind cornices, parapets and balconies.

· Damage to, or removal of, projecting features, such as drips, strings or cornices, designed to throw water away from the wall surfaces. Where, for instance, a string course is cut to take a downpipe, rainwater will be channelled onto the wall below, causing localized saturation. This is often indicated by an area of moss or algal growth on the surface of the affected wall.

· Where the upper surfaces of projecting features have become eroded, rainwater may collect in such depressions and form localized points of moisture penetration.

· Direct penetration of rainwater down an open flue. This will usually show as a damp patch on a chimney breast, often with staining caused by the take-up of soluble soots and tars deposited on the walls of the flue.

· Absence or failure of a damp-proof course beneath copings, such as found on parapet walls and gable parapets.

· Absence or failure of flashings and weatherings to features penetrating the roof covering, such as soil and vent pipes, dormer windows, skylights and chimney stacks.

· Absence or failure of damp-proof trays in cavity walls.

· Absence or failure of drips to copings.

· Defective window cills where a drip to the underside is absent or bridged, or the upper surface is angled back towards the building. Where windows are set in battered masonry, such as with tower mills, the cills to standard window units are often found to be angled backwards towards the wall unless they have been cut to take account of how the window is to be set.

· Saturation of a wall may result from inappropriate washing techniques or direct water discharge.

*Surface and interstitial condensation*

Moisture vapour (% relative humidity) is directly related to the temperature of the air, so that a drop in temperature will increase the relative level of humidity to a point where the vapour will condense out (dew-point). When air becomes saturated (100% relative humidity) water droplets will condense out on cold surfaces, such as glass, tiles, impermeable gloss paint and vinyl wallpaper. This is surface condensation. Where the dew-point temperature is reached within the thickness of the construction, condensation will form at that point. This is interstitial condensation.

High levels of moisture vapour are generated by washing, cooking, bathing, rising damp, rain penetration, leaks, spillages and the use of flueless gas and paraffin heaters. Natural ventilation may be reduced by the installation of double glazing and draught-proofing, and the blocking of open flues and air bricks.

Some of the more common reasons for the presence of condensation to consider when inspecting a traditional building include:

- Mould growth, often found in poorly ventilated areas such as within cupboards or behind furniture, causes damage to finishes, furnishings and clothing, and poses a threat of respiratory problems through the presence of spores.
- High humidities will increase the risks of corrosion and damage to textiles.
- Saturation of thermal insulation will reduce its efficiency and lead to an increase in heating costs.
- Condensation may form on the underside of roofing felt in an inadequately ventilated roof space. The installation or presence of fire stopping, cavity closers and insulation may also restrict ventilation.
- In lightweight modern constructions heating is typically provided only during the hours of occupancy, raising the ambient temperature in a relatively short period of time.
- In traditional constructions walls and ground floors often have a high mass and therefore will have a slow thermal response, that is they warm and cool slowly. If the building is only heated intermittently the fabric of the building tends to remain cold. The air, although capable of holding the moisture vapour generated by occupation while the heating system is on, quickly drops to dew-point when the heating is turned off and deposits condensation on cold internal surfaces. Where building fabric has a slow thermal response, constant low output heating systems are to be preferred.

## FUNGAL ATTACK

## Typical forms of fungal infection

All fungal attack in buildings starts with the spores of the fungus landing on timber surfaces. If the timber is damp, these spores germinate and send out hyphal threads to form the mycelium, which feeds on the organic matter in the wood causing it to decay. Within the mycelium a sporophore or reproductive fruiting body will develop in time and release further spores which, travelling on air currents, spread the infection to other susceptible timbers.

Wood-rotting fungi are commonly classified as either dry or wet rots, and may be further designated as brown or white rots, the former consuming only the pale-coloured cellulose causing the affected wood to darken in colour and the latter consuming both cellulose and lignin, giving a bleached appearance to the affected wood.

It is important to make a clear distinction between the true dry rot fungus, *Serpula lacrymans*, and other wood-rotting fungi, both for its ability to spread by sending out strands in search of further timber, and for the damage it can cause to structural timbers.

The term wet rot is used to describe a number of wood-rotting fungi, the two most common forms of which are *Coniophora puteana* and *Fibroporia vaillantii*. Other wet-rot fungi include *Amyloporia xantha, Poria placenta, Phellinus contiguus, Donkioporia expansa, Pleurotus ostreatus, Asterostroma* spp, and *Paxillus panuoides*.

There are, in addition, various moulds and slime moulds, blue stain fungi and plaster fungi that should be considered when assessing the condition of timber or masonry, and numerous moulds and mildews that will attack organic materials such as leather, fabrics and paper.[1]

## Symptoms and diagnosis

### Dry rot (Serpula lacrymans)

- Brown rot.
- Attacks mostly softwoods.
- Requires timber with a moisture content of about 22%.
- Needs unventilated space with ambient and surface temperatures of 18–24°C (65–75°F).
- Deep cross-cracking of timber into cuboidal pieces about 50 mm in size.

- Branching white or grey surface strands up to 5 mm thick, which become brittle when cut and dried.
- Fruiting bodies rusty-red in colour due to spores, with white or grey margin. Texture soft and tough.
- Mycelium forms as soft white cushions or thick grey sheets with yellow patches.

### Cellar fungus (Coniophora puteana)

- Brown rot.
- Attacks hardwoods and softwoods.
- Requires timber with a moisture content greater than 25%.
- Needs unventilated space with ambient and surface temperatures of 18–24°C (65–75°F).
- Most common form of decay found with saturated timber.
- Cross-cracking with visible darkening

of wood. The surface of the timber may appear sound.
- Slender dark-brown or black surface strands.
- Fruiting bodies are rare, but olive-brown in colour, and surface raised in lumps and pimples.
- Mycelium rare except in conditions of high humidity, forms as a thin skin-like growth.

## White pore or mine fungus (Fibroporia vaillantii)

- Brown rot.
- Attacks softwoods.
- Requires timber with a moisture content greater than 25%.
- Needs unventilated space with ambient and surface temperatures of 18–24°C (65–75°F).
- Cuboidal-cracking of timber as seen with *Serpula lacrymans*, but less deep.

- White surface strands up to 2.5 mm thick, which remain flexible when cut and dried.
- White or pale-coloured fruiting bodies forming as irregular sheets or plates.
- Mycelium white or cream coloured sheets.

## BEETLE INFESTATION

## Typical forms of beetle infestation

The life cycle of the wood-boring insects found in buildings starts with eggs laid on the surface of the timber. The resulting larvae tunnel into the timber to feed on the available organic material and, depending on the species and the prevailing conditions, may spend between one and eleven years there. Eventually, the larva forms a pupal chamber close to the surface of the timber, from which the adult beetle emerges causing the characteristic flight hole and bore dust.

Other insects that can cause damage to structural and non-structural timbers used within a building include weevils, wasps and borers.[1]

## Symptoms and diagnosis

### Common furniture beetle (Anobium punctatum)

- Attacks softwoods and European hardwoods.
- Commonly referred to as 'woodworm'.
- Requires timber with a moisture content in excess of 12%.
- Flight holes circular, 1–2 mm in diameter.

- Adult beetle 3–5 mm in length.
- Flight season April to August.
- Three-year life cycle.
- Bore dust fine, white and granular or cylindrical pellets pointed at one or both ends.

### Death watch beetle (Xestobium rufovillosum)

- Attacks decaying hardwoods, mostly oak, and adjacent softwoods.
- Flight holes circular and 3 mm diameter.

- Flight season April to June.
- Adult beetle 6–9 mm long.
- Five to twelve-year life cycle.
- Bore dust coarse, bun-shaped pellets.

### House longhorn beetle (Hylotrupes bajulus)

- Attacks sapwood of most softwoods.
- At present found only in the south-east of England, where special provisions within the Building Regulations apply. Records of infestations in the United Kingdom are maintained by the Building Research Establishment.

- Flight holes oval, often ragged, 6–10 mm in diameter.
- Flight season July to September.
- Adult beetle 10–20 mm long.
- Three to eleven-year life cycle.
- Bore dust large, cylindrical sausage-shaped pellets.

### Powderpost beetle (Lyctus brunneus and L. linearis)

- Attacks sapwood of new hardwoods, particularly oak and elm.
- Flight holes circular 1–2 mm diameter.
- Flight season June to August.

- Adult beetle 4–7 mm long.
- Ten-month life cycle.
- Bore dust soft and silky, very fine powder.

### Ptilinus beetle (Ptilinus pectinicornis)

- Attacks certain European hardwoods, particularly beech, elm, hornbeam and maple, and found mainly in furniture.
- Flight holes circular 1–2 mm in diameter.

- Flight season May to July.
- Adult beetle 4–6 mm long.
- Two-year life cycle.
- Bore dust fine powder.

### Wood-boring weevil (Pentarthrum huttoni and Euophryum confine)

- Attacks decaying hardwoods and soft-woods.
- Flight holes small and ragged 1 mm in diameter.

- Flight season any time.
- Adult weevil 3–5 mm long.
- Seven to nine-month life cycle.
- Bore dust fine round cylindrical pellets.

## CHEMICAL AND PHYSICAL CHANGE

### Typical causes of chemical and physical change

A chemical change is the term used to describe the rearrangement of atoms among the molecules to create new molecular structures whether in solids, liquids or gases. Examples of chemical changes include sulphate attack, carbonation of concrete and ultraviolet degradation. The corrosion of metals is also a chemical change, and is described in more detail below.

A physical change involves the rearrangement of the molecules, without altering the structure of the individual molecules, and typically involves a change in volume. Such changes includes frost damage, the crystallization of soluble salts and mechanical wear.

These changes can come about as a result of poor material selection, poor site storage, inappropriate material handling or through the use of incompatible materials. They may also arise for less obvious reasons, such as exposure to sun, wind and rain; the use of different cleaning materials; changes in environmental conditions; or changes in user activities.

## Symptoms and diagnosis

### Sulphate attack

When water-soluble sulphates present in natural clays and stones, or found in contaminants, come into contact with concrete or ordinary Portland cement-based mortars and renders they react with the tri-calcium aluminate within the cement to form the compound ettringite. This reaction causes the expansion of the tri-calcium aluminate, leading to the breakdown and failure of the cementitious product.

### Carbonation

A concrete matrix is naturally alkaline due to the presence of calcium hydroxide, and this alkalinity (pH 12.5 to 13.5) confers a level of chemical protection to embedded steel reinforcement. Where acidic atmospheric oxides, such as carbon dioxide, sulphur dioxide and sulphur trioxide, enter the matrix through pores, cracks and damaged areas this alkalinity decreases and carbonation takes place. Carbonated concrete offers little protection to embedded metal, and corrosion may occur.

### Electro-magnetic radiation

Visible light forms that part of the spectrum of electro-magnetic radiation with a wavelength of between 100 nm and 1μm to which the human eye is sensitive. Other wavebands within the spectrum, such as radio waves, infrared, ultraviolet and X-rays, have differing wavelengths and different characteristics.

Light provides a source of energy by which chemical changes occur. This energy is greater at the ultraviolet end of the spectrum, while light at the infrared end produces more heat, which itself can be the cause of problems for sensitive objects. Ultraviolet radiation, having a wavelength of between 1 nm and 100 nm, will affect many materials, causing oxidization or embrittlement of plastics, and the breakdown and weakening of long-chain molecules as found in fibrous products.

Infrared radiation, with a wavelength of between 1μm and 1mm, is present in both sunlight and artificial light sources as radiant heat. Such direct heat will reduce the relative humidity of the air around an object, causing embrittlement and shrinkage of organic materials as moisture is lost. This can often be seen with warped and split window shutters, and distorted veneers. Fluctuating humidities, as between winter and summer, and day and night, can cause particular problems due to the stresses set up by cycles of swelling and shrinkage associated with high and low relative humidities.

The energy in visible light is also sufficient to bring about photochemical change, particularly with certain sensitive objects. Pictures, paintings, fabrics, dyes and stains will typically fade and weaken as they undergo chemical change, depending on the levels of light and length of exposure.

## Frost damage

When water that has been absorbed into a porous material freezes it exerts a pressure on the internal structure of the material, causing fracturing and disintegration (Figure 7.1). This is commonly seen in brickwork, when the face of the brick fails (spalls) and becomes detached. The susceptibility of a material to such damage is related to the size and distribution of its internal structure of capillaries and pores. In order for water to freeze it requires sufficient space in which the ice crystals can nucleate. Materials with a fine pore structure will thus suffer less damage than those with larger pores in which ice crystals can grow.

## Crystallization of salts

Where soluble salts in solution are present within a porous material, evaporation of the liquid will tend to concentrate the salts at the surface, where they will crystallize and form the white deposit known as efflorescence. Where the salt crystals form within the pores of the material the resulting pressure can set up internal stresses that cause the failure and disintegration of the surface layer. This is known as crypto-efflorescence.

Clay bricks typically contain sulphates of calcium, sodium, potassium, magnesium and iron, while contamination from ground water and other sources can also introduce nitrates and chlorides. Natural stones also contain salts, and these can react with atmospheric pollutants to form sulphates that can affect both limestones and sandstones.

## Pollution

Aside from the documented effects of atmospheric pollutants on major building materials, there are also many other forms of pollution that can affect buildings and their contents. Sulphur dioxide will tarnish metals, weaken leather, damage paints and dyes, cause the defibration of timber

*Figure 7.1* Medieval stone cross at Aylmerton, Norfolk, rebuilt during the 1930s using hard, cement-based mortar. The stone has eroded at the joints, and the surface spalled as a result of frost damage and salt crystallization.

surfaces and the embrittlement of paper. Ozone, given off by certain photocopiers, will crack rubber, fade dyes and cause damage to books and manuscripts. Hydrogen sulphide, a product of woollen fabrics, will tarnish metals. Formic acid vapours, given off by certain woods and glues, will attack photographic emulsions and lead-based objects.

Pollution can also occur as a result of particles being dispersed into an internal environment. The acidic soots and smoke given off in an open fire are an obvious pollutant, while the alkaline spray given off by drying concrete and plaster, which can damage paintings, is perhaps less so. Direct soiling, by inappropriate handling of objects, will introduce damaging moisture, salts, fats and dirt.

## CORROSION OF METALS

### Typical causes of metal corrosion

Corrosion occurs due to a reaction between a metal and its environment, and as such can be affected by levels of atmospheric pollutants, and the presence and proximity of dissimilar metals and other materials. The two basic mechanisms of corrosion are direct oxidization and electro-chemical reaction.

It is important to note that the rate of oxidization and electro-chemical corrosion is greater where the metal is subjected to high concentrations of acids and salts. The corrosion of iron or mild-steel wall ties will, for example, be greater when in contact with mortars containing high levels of sulphates or chlorides, or when used with sulphide-rich black-ash mortars.

### Symptoms and diagnosis

#### Direct oxidization

When moisture comes into contact with ferrous metals, such as mild steel and cast iron, the surface becomes anodic and oxidizes, forming the well-known red-brown oxide layer of rust. This gives a level of protection, but tends to flake off so exposing more of the metal to corrosion. The exposed surfaces of non-ferrous metals also oxidize, forming a protective layer typically seen as the grey carbonate patina on lead and zinc roofs, and the green oxide film on copper roofs.

#### Electro-chemical reaction

The corrosion of ferrous and non-ferrous metals is also caused by an electro-chemical reaction that takes place when the metal is exposed to air and water. Typically, a galvanic cell is formed where a current passes from one part of the metal to another. The metal that is anodic corrodes in preference to that which is cathodic. Each metallic element reacts differently to exposure, and to the presence of other metals, according to its position in an electro-chemical series (Table 7.1).

*Table 7.1* Standard electrode potentials (volts) with reference to hydrogen electrode

| Magnesium | -2.37 | Hydrogen | 0.00 |
|-----------|-------|----------|------|
| Aluminium | -1.66 | Copper | +0.34 |
| Zinc | -0.76 | Mercury | +0.80 |
| Iron | -0.44 | Silver | +0.80 |
| Tin | -0.14 | Platinum | +1.20 |
| Lead | -0.13 | Gold | +1.42 |

## Differential aeration

Metal that is starved of oxygen, such as by water held within a crevice, under a particle of dirt, in a joint or at a point of damage in a protective coating, will become anodic in what is termed a differential aeration cell, and will corrode in preference to the cathodic area at the edges of the water droplets. This anodic reaction will proceed at a faster rate in an acidic environment.

## Bi-metallic corrosion

When two metals come into contact with one other in an electrolyte the difference between their electro-potentials will mean that one metal will act as an anode, and the other a cathode. This potential difference between dissimilar metals sets up an electrical current, or galvanic cell, and results in the corrosion of the metal with the lower potential (the anode).

Examples of such bimetallic action include the corrosion of an aluminium flagpole (-1.66 V) by an uninsulated copper lightning conductor (+0.34 V), a zinc-galvanized steel water cistern (-0.76 V) by connected copper piping, a zinc or aluminium covered roof by rainwater run-off from a copper-covered roof, zinc nails used to fix copper roofing sheets, and steel or galvanized-steel nails used in moist timbers treated with a copper-based preservative.

Protection against corrosion can be given by coating the object with a layer of a metal having a lower potential that will act as a sacrificial anode, such as the zinc galvanizing on a steel water cistern. Anodes of zinc, magnesium or aluminium are also used on larger items, such as ships' hulls, the immersed sections of oil rigs and pipelines, to give cathodic protection.

DIMENSIONAL STABILITY

## Typical causes of dimensional movement

The response of materials to changes in temperature and humidity is an important cause of defects in traditional buildings brought about by changing patterns of usage and varying levels of heat and humidity. It is therefore important that the basic mechanisms of change are understood so that dimensional movement can be minimized or countered.

## Symptoms and diagnosis

*Thermal movement*

Materials exposed to varying thermal conditions will undergo dimensional change as a result of the vibration and movement of their atoms and molecules. The extent of this movement is related to the strength and character of the bonding between these atoms or molecules, and to the increase or decrease in temperature. The measurement of movement in a particular material is known as its coefficient of thermal expansion (Table 7.2). Unless restrained most materials will contract in response to a decrease in temperature.

Where materials are exposed to cycles of high and low temperatures, as experienced during the course of the day, between day and night, and between summer and winter, the material will experience corresponding cycles of expansion and contraction. Within a homogeneous material, such as stone, such cyclical movement between the surface and the body of the stone can lead to shear failure and the detachment of the surface layer.

Where materials with different coefficients are bonded or secured together, differential expansion and contraction will cause the bond or weaker of the two materials to fail. Similarly, the internal stresses that are generated within a material that is unable to expand or contract due to the use of inappropriate fixings or other forms of restraint will cause it to crack or distort.

*Moisture movement*

The absorption of water into porous materials takes place due to a weak chemical/physical bond between the surface of the material and free molecules of water. This absorption typically causes an increase in the volume of the material, as shown in Table 7.3. A loss of moisture from a

*Table 7.2* Coefficients of thermal expansion (m/m°C), with approximate unrestrained thermal movement for a 30° change in a material length of 3 m (mm)[2, 3, 4]

| | | |
|---|---|---|
| Marble | $4 \times 10^{-6}$ | 0.360 mm |
| Limestones | $4–7 \times 10^{-6}$ | 0.360–0.630 mm |
| Clay bricks | $5–8 \times 10^{-6}$ | 0.450–0.720 mm |
| Sandstones | $5–12 \times 10^{-6}$ | 0.450–1.080 mm |
| Granite | $8–11 \times 10^{-6}$ | 0.720–0.990 mm |
| Concrete | $10–12 \times 10^{-6}$ | 0.900–1.080 mm |
| Sand-lime bricks | $12–22 \times 10^{-6}$ | 1.080–1.980 mm |
| Lime mortar | $8–10 \times 10^{-6}$ | 0.720–0.900 mm |
| Cement mortar | $10–11 \times 10^{-6}$ | 0.900–0.990 mm |
| Gypsum plaster | $10–12 \times 10^{-6}$ | 1.900–1.080 mm |
| Cast iron | $10.6 \times 10^{-6}$ | 0.954 mm |
| Steel | $10–14 \times 10^{-6}$ | 0.900–1.260 mm |
| Iron | $11–12 \times 10^{-6}$ | 0.990–1.080 mm |
| Copper | $16.8 \times 10^{-6}$ | 1.512 mm |
| Brass | $18 \times 10^{-6}$ | 1.620 mm |
| Bronze | $19.8 \times 10^{-6}$ | 1.782 mm |
| Aluminium | $23.8 \times 10^{-6}$ | 2.142 mm |
| Lead | $29.4 \times 10^{-6}$ | 2.646 mm |
| Zinc | $31.2 \times 10^{-6}$ | 2.808 mm |
| Glass | $7–9 \times 10^{-6}$ | 0.630–0.810 mm |
| Oak, along fibres | $3.4 \times 10^{-6}$ | 0.306 mm |
| Pine, along fibres | $5.4 \times 10^{-6}$ | 0.486 mm |
| Wood laminates | $10–40 \times 10^{-6}$ | 0.900–3.600 mm |
| Oak, across fibres | $28.4 \times 10^{-6}$ | 2.556 mm |
| Pine, across fibres | $34.1 \times 10^{-6}$ | 3.069 mm |
| Plastics | $14–97 \times 10^{-6}$ | 1.260–8.750 mm |
| Epoxy resins | $60 \times 10^{-6}$ | 5.400 mm |
| Acrylic resins | $70–80 \times 10^{-6}$ | 6.300–7.200 mm |
| Polyester resins | $100–150 \times 10^{-6}$ | 9.000–13.500 mm |

*Table 7.3* Approximate unrestrained moisture movement from dry to saturated for a material length of 3 m (mm)[3]

| | |
|---|---|
| Marble | minimal |
| Clay bricks | 0.075–0.300 mm |
| Sand-lime bricks | 0.300–1.500 mm |
| Concrete | 0.600–1.800 mm |
| Gypsum plaster | minimal |
| Sand plaster | minimal |
| Aluminium | nil |
| Copper | nil |
| Steel | nil |
| Glass | nil |
| Wood, along grain | 0.025 mm |
| Wood, across grain | 3–5% radial and 5–15% tangential |
| Plastics | minimal |

porous material will typically cause a decrease in volume and corresponding shrinkage.

Materials, such as brick, may suffer from both thermal and moisture-related movement, and thus be particularly susceptible to deterioration and decay.

Materials that require the addition of moisture during their manufacture, such as mortars, renders and plasters, will contract during setting, and respond little to later wetting. Other materials, such as unseasoned timber, will suffer continual expansion and contraction due to changes in moisture content.

Moisture absorbed into a porous material may carry with it other ions that can form chemical compounds, leading to varying rates of irreversible expansion. An example of this is the expansion of cement-based products under the action of sulphates.

# Chapter Eight

# Building element I: Roofs

## INTRODUCTION

For a roof to fulfil its function as a weathershield it requires a durable weather-resisting covering and associated flashings, supported by a suitable structural system. The variations in roof geometry, colour and texture impart an important sense of local character.

Any survey to assess the condition of a roof must be conducted as two linked inspections – internal and external. The roofspace should be inspected first to give the surveyor the opportunity to consider the construction of the roof, and gain an insight into the causes of defects visible externally and in relation to other parts of the building, particularly the walls. The roof structure also provides some of the best evidence on which to date a building and to uncover changes that have taken place in the past.

## ROOF STRUCTURE

### Typical forms of construction

- **Single roof**: couple, close couple or, typically, collar construction used for simple roofs. Longitudinal rigidity was introduced with the use of ridge pieces and purlins in the thirteenth century, and transverse rigidity with parallel rafters and scissor bracing from the thirteenth and fourteenth centuries.
- **Crown-post truss**: supporting a collar purlin. First used during the early thirteenth century for churches, and from the late thirteenth century to the early fourteenth century for high-status domestic buildings, persisting into the sixteenth century for smaller houses. Common in the south-eastern counties, and spreading later to the north and west.
- **Arch-braced roof**: popular, together with the use of wind bracing, from the fourteenth century for decoration in roofs of increased height.

- **Hammer-beam roof**: increasingly used from the late fourteenth century for open and decorative roofs, progressing to double and false hammer-beam roofs.  ·
- **King-post truss**: supporting a ridge piece. Used from the fourteenth century to sixteenth century in northern counties where favoured for low-pitched and undecorated roofs, and later in the eighteenth and nineteenth centuries. A king strut supports the apex joint of the principal rafters, rather than a ridge piece.
- **Queen-post truss**: supporting a collar. Increasingly used from the mid-sixteenth century with the abandonment of the open hall and need to utilize the roof space. Queen struts support the side purlins where there is no collar.
- **Cruck roof**: cruck forms, such as

*Figure 8.1* Varied roofscape to a Tuscan villa.

raised, middle and upper crucks, were used in high-status houses and farm buildings in the fourteenth and fifteenth centuries, and for humble dwellings until the eighteenth or nineteenth century.

• **Mansard truss**: used from the eighteenth century in order to make use of the attic space.

• **Long-span roof**: new structural arrangements were required from the late seventeenth century to roof the new double-pile houses, and later industrial buildings. Modified king and queen-post trusses, with secondary struts and posts, allowed long-span roofs to be formed, often with shallow pitches and low ridge lines. Alternative roof forms were also developed, such as the hipped roof with central flat area, the M-shaped or 'butterfly' roof, and the multiple-pitch or 'saw-tooth' roof.

• **Composite roof**: combination of timber, iron or steel members, common from the late nineteenth century, making best use of the structural qualities of the materials.

• **Iron or steel roof**: from the early nineteenth century iron, and later steel, were used for large spans, with various truss arrangements common from the mid-nineteenth century until the adoption of portal frame construction in the 1950s.

• **Clinker-based concrete**: unreinforced concrete fill between iron or rolled steel joists used for fire-proof flat-roof construction from the late nineteenth century.

## Roofspace inspection

Items to check:

• Construction; examine the roof framework for the adequacy of its structural arrangement:
  – proper triangulation of structural members;
  – intermediate support to purlins to prevent overspanning;
  – joints for signs of opening up indicating movement;
  – member sizes related to load and span (The Building Regulations *Approved Document A Structure* provides guidance for softwood structural members used in single family houses);
  – plumbness of trusses.

• Evidence of overloading or careless adaptation;
• Support for cold water storage tank(s)
• Fungal attack and/or beetle infestation
• Dampness:
  – penetration;
  – leaking services;
  – condensation.
• Battens and the condition of the underside of the roof covering and its fixings (where absence of roofing felt permits).
• The nature of the ceiling construction.
• Level of thermal insulation/ ventilation.

## Symptoms and diagnosis

### Sagging in plane of roof

• Deflection of rafters or purlins caused by inadequate scantlings for original or current roof covering.
• Ground movement causing loss of support and restraint to wall plates and purlins.
• Spread of roof at eaves. This may result from a lack of triangulation in the

roof structure, as with the absence, failure or removal of a tie member in a couple or collar roof, or an inherent design weakness as with a raised tie roof, and lead to the outward movement of the wall plate(s) and wall heads.

- Inadequate support to purlins by struts or masonry piers. Where a purlin is supported by later brickwork, check for slippage occurring where the uppermost brick is laid frog up or small pieces of cut bricks are used around the member.

- Beetle infestation, particularly to areas of sapwood and retained bark. It is important to check sections of timber in areas subject to maximum compressive and tensile forces to ensure adequate strength.
- Fungal infection, particularly to timbers built into or surrounded by masonry such as the ends of purlins, ridge beams, wall plates or corbels for wall posts.
- Warping and twisting of unseasoned timber, both original or inserted for repair.

## Movement of roof structure

- Excessive dead loading caused by replacement of roof coverings with heavier material.
- Excessive loading, such as snow or in extreme cases the accumulated weight of bird or bat droppings. Ceiling joists can become overloaded by the storage of goods or the introduction of water-storage cisterns into the roof space without localized strengthening of joists.
- Load redistribution following failure, removal or modification of roof members, suppression of movement at joint(s), or freeing of joints due to failure of pegs, keys or iron cotters. The identification of missing members through clues such as empty mortises and peg holes can help in the explanation of present symptoms. It is worth noting that bats find empty mortise holes and other cavities ideal places for summer or maternity roosts.
- Longitudinal movement of structure caused by absence or failure of bracing or supporting structure, such as a

gable chimney stack. In a terrace of properties this movement will have a 'domino' effect, placing reliance on the ability of the end structure to offer adequate restraint.
- Lateral movement of structure caused by absence or failure of ties or outward movement of walls.
- Failure of joints and loss of end bearing, leading to risk of overloading.
- Absence or failure of trimming around dormer windows and chimney stacks.
- Failure of remedial measures. Iron braces, rods, stirrups and ties can corrode and either fail completely or partly causing a redistribution of load.
- Wholesale removal of battens or sarking boarding during reroofing, which previously conferred a degree of rigidity to the roof structure.
- Past damage associated with storms, lightning strikes or explosions revealed in later repairs, modifications or misalignment of members.

## Excess moisture

- Inadequate ventilation to roof void. Where a roof is felted, ventilation is reduced; where sarking boarding is employed without special provision for ventilation, air movement is almost absent. Ventilation will also be restricted by insulation material being packed into eaves, spray-on insulation applied to the underside of the roof covering, or waterproof coatings applied over

the roof covering. Compartmentation to limit spread of fire may also restrict airflow.
- Condensation forming on the underside of roofing felt and dripping onto timbers, insulation and ceiling. Air movement may be restricted by the introduction of insulation, or firestopping above separating walls in roof spaces or in boxed eaves.

- Inadequate maintenance of gutters, particularly those difficult to reach as on hipped roofs with central flat area, M-shaped or 'butterfly' roofs, and multiple-pitch or 'sawtooth' roofs.
- Rainwater pounding on roofing felt behind fasciae where tilting fillets have been omitted.
- Rainwater channelled to wall head where roofing felt has not been taken into the gutter.
- Absence of counter-battens to roof with sarking boards laid over rafters, causing rainwater to become trapped behind battens.
- Water held in contact with timbers by torching, leading to fungal infection.
- Presence of hygroscopic salts, leading to an increased moisture content of affected timbers. During the 1950s and '60s magnesium fluorosilicate was an approved water-soluble preservation treatment, from which the white deposit magnesium sulphate may sometimes be found on treated timbers. Such salts may cause irritation of the eyes and nasal passages.

## Cracking and spalling to beam and clinker flat roofs

- Penetrating moisture through a defective roof finish, such as asphalt, will cause the clinker to expand and exert pressure, leading to cracking and bulging of perimeter parapets and walls.

## Movement in timber flat roofs

- Cupping and curling of decking boards.
- Moisture-related movement of wood-wool slabs.
- Deflection of chipboard decking used for repairs or reroofing.

## ROOF COVERING

## Typical forms of covering

- **Tiles**: clay tiles were used by the Romans, and were popular as a fire-proofing material by the twelfth century. Single-lap tiles, such as pantiles, are found from the seventeenth century; Roman and Spanish tiles from the nineteenth century. Double-lap tiles, such as plain tiles, are found from the twelfth century. Concrete tiles were available from the late nineteenth century, and asbestos-cement tiles from the early twentieth century. Clay tiles have a life of 60–70 years if handmade and 40–60 years if machine-made. Concrete tiles may be expected to give 50–60 years of life.
- **Slates**: natural riven slates, such as from Cumberland, Delabole, Swithland and Westmorland, were used close to the quarries from the fifteenth century. Increased usage followed the introduction of canal and rail transport in the eighteenth and nineteenth centuries. Laid in diminishing courses, often to steep pitches.
- **Welsh slate**: popular as a lightweight and readily available material as a result of improved rail transport in the nineteenth century. Usually laid in regular courses, often to low pitches. Good-quality slate has a life expectancy of 60–90 years.
- **Stone flags and tiles**: flags are thick, heavy slabs, usually of sandstone and found mainly in the Pennine area, while stone tiles, or slates, such as Collyweston and Stonesfield, are a thinner, lighter material usually of limestone. Laid to diminishing courses and hung from battens using bone or wooden pegs with or without mortar

torching. Available since Roman times, their use has now almost ceased due to limited production. Stone flags and tiles have an average life of 100 years.

- **Thatch**: used in various forms throughout history, but restricted in urban centres due to the risk of fire. Remained in use for humble dwellings into the seventeenth and eighteenth centuries, with a revival in use in the nineteenth and twentieth centuries. Water reed (*Phragmites communis* or *P. australis*), often called Norfolk reed, can last up to 100 years, with reridging required every 10–15 years. Long straw has a life of 15–20 years, while combed wheat reed, often termed Devon reed, has a life of 30–50 years. Flax, heather, broom, sods and marram grass are also used to form a covering, and sedge (*Cladium mariscus*) used to form the ridge to reed thatch. Recent changes in agricultural practices have introduced high levels of chemicals, particularly nitrogen, into thatching materials, with a serious effect on their potential lifespans.
- **Shingles**: used from Roman times until replaced by cheaper and less flammable tiles in the twelfth century. Originally of cleft oak, or occasionally elm, but lately of western red cedar. Oak shingles have a life of 60–100 years.
- **Lead slates**: sometimes used to cover complex roof forms, such as domes, from the nineteenth century (Figure 8.2).
- **Cast-iron tiles**: used from the mid-nineteenth century on buildings such as the Clock and Victoria Towers, Palace of Westminster.
- **Corrugated iron**: wrought-iron sheets were available from the mid-nineteenth century.

- **Lead**: used from the seventh century for pitched, and later flat, roof coverings, and also for covering and weathering many roofscape features. Early lead was cast on a bed of sand, typically to a weight of 8–10 lbs/sq ft (39–49 kg/m$^2$), and possessing a stippled finish that was quick to oxidize. Thinner and smoother factory milled lead was available from the early nineteenth century.
- **Copper**: strong and lightweight sheet covering used from the eighteenth century, particularly for visible roof slopes where the typically green oxide layer forms an attractive patina. A well-laid cooper roof can last between 150 and 200 years.
- **Zinc**: available from the late eighteenth century as a cheap sheet metal substitute for lead, having a typical life of between 40 and 50 years, which can be much reduced by atmospheric pollution.
- **Asphalt**: a mixture of bitumen and inert mineral matter available either as natural mined rock or lake asphalt, or as a mechanical blend of the two materials. Used since Roman times as a waterproof covering, it only became commercially available for use as a flat-roof covering from the mid-nineteenth century. Typically an asphalt roof covering will last between 25 and 30 years, and may be used with either a timber or solid substrate.
- **Bituminous felt**: used as a flat-roof covering from the 1940s, with a life of only 15–20 years. Built-up roofing was usually laid with three bitumen-bonded layers of felt, but has now been superseded by modern high-performance felts and single-layer membranes.

## Symptoms and diagnosis

### Water penetration into tiled or slated roofs

- Slipped or missing tile or slate.
- Broken tile or slate caused by window cleaners, workmen or storm damage. Evidence for localized water penetration can often be seen as spotting and

streaking on insulation, stored goods and timbers.
- Lack of roofing felt allowing rain, snow and leaves to be blown in.
- Breakdown and detachment of mortar

*Figure 8.2* Lead fish-scale slates to the dome of the gazebo (c. 1845) at Kelham Hall, Nottinghamshire. Photograph by David Watt, courtesy of Newark and Sherwood District Council.

torching. Half torching or 'shoulder-ing' was used at just the head of the tile or slate, whereas full torching in-volved bedding the tile or slate in mortar held in place by various means. In Norfolk, reeds were commonly laid over the backs of the rafters and held in place with a lath sprung under the battens, or riven laths were laid be-tween the battens to form a sarking.

• Changes in pitch with single-lap tiles, as at sprocketed eaves, dormer win-dows or outshuts, where the head lap is opened. Such changes should be weathered with a lead apron.

• Defective sheet metal flashings. Bime-tallic corrosion can occur where dissimilar metals are used to form soakers and flashings.

• Cracking and failure of mortar fillets.

• Absence of lead soakers with flashings and mortar fillets.

- Failure of applied remedial coatings, such as hessian and bitumen.
- Snow holding on rough tile surfaces longer than smooth slate surfaces. Snow guards may hold snow for long periods at the eaves.
- Condensation forming on the underside of roofing felt caused by a lack of ventilation.
- Inappropriate covering for pitch of roof.
- Inappropriate pitch or lap for location of building and level of exposure.
- Defective parapet wall causing penetration of moisture that appears as a roof defect.

## Slipped or displaced tiles or slates

- Corrosion and breakage of fixing nails, sometimes referred to as 'nail sickness'. Tingles of copper or lead, or copper wire, used to resecure slipped slates, can indicate the extent of the problem.
- Decay of timber peg fixings sometimes found with early tiling.
- Broken nibs to tiles, often resulting from salt crystallization.
- Accumulated dirt and debris wedging tile nibs off battens. Where torching is deteriorating loose mortar can slide under the tile.
- Enlarged fixing holes to slates resulting from excessive movement or damage from thin-shanked nails.
- Broken, loose or decayed battens. Early roofing battens were riven, as opposed to being sawn, which gives a pleasant variation to the line of the tiles or slates.
- Tiles or slates laid on roof of inappropriate pitch. Also changes of pitch and roof shape as with mansard roofs and extensions.
- Wind uplift and storm damage, particularly at verges, eaves and ridges.
- Breakage and displacement caused by window cleaners, workmen and fallen branches.
- Disturbance related to movement of roof structure.
- Disturbance caused by low-flying aircraft.
- Blown insulation to the underside of the roof covering may be holding the tiles or slates in place, and will preclude detailed inspection.

*Table 8.1* Minimum pitches required for a range of roof coverings

| | |
|---|---|
| Clay, double-lap plain tile | 40° |
| Clay interlocking tiles | 30° |
| Clay pantiles | 25° |
| Concrete double-lap plain tile | 35° |
| Concrete single-lap tile | 17.5° |
| Western red cedar shingles | 25° |
| Oak shingles | 45° |
| Natural slates | |
|    large | 22.5° |
|    ordinary | 26° |
|    small | 33° |
| Fibre-cement slates | 20° |
| Cotswold stone tiles | 55° |
| Stone flags | 33° |
| Thatch | 45° |
| Patent glazing | 15° |

## Slipped or displaced ridge and hip tiles

- Wind uplift and storm damage.
- Failure of bedding mortar.
- Absence, or corrosion and failure, of hip irons or fixings, causing hip tiles to slip.
- Deflection or movement in ridge board or hip rafter, or sagging in plane of roof.

## Excessive weathering of exposed surface of tile

- Saturation of tile, with increased risk of frost damage and eventual disintegration. This can be a particular problem beneath overflow pipes. Glazed tiles can suffer where the glaze has become damaged.
- Moisture retained in contact with surface. Mosses and lichens retain water, and produce acidic secretions.

- Old age, often seen with second-hand materials.
- Poor quality or substandard tiles.
- Atmospheric pollution.
- Blown insulation to the underside of the tiles will preclude detailed inspection.

## Excessive weathering of exposed surface of slate

- Delamination of slate with risk of water penetration and eventual disintegration. It is important to distinguish natural slate from asbestos/fibre cement slates which can, at a distance, sometimes be mistaken for true slates.
- Moisture retained in contact with surface. Mosses and lichens retain water, and produce acidic secretions.
- Old age, often seen with second-hand materials.

- Poor quality or substandard slates, such as those with an excessive carbonate content that will react with acidic atmospheric gases (e.g. sulphur dioxide) to form calcium sulphate.
- Atmospheric pollution.
- Failure of externally applied hessian and bitumen remedial coatings.
- Blown insulation to the underside of the slates will preclude detailed inspection.

## Defective stone flag and tile covering

- Decay and breakage of wooden pegs. Pegs are liable to twist under the weight of the flag or tile, unless restrained by the use of double battens.
- Deflection of roof timbers caused by the weight of the covering.
- Breakdown and detachment of mortar bedding used with certain types of tile, such as Collywestons.

- Breakdown and loss of early torching materials, such as sphagnum moss, used to prevent entry of rainwater.
- Frost damage, particularly to the upper half of the flag or tile where moisture is retained by the head lap.
- Failure of externally applied remedial coatings, such as cement slurries.

## Defective thatch covering

- Localized settlement of thatch, particularly adjacent to hard features such as chimney stacks, forming hollows which hold rainwater.
- Localized deterioration of thatch and fixing spars, particularly at valleys, ridges, verges and eaves, allowing rainwater to collect and soak into the material and roof timbers.
- Failure of sedge or heather ridges.
- Loss of material due to rats, squirrels and birds. Wire netting is often used to prevent such loss, particularly to

long-straw roofs, but may itself hold snow and prevent shedding of rainwater.
- Corrosion and breakage of wire netting, leading to loss of material.
- Inappropriate environment and orientation with respect to site features. The little water-powered sawmill at Gunton in Norfolk is thatched in water reed, the roof being in a poor environment for the material. The building lies close to a lake, with a continual fine spray rising from the outflow.

There are mature trees close by, and air movement is restricted.

- Moisture retained in contact with surface. Mosses and lichens retain water and produce acidic secretions, while fungi will thrive in areas of high humidity.
- Inappropriate pitch, causing thatch to remain damp. In East Anglia the pitch for a thatched roof is usually in excess of 50°.

- Use of fire retardant treatments or finishes. Chemical retardants are applied by soaking the thatch in the solution prior to fixing. Recent research suggests that the quantities of water and chemicals taken up may have a deleterious effect on the material. Water reed should be cut and stored in dry conditions, and such a treatment is thus considered contrary to best practice.

## Defective shingle covering

- Decay of original timber pegs.
- Corrosion and expansion of fixing nails.
- Lack of adequate fixing nails to prevent warping.
- Inadequate seasoning of replacement sawn or split cedar shingles.
- Moisture movement in sapwood of replacement shingles.

- Inappropriate pitch. The pitch should be no less than 45°.
- Inappropriate lap.
- Retention of moisture by mosses and lichens.
- Displacement caused by woodpeckers, where attracted by insects behind shingles.

## General defects in sheet metal and flat-roof coverings

- Fatigue. Sheet metals can become overworked during laying, causing micro-fractures and possible anodic areas susceptible to corrosion.
- Surface pitting, distortion, tearing and penetration caused by overworking, thermal movement, pollution, excessive or heavy traffic, and pressure of heavy items such as urns and statues.
- Excessive sheet size. Adequate allowance must be made for thermal movement, particularly in the case of lead which will expand or 'creep' without any subsequent contraction, and zinc which has a high coefficient of thermal expansion.
- Excessive fixings for size of sheet. This will restrict thermal movement, setting up excessive stresses and leading to eventual failure.
- Inadequate and failed fixings for size of sheet. This will allow excessive movement and subsequent slippage.
- Inadequate or distorted falls. This may result from movement of the roof decking or structure, and lead to inadequate rainwater disposal with ponding and the risk of localized penetration.

- Poorly designed or executed drips and rolls.
- Movement in substrate. Timber boards should be laid to follow the slope of the roof so that any distortion will not impede the flow of water.
- Underlays with high bitumen or resin content will adhere to the underside of sheet metals in hot weather and restrict thermal movement.
- Lack of adequate ventilation or vapour barrier, allowing build-up of moisture vapour and subsequent decay of decking, insulation and substrate.
- Condensation forming on the underside of fully-supported sheet-metal coverings leading to localized corrosion and eventual failure.
- Bimetallic corrosion of metals, such as copper affecting aluminium and zinc. Run-off from lead roofs or flashings onto aluminium in a marine environment will cause severe corrosion of the aluminium.
- Surface corrosion due to acidic water run-off from mosses and lichens, and atmospheric pollution.
- Wind uplift and subsequent damage affecting lightweight coverings.

*Figure 8.3* Copper sheet used as a covering for the pediment and dormer roof, and lead for the dormer cheeks and as a weathering to the timber cornice. The pitch is covered with Westmorland slates. Both sheet metals have suffered from thermal movement to this south-facing section of the roof, and patch repairs are in evidence.

## Defects in lead sheet covering

- High coefficient of thermal expansion. Where lead is unrestrained it will 'creep' under its own weight, causing localized distortion. Continuous cycles of expansion and contraction will cause eventual failure of the sheet.
- Failure or absence of supporting soldered dots, lead-burned dots or lead tacks to lead used on slopes and roof pitches.
- Rolls and drips. Timber rolls may be rotten or distorted, and hollow rolls distorted or torn. Drips may be poorly formed without anti-capillary grooves.
- Condensation and corrosion. Where heating levels inside a building are increased, and natural ventilation decreased, condensation may form on the underside of lead sheets leading to localized corrosion and eventual failure. In the absence of carbon dioxide the protective layer of lead carbonate cannot form, and the distilled condensate will corrode the lead. Such condensation will also cause the decay of organic materials found in traditional underlays.
  - Corrosion was also thought to be caused simply by the acid-bearing timber being in contact with the lead, but experience has shown that corrosion can be exacerbated by some kinds of timber, such as oak boarding and plywood decking, where acids are taken up by the condensate.
  - As a means of reducing the risk of condensation, and in an attempt to avoid the problems of ensuring effective vapour checks and adequate ventilation in a cold roof construction, the unventilated warm roof construction became popular during the late 1970s. It has since been found that moisture can be drawn in at joints by the action of pressure differentials set up by temperature cycles. This phenomenon, known as 'thermal pumping', has brought about an increase in the use of the ventilated warm roof construction for roofs to existing buildings.
- Bimetallic corrosion caused by the use of galvanized, zinc or copper nails and tacks.
- Corrosion of lead sheet caused by contact with cement mortar without protection of bituminous paint.
- Inappropriate patch repairs. Repairs should be carried out with lead-welded patches rather than soldered or fabric patches. Solder will have a different coefficient of thermal expansion, and lead to fatigue cracking in the lead.
- Theft of lead sheets and/or flashings. Where theft is a persistent problem terne-coated stainless-steel sheet may have be used as a substitute. This lightweight material needs to be adequately fixed to avoid wind uplift and drumming.

## Defects in copper sheet covering

- Fatigue caused by drumming of inadequately supported or overworked sheets.
- Failure or damage to standing seams or wooden rolls with the fall, or welted seams across the fall.
- Failure of soldered joints due to expansion and contraction.
- Absence or failure of expansion clips to standing seams in long-strip copper roofing.
- Absence or failure of capping pieces to ridge, hip and common rolls.
- Breakdown or melting of unsuitable underlays restricting thermal movement of copper sheets.
- Corrosion of other metals caused by contact with or run-off from copper roof. This may include nails and screws.
- Corrosion of copper caused by contact with cement.

## Defects in zinc sheet covering

- Distortion and failure of drips to low-pitched roofs and rolls.
- Absence or failure of capping pieces and clips to rolls.
- Excessive fixings for high coefficient of thermal expansion.
- Bimetallic corrosion when zinc is in contact with copper, such as rainwater run-off from a copper roof or contact with a copper lightning conductor.
- Corrosion due to atmospheric pollution. Zinc is particularly susceptible to acidic deposits, and will become pitted by run-off from certain timbers, secretions from mosses and lichens, and when in contact with salt-laden masonry.

## Defects in asphalt roof covering

- Oxidation and eventual crazing of the surface caused by ultraviolet degradation, particularly affecting bitumen-rich surface layer caused by overworking of asphalt.
- Thermal expansion and contraction causing crazing, fractures and lifting of the surface.
- Bubbling and cracking due to trapped moisture.
- Failure of abutment upstands due to the absence or failure of bond with wall, and cracking at angle due to movement or absence of reinforced angle fillet.
- Cracking and failure at acute angles such as upstands and downstands.
- Condensation beneath impermeable asphalt covering, with risk of decay to decking, insulation and substrate.
- Inappropriate substrate. Sometimes lead sheet has been replaced with asphalt over a timber decking, where movement sets up stresses in the asphalt leading to cracks and failed abutment junctions.
- Fracture of brittle finish due to movement in substrate or building.
- Inappropriate repair of cracks using bitumen.

## Defects in bituminous felt roof covering

- Decay of early felts based on organic fibres.
- Embrittlement due to ultraviolet degradation, leading to splitting and tearing in response to movement in substrate and traffic.
- Cracking at abutments where angle formed without fillet.
- Failure of abutment where the felt is dressed directly into the wall.
- Inadequate number of layers in built-up system and failure of bonding between layers.
- Separation or breakdown of bond between layers due to overheating of bitumen during application.
- Absence of vapour barrier allowing insulation and decking to decay.
- Inappropriate patch repairs.

## FLASHINGS AND WEATHERINGS

## Typical forms of construction

Sheet-metal flashings or weatherings, and simple fillets of mortar, are relied on to prevent the penetration of rainwater at various points on a traditional roof. They fulfil an important function, and should never be overlooked or considered in isolation during an inspection of a property, however difficult they may be to reach.

- **Abutment flashing**: used to prevent water penetration at the junction between a wall and roof. Typically it is formed as a step flashing covering soakers sandwiched between double-lap slates or tiles, or as a combined step and cover flashing for a single-lap covering.
- **Soakers**: used between double-lap slates or tiles at abutments or with mitred hips.
- **Secret gutter**: used with either an abutment flashing or an abutment step and cover flashing, where there is a risk of moisture penetration at the abutment in exposed locations.
- **Mortar fillets**: used instead of an abutment flashing with or without soakers.
- **Cover flashing**: secured into a masonry joint and used to cover an upstand.

- **Chimney flashings**: a stack penetrating a roof slope will need a front apron, side flashings and a back gutter with cover flashing, whereas a stack on the ridge will need two front aprons, side flashings and two saddle pieces.
- **Valley gutters**: used to protect and weather the junction between two roof slopes.
- **Saddles**: used to protect and weather the junction between roof slopes at a ridge or hip.
- **Aprons**: used to protect and weather changes in roof pitch on mansard roofs and at the upper edges of tile hanging.
- **Rolls**: used to cover wood rolls at ridge or hip.
- **Lead slates**: small lead sheets used to weather a projection through the roof covering, e.g. a flue.

*Figure 8.4* Fungal attack and beetle infestation to modillion cornice. Notice the detached section of moulding and condition of paintwork to this south-facing section of roof.

- **Protective weatherings**: used to protect exposed masonry, such as cornices, copings, parapets and other projections, and to shed rainwater from such surfaces.

- **Listings:** projecting courses at the base of a chimney stack intended to throw rainwater away from the point of roof penetration.

## Symptoms and diagnosis

### Defects in flashings, weatherings or fillets

- Sheet-metal flashings. Inadequate depth of upstand; poorly secured flashing; excessive flashing length; and loose or missing wedges, tacks and clips, allowing water to penetrate behind the upstand.
- Leakage through tuck-in of abutment or cover flashing where lead wedges have become loose, such as where a joint coincides with a cavity tray, or where it is turned into a rendered wall.
- Wind-lift and distortion caused by inadequate or inappropriate clipping of free edges. Lead should not be used for clips in exposed locations due to its low mechanical strength.
- Inadequate soakers fitted with double-lap tiles.

- Fatigue at angles in sheet metal flashings and cover strips.
- Failure or blockage of back gutters to chimney stacks.
- Staining on materials below flashings and weatherings due to run-off from lead. New lead should be coated with patination oil to prevent such staining.
- Failure of brittle mortar fillets to rigid elements, such as chimney stacks and parapets, resulting from movement in the roof structure and covering, or initial drying shrinkage. Failed and displaced fillets can allow rainwater to run down into the spaces below, and cause the blockage of gutters and valleys.
- Broken or open-jointed listings concentrating rainwater onto flashing or fillet.

### Water penetration at valleys

- Inadequate lap between valley and roof covering.

- Deflection or movement in valley boards or bearers.

## ASSOCIATED JOINERY

## Typical roof joinery

External joinery associated with a pitched roof performs both a protective and decorative role, and disrepair of items such as bargeboards, cappings, finials, fasciae and soffits may affect the performance of the roof as a whole.

## Symptoms and diagnosis

### General defects in roof joinery

- Fungal decay, particularly at joints,

leading to movement and displacement of roof covering.

- Beetle infestation, particularly to protected surfaces.
- Failure of bargeboards, exposing ends of purlins to deterioration.
- Failure of cappings, forming the weathering to a roof covering abutting a bargeboard.
- Movement of fascia boards, affecting falls of gutters.

*Figure 8.5* Defects to glass dome include failed gaskets, corroded cover strips and cracked glass.

ROOFSCAPE FEATURES

## Typical roofscape features

The features that are to be found on, or forming part of, the roof of a building are many and varied, and include bellcotes, belvederes, cupolas, flèches, skylights, lantern lights, dome lights, dormer windows, patent glazing and clock towers. Chimney stacks are considered in detail in Chapter Thirteen.

## Symptoms and diagnosis

### General defects in roofscape features

- Direct moisture penetration through broken glass, slipped or displaced tiles or slates, or poor-fitting opening lights. Tile or slate coverings to steep pitches, such as those on cupolas and flèches, are particularly at risk from defective fixings.
- Indirect moisture penetration through defective flashings, failed glazing gaskets and putties, and missing or defective cover strips.
- Corrosion and distortion of iron curb plates, ribs and other roofing members, leading to failure of seals and flashings, and cracked glass.
- Missing or defective mechanical linkages and adjusters for high-level opening lights.
- Defective mechanisms and associated equipment, as found in bellcotes and in clock towers.

# Chapter Nine

# Building element II: Walls and structural frames

## INTRODUCTION

The load-bearing walls or structural frame of a building often display symptoms from which the surveyor will recognize and diagnose a defect. These symptoms may be clearly visible, as a crack in a brick wall, or be hidden, for example, by ivy, cladding or render. What, at first glance, appears to be brickwork may turn out to be mathematical tiles, and the rendered wall assumed to have been of brickwork may prove on closer examination to be of timber-framed construction, or another material such as shuttered clay or clay lump. The surveyor must therefore not accept things at face value.

## FOUNDATIONS

### Typical forms of construction

- **Footings**: the principle of spreading the load of a building by increasing the width of the wall below ground level was known to the Romans, and used almost continuously from the twelfth century up to the early twentieth century. Preparation of the ground might have included trenching, compaction and the introduction of large stones. The footings may also be built off a grillage of timber to assist in stiffening and strengthening the masonry substructure.

- **Piles**: individual or grouped timber

*Figure 9.1* Flint-faced house with clay-lump backing in south-west Norfolk. The key between the two materials was minimal, and the house appeared as a conventional flint building.

piles were used when building on poor ground from the eleventh century and probably before. These were driven into the ground and often capped with horizontal timbers designed to spread the load and provide a suitable base to build up from.

• **Rafts**: many medieval structures were built off simple rafts made up from layers of rubble, pebbles, gravel, clay or mortar. Concrete rafts were used from the early nineteenth century.
• **Concrete**: trench-filled foundations, formed with similar materials as for

early raft construction, were in use by the eleventh century, and continued up to the sixteenth century. Concrete as we know it began to be used from the early nineteenth century, and was made compulsory for foundations in 1878 with the London Building Act of that date. By the late nineteenth century brick footings were being built off concrete strip foundations rather than timber grillages.

- **Foundation arches**: the practice of spanning poor ground with arches built between piers was seen from the fourteenth century, whilst inverted arches were used from the nineteenth century to spread high loadings along the length of the foundation between intermediate piers.
- **Below-ground masonry**: puddled clay, dry-packed sand and dry-bedded masonry were used by medieval builders for building on waterlogged, marshy and poorly consolidated land. With the growth in civil engineering projects in the eighteenth century use was increasingly made of hydraulic mortars. The writings of the Roman architect Vitruvius were studied for their advice on concretes and pozzolanic materials, and much work was done by John Smeaton and others to develop hydraulic cements.
- **Basements, cellars and pavement vaults**: commonly used with better-quality housing from the eighteenth century up to the early twentieth century. Masonry was kept dry, and dampness excluded, by the use of open or dry areas around the outside of the house, cavity-wall construction, vertical damp-proof courses and basic asphalt tanking.

## Symptoms and diagnosis

### Ground movement

- Settlement, brought about by initial or additional loading. Differential settlement may occur where a structure is founded in varying ground conditions or over 'hard shoulders' such as part basements, or has foundations imposing unequal loads as may occur with extensions, projecting bays or porches.
- Subsidence, resulting from mining, extraction, landslip, erosion of fines due to defective drains or underground streams, shrinkage of clay soils and changes in the water table as a result of abstraction or land drainage (Figure 9.2). It should be remembered that records of early mining and extraction of coal and minerals, such as gypsum, iron ore, lead, salt and tin, either do not exist or are less than accurate in location and extent.
- Site features, such as trees and shrubs, former ditches and watercourses, inadequately compacted fill, underground streams, slope instability, and vibration from traffic and machinery will all have an effect on the initial and continuing stability of a building.
- Soil characteristics. Clay soils suffer volumetric changes in relation to changes in moisture content. This may be effected by seasonal shrinkage or swelling, take-up of moisture by trees and shrubs, felling and removal of trees and shrubs, or leakage from below-ground pipes and drains. Clay hillside soils will often exhibit a downhill creep associated with seasonal changes in moisture content.
- Geological faults.
- Freezing of ground water and formation of ice lenses in frost-susceptible soils, such as chalk. Damage can occur due to both the initial heave of the ground and later settlement as the ice thaws.
- Swallow holes, caused by the localized erosion of chalk or limestone.

### Foundation failure

- Inadequate depth and spread of footings, making them susceptible to mois-ture-related movement of clay soils, overloading and damage by tree roots.

*Figure 9.2* Church of St Mary and St Laurence in Bolsover, Derbyshire. Coal-mining subsidence has caused severe distortion to the windows to the south aisle.

- Failure of foundation arches caused by localized subsidence or loss of abutments.
- Decay of timber piles. Elm was traditionally used for piling in wet ground, but will decay when exposed and subjected to drying, often as a result of changes to drainage patterns or excavations.
- Chemical attack on concrete, caused by aggressive acidic and sulphate-bearing ground-waters or localized contaminants.
- Lateral loading on walls of basements, cellars and vaults, caused by vibration and localized compaction.
- Corrosion and subsequent expansion of embedded ironwork.

## WALL CONSTRUCTION

### Typical forms of construction

- **Solid**: a wall constructed of structural units, such as brick or stone, bedded one on top of the other in a pattern or bond to ensure strength and stability.
- **Mass**: a wall constructed of a homogeneous material, such as earth, clay or concrete, usually formed between shuttering.
- **Faced wall**: a wall in which the facing and backing are so bonded as to result in a common action under load.[1]
- **Veneered wall**: a wall having a facing that is attached to the backing, but not so bonded as to result in a common action under load.[1]
- **Double leaf wall**: a wall of two parallel single-leaves, with the space between not exceeding 25 mm, filled

solidly with mortar and so tied as to re-sult in common action under load.[1] Also termed a collar-jointed wall.

- **Cavity wall**: a wall comprising two single leaves, usually at least 50 mm apart, and effectively tied together with wall ties, the space between being left as a continuous cavity or filled with non-loadbearing material.[1]

- **Framed**: A wall based on a structural frame with either external cladding or non-loadbearing infill walling.

## Symptoms and diagnosis

### Bowing and bulging of solid and mass wall panels

- Original defects, such as premature loading of new brickwork, lack of lateral restraint and non-uniform sections of wall. It should be noted

*Figure 9.3* Remains of North Mill on Reedham Marshes, Norfolk. Drainage mills, such as this, were built on poor ground with shallow brick footings or timber piles, and can often be seen leaning.

that some early walls were built with a deliberate batter, and this should not be confused with an original or progressive defect.

- Expansion and contraction: this can result from changes in moisture content and/or temperature, and is dependent on location, level of exposure, materials, use of the building, provision of movement joints and restraint to movement. Parapet walls are particularly vulnerable, and will exhibit distortion if movement is restrained.

- Irregular plan forms, with temperature and moisture-related expansion and contraction causing eccentric forces.
- Eccentric loading, such as balconies, overhanging eaves, asymmetrical roofs, party walls or the presence of voids within a wall. The number and area of flues within a gable or cross wall may be considerable, and be the cause of localized deterioration and distortion.
- Removal or partial removal of chimney breast(s) without adequate support for the remaining stack.

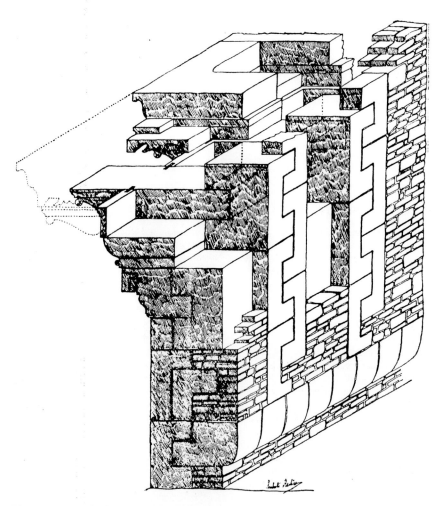

*Figure 9.4* Interlocking system of construction for stone cornice to the late 15th-century Palazzo Strozzi, Florence. Used to resist overturning of heavy eccentric mass. Reproduced from *Palazzo Strozzi di Guido Pampaloni,* credited to Istituto Nazionale delle Assicurazioni.

- Cutting of chases can lead to eccentric loading and rotation.
- Imposed loads: heavy cornices are often counterweighted by the parapet above; where the parapet is removed the cantilevered cornice is liable to rotate and impose increased loading on the front edge of the wall below.
- Decay and subsequent compression of embedded timber, such as bonding timbers (to reinforce brickwork), spreaders and fixing grounds, leading to eccentric loading and the wall rotating about this line. Bonding timbers may also act as bearers for floor members, and provide reinforcement against brick settlement.
- Concentrated load: the stresses present at the bearing of a bressumer onto a narrow masonry pier may be sufficient to cause distortion and crushing.
- Lack of restraint: where gable or party walls are not properly bonded into the flank walls, or roofs and floors are not tied to the wall, outward movement may result from ground movement, roof spread or lateral loading from stored goods. Insertions, such as stairways, can have a significant effect on the restraint offered by the floor construction. Such movement is often evidenced by displacement of door and window frames, gaps around floors and ceilings, and subsequent failure of finishes.
- Outward movement of gable masonry caused by the loss of buttressing elements, such as chimney stacks, or a lack of adequate bracing in the event of wind suction. This may result in a loss of bearing for supporting members such as purlins.
- Remedial tying of an outward bulging wall may cause a corresponding inward movement of the restraining opposite wall. Movement may also be triggered by the temperature-related expansion or contraction of long iron tie rods.
- Decay of joist and beam ends that offered lateral restraint to walls.
- Decay and deflection of solid, built-up or jointed timber bressumers and lintels.

## Bowing and bulging of faced and veneered wall panels

- Inadequate restraint: facing of buildings with a veneer or skin of quality masonry was often carried out onto a backing of common brickwork or random rubble, with little opportunity for tying the two together. Timbers might be built into the backing at intervals to align the courses for a tie, but these are liable to decay. Where a brick bond indicates a solid wall the headers might be snapped and used for appearance only.
- Absence or failure of ties: where facing and backing are tied together with header bricks, through-stones or proprietary ties these may fracture as a result of differential movement or pull out due to poor mortar adhesion. This will lead to an increased slenderness of the masonry facing and greater instability.
- Expansion of restrained outer facing: this may be caused by the expansion of mortar joints as a result of sulphate attack, thermal movement, or the corrosion and expansion of embedded ironwork.
- Shrinkage or consolidation of backing: this may be caused by the decay and subsequent compression of embedded bonding timbers, fixings grounds or settlement under load.
- Settlement of core material: this may result from the presence of unconsolidated or poor-quality material, and the action of water or vibration. The wedging or slumping action of loose material falling down between the inner and outer facing will lead to lateral thrust and increased instability, with bulging of the inner and/or outer facing and eventual collapse.
- Corrosion of iron or steel cramps and dowels used between a later facing and backing.
- Openings too close together: inadequate masonry for the load, leading to localized distortion and loss of bearing for lintels.

## Bowing and bulging of cavity-wall panels

- Corrosion of early or proprietary iron ties.
- Fracture of early or proprietary brick or stoneware ties due to structural movement.
- Corrosion of metal ties due to poor galvanising, site damage, aggressive mortars such as those including sulphur-rich black ash, or exposed coastal location.
- Inadequate number and/or distribution of ties.
- Incorrect placing of ties.
- Wind suction on untied outer leaf.

## Cracking in wall panels

- Irregular plan forms, with temperature and moisture-related expansion and contraction causing eccentric forces.
- Expansion and contraction: this can result from changes in moisture content and/or temperature, and is dependent on location, level of exposure, materials, use of the building, provision of movement joints and restraint to movement. Movement is particularly prevalent in exposed parapet walls and walls facing south or south-west.
- Ground movement.
- Foundation failure.
- Vertical cracking caused by overloading of masonry, usually as a result of the removal of buttressing elements, roof spread or an excessive combination of live and dead loads.
- Concentration and change to load paths as a result of alterations or failure of structural members, such as lintels or bressumers.
- Cracking and open joints to arches over openings caused by the slippage or failure of voussoir(s), failure of abutments, or decay and movement in timber backing lintel.
- Sulphate attack on joints: the affected joints expand, causing tensile forces to develop that may result in horizontal cracking patterns.
- Impact damage.
- Corrosion and expansion of embedded ironwork, such as hoop-iron reinforcement, and cavity wall ties.
- Calcium silicate bricks, also known as sand-lime or flint-lime bricks, suffer from drying shrinkage more than clay bricks. Such movement can result in cracking unless movement joints are provided.

## WALL MATERIALS

## Typical forms of material

- **Mortar**: early mortars were based on locally burnt and slaked chalk or limestone and local aggregates, which, from the evidence of mortar analysis, were typically in proportions of one part lime putty to two and a half or three parts of graded aggregate. By the mid-eighteenth century research by John Smeaton and others had led to a greater understanding of materials and the use of hydraulic limes for engineering applications. Cement:lime or compo mortars, and those based purely on cement, became popular from the early twentieth century. Other cementitious materials used in mortars included fly-ash and natural pozzolans.
- **Pointing**: the manner in which the masonry joint is finished is both a product of practical necessity and visual appearance. Early stonework joints were wide and full, intended to blend with the stone or be covered with plaster or render. Later, finely-cut ashlar stone was laid with thin joints of pure lime putty, using pinnings of slate or shell to achieve a uniform thickness.

With brick, various pointing techniques were employed, of which the use of tuck pointing, introduced in the eighteenth century to imitate the fine joints of high-quality gauged brickwork with bricks of a lower quality, is perhaps the most distinctive.

- **Brick**: bricks were first used in this country during the Roman occupation in the form of broad, flat wall tiles, and afterwards, when salvaged, for medieval structures. Brick making was re-established in the late twelfth century with the help of Flemish craftsmen, and afterwards became a principal material in urban building for fire-resistant construction.
  – Brick sizes were controlled by statute during the reigns of Edward IV and Elizabeth I, and later with the introduction of mechanical production in the late nineteenth century. Brick manufacture was first taxed in 1784, this eventually being repealed in 1850.
  – Methods of manufacture and choice of clays resulted in various brick types including commons, stocks, rubbers, engineering, glazed, gaults, Flettons, sand-lime, and later concrete in the early twentieth century. The use of contrasting materials can be seen in the diaperwork of the Tudor period, early polychromatic brickwork of the late seventeenth century, and later in the nineteenth century.
  – Early brick bonding was erratic, but by the mid-sixteenth century English bond was common and later, in the seventeenth and eighteenth centuries, Flemish bond became popular. Variations include English and Flemish garden-wall bonds, English cross bond, Monk or Yorkshire bond, rat-trap or Chinese bond, and Dearne's bond.
- **Cavity wall construction**: while early nineteenth century brick bonds, such as rat-trap and Dearne's, and mid-nineteenth century patent hollow bricks, were used to reduce direct penetration of moisture, particularly in coastal locations, cavity walls were not common until the early twentieth century. Late nineteenth century cavity ties were constructed from wrought and cast iron, patent stoneware or specially-shaped clay bricks. Early mild-steel ties were either galvanised or bitumen coated.
- **Damp-proof courses**: the use of damp-proof courses was made mandatory for new housing by the Public Health Act of 1875, with early courses made from slate, blue bricks, asphalt and bitumen-saturated hessian.
- **Stone**: the earliest use of stone was for ecclesiastical and military buildings, and relied on either suitable local quarries or transport from distant sources. By the fifteenth and sixteenth centuries building in stone was seen as a sign of prosperity, and houses were built using the various native lime and sandstones, and stones taken from the monasteries and religious houses at the time of the Dissolution. Tastes and fashions during the seventeenth and eighteenth centuries dictated that stone remained the material for the great houses, but from the mid-nineteenth century cheap bricks and improved transport led to a decline in usage. Stone can be used for rubble work, whether coursed or uncoursed, ashlar or as a cladding.
- **Cobbles and pebbles**: cobbles, and the smaller pebbles, can be formed from various types of stone, but have usually been transported and rounded by glacial ice or water.
- **Flint**: formed as nodules of silica within a bed of chalk, flint is used whole, knapped or polled in the Eastern counties, and also in Cambridgeshire, Hertfordshire, Essex, Sussex, Kent, Surrey, Berkshire, Wiltshire and Dorset.
- **Chert**: similar to flint, but usually larger and brown in colour, and found in south Somerset and east Devon.
- **Terracotta**: glazed or unglazed moulded blocks of selected fired clays used typically in a structural capacity. Imported from Italy in the early sixteenth century, and later manufactured in England from the eighteenth century. Used extensively during the nineteenth century both as a plain building material and as a source of repetitive decoration, particularly in heavily polluted areas where it was less prone to decay than natural stone.
- **Coade stone**: a hard, durable material resembling stone made up of a mix of

clay, water, ground terracotta, flint, fine sand and crushed soda-lime-silica, used for decorative features in the second half of the eighteenth century.

- **Faience**: a term used either to describe glazed terracotta in a structural or non-structural context, or as a cladding to a structural frame. Used predominantly in the early twentieth century as a cladding for new and refurbished buildings.
- **Glazed ceramics**: used from the mid-nineteenth century as a durable means of adding colour and texture to a façade.
- **Stoneware**: a mix of fire-clay and glass which, when fired, becomes fully vitrified. Used from the mid-nineteenth century as a durable cladding, with the introduction of colours in the late nineteenth century.
- **Cob**: made from clay, straw and aggregate, and built up without shuttering in lifts usually off a masonry plinth. Found principally in the south-west, but also in the East Midlands and Cumbria.
- **Clay lump**: un-fired moulded blocks of chalk, clay and straw found particularly in East Anglia from the late eighteenth century to early twentieth century. The term 'adobe' is used in other countries to describe a similar form of construction.
- **Pisé de terre**: introduced in the late eighteenth century from Continental Europe, and formed by compacting layers of suitable dry earth between shutter boards. Also known as rammed earth.
- **Shuttered clay**: similar to pisé, but using chalk, clay and straw, and found particularly in East Anglia.
- **Wychert**: a mix of earth and straw built up from a plinth with no shuttering. Found principally in Buckinghamshire. Also spelt wychert and witchit.
- **Concrete**: the earliest unreinforced concrete was used by Roman engineers, and made up of lime, pozzolans and water. It is from this that we can trace today's use of reinforced and precast concrete in construction and civil engineering. Advances came with the production of Joseph Aspdin's Portland cement in the early nineteenth century, the use of basic reinforcement by the middle of the century, and the introduction of ferro-concrete at the start of the twentieth century. The earliest concrete house was built in Swanscombe (Kent) in 1835. For those now involved with the repair and maintenance of the pioneering buildings and structures constructed of reinforced concrete, it is evident that the characteristics of the materials were not fully appreciated, and that many of the present defects relate to poor detailing and workmanship.
- **Mundic**: local mine waste rich in iron pyrites used as aggregate for *in situ* concrete and blockwork, particularly in Cornwall during the early to mid-twentieth century.

## Symptoms and diagnosis

### Open and defective masonry mortar joints

- Poor mortar, with inadequate matrix and poorly-graded aggregate. Defective mortar will increase the risk of moisture penetration and adversely affect the bearing for masonry units or fixings.
- Cement gauging: research carried out under the English Heritage 'Smeaton' research project, itself linked with the European EUREKA Eurocare Eurolime programme, has offered preliminary indications that cement gauging of lime mortars can have a negative effect on the strength and durability of the mortar, by increasing mortar density and decreasing porosity, and that the presence of porous particles of unburnt lime and chalk may aid the setting of the mortar and increase frost resistance.[2]
- Frost damage: evaporation of moisture from within a wall occurs mainly through the joints, which make up approximately 17 per cent of the surface

area. Reduced permeability, resulting from the addition of cement, will limit this evaporation and result in an increased susceptibility of the walling material to frost action.

• Sulphate attack caused by the expansive reaction between tricalcium aluminate (one of the constituents of Portland cement) and soluble sulphate salts.

• Wind erosion: in exposed situations, and particularly where abrasive particles can be carried, the wind can have a scouring action affecting both masonry and mortar joints.

• Concentrated water action, as seen with defective gutters or outlets, can erode joints and wash out soft mortars.

• The mortar has lost its adhesive characteristics and reverted to its constituent parts. This phenomenon, sometimes known as 'de-naturing', seems to result from a combination of factors relating to the nature of the materials, workmanship and exposure of the mortar.

• Root action: the smaller roots and tendrils of plants such as ivy will penetrate joints, often seeking nutrition from the lime in the mortar.

• Birds pecking out the mortar for grit and lime content.

• Masonry bees: wild bee species, including the most common *Osmia rufa*, that usually live in earth banks and soft exposed rocks, can cause damage to buildings by burrowing. The female burrows into soft mortar during the spring to form a system of galleries or tunnels for the pupae, and over a period of time these can be extended until joints are severely eroded and masonry becomes unstable.

• Dark-coloured acidic black-ash mortars, used in industrial areas such as south Wales from the nineteenth century to 1930s, causing corrosion of wall ties.

## General surface disintegration of wall materials

• Excessive weathering caused by aggressive environmental conditions, and erosion by water or wind. Soft bricks, such as rubbers used in gauged work, are particularly susceptible to damage and erosion. Wind-borne grits and sands can scour and abrade softer stones, as often seen in exposed coastal locations and where winds are channelled and form vortices around standing ruins and through the arches of bridges.

• Localized saturation
– Saturation of projecting features, such as stone string courses and drip moulds. Weatherings used to protect such features may be defective and hold water in contact with the stone.
– Saturation of walling, such as brickwork under a projecting feature without drips or water checks.
– Removal of copings, cornices, drips, label moulds or other projecting courses, often for reasons of economy in repair, causing rainwater to run down the face of the wall rather than be thrown clear. Projecting courses are often seen cut for downpipes, together with the resultant localized saturation and staining. Replacement with an incorrect profile, following the eroded line of others, can prove ineffectual and channel the water rather than disposing of it.

• Efflorescence: soluble salts in solution migrate to the surface where the liquid evaporates and salts crystallize out. Such salts are present in the walling materials or ground, or are introduced by activities such as former meat salting, animal urine or road salting, and can be set in motion by leaking services or a failed damp-proof course.

• Crypto-efflorescence: soluble salts may crystallize within the body of the walling material, setting up internal stresses and causing surface spalling.

• Frost action: moisture within porous walling materials expands on freezing, setting up internal stresses and causing surface spalling. Where dense mortars based on artificial cements are used, evaporation is forced to take place through the walling material rather than the joint, giving an increased risk of surface disintegration through salt crystallization and frost action. Projecting 'strap' or 'ribbon' pointing,

*Figure 9.5* Deeply-eroded joints to 15th-century masonry, resulting in the loss of individual bricks and subsequent erosion of exposed corework.

together with surface vegetation, will also retain water. Damage will often be worse where the walling is exposed on both sides, such as parapets and free-standing structures. Damage will be related to the amount of moisture taken up by the pore structure of the walling material. Soft and porous bricks, such as Norfolk red bricks, are particularly susceptible to frost action, whereas dense or vitrified bricks, or those with vitrified surfaces, are less so.

- Localized decay caused by a build-up of dirt and fine surface moisture in sheltered areas.
- Ivy or creeper growth, with roots and tendrils entering cracks and open joints. Elder and buddleia are lime-loving plants and will enter defective mortar joints. Vegetation will retain moisture, and root systems can jack sections of walling up (Figure 9.6).
- Concentrated loads causing local crush-ing and disintegration, particularly to overstressed piers.
- Corrosion and expansion of embedded ironwork.
- Damage caused by grinders and disc cutters during preparation for re-pointing.
- Damage caused by inappropriate surface cleaning, particularly associated with the removal of graffiti and paint finishes.

## Surface disintegration of brick

- Inherent weaknesses, brought about by poor firing, inclusion of foreign materials such as pebbles and organic matter, and high levels of salts.

## Surface disintegration of stone

- Incorrect selection of stone for use and/or location. The Mansfield red do-lomitic sandstone chosen by Sir George Gilbert Scott for the tall one-piece shafts to St John's College Chapel, Cambridge (1866–69) failed as the stone had to be used with the bedding planes set vertically due to the

*Figure 9.6* Action of tree roots to parapet of early 19th-century viaduct in Mansfield, Nottinghamshire.

shallow stratum from which the stone was taken (Figure 9.7).
- Inherent weaknesses, such as soft clayey or poorly-bound beds.
- Moisture retained by mosses and lichens, causing localized saturation and staining.
- Build-up of droppings from feral

pigeons. Chemical compounds within the faeces can attack the stone.
- Atmospheric pollution, including tars and chemical compounds, can lead to surface deposits that block the pores of the stone and attack calcite binders. The effects of historic pollution are only now being fully realized, but

*Figure 9.7* Spalling of sandstone shafts to St John's College Chapel, Cambridge as a result of inappropriate bedding.

current problems stem from industry and exhaust emissions. Limestones and sandstones react differently to such conditions, and it is thus essential to correctly identify the principal and secondary decay mechanisms before taking action.

- Delamination of sedimentary stones where bedding planes are not in compression. For walling the bedding planes should be horizontal and parallel to the foundations; for arches the planes should be at right angles to the face of the building and to the direction of thrust; for cornices, copings and other projecting courses the planes should be at right angles to the face of the building, set vertically, and parallel to the perpend joints. Incorrect bedding may result from error or in order to make up a course height.
- Formation and subsequent 'contour scaling' of skins formed on washed areas of sandstones, caused by the cyclical wetting and drying of surface zones, and blocking of pores by particulate pollutants.
- Formation of crystalline skins of calcium sulphate on unwashed areas of limestone leading, particularly with certain stones such as magnesian limestones, to splitting, spalling and deep pocket or 'cavernous' decay.
- Localized degradation of sandstone caused by the run-off from limestone where carbonates attack the binding matrix.
- Localized erosion of sandstone induced by interaction with lime mortar.[3]
- Corrosion and expansion of embedded ironwork. This is often seen with iron cramps securing facing stones and in church windows where the ferramenta has spalled sections of the jambs or mullions.
- The temperature differential between the surface and body of a stone may be such that internal stresses are set up

that result in the failure of the surface by cracking and spalling.
- Differential rates of expansion and contraction with closely set contrasting stones, such as decorative Purbeck shafts, causing internal stresses and local disintegration.
- Concentrated loads causing local crushing and disintegration.
- Fracture of stone set over a hard spot in the mortar bed, such as caused by the presence of a stone or pebble.
- Compression fractures at the face joint, particularly with hollow-bedded work.
- Abrasion and wear, such as seen on steps and pavings.
- Erosion of soft stones caused by the action of masonry bees or the removal of grit from eroded surfaces by birds.
- Coloration of surface caused by fire. Usually the stone takes on a pinkish tinge, the depth of colour relating to the intensity of the heat. Intense heat can also cause cracking and delamination of surface layers (Figure 9.8).
- Surface staining, such as copper salts washing off a roof.
- Aggressive surface cleaning: grit or sand blasting, whether wet or dry, can cause damage in varying degrees to the surface of the stone through the impact and abrasion of the particles, and blur or destroy fine detail. Mechanical cleaning can cut into the surface and leave scour marks. Acid and alkali cleaning techniques can each leave surface staining, and cause damage to surrounding fabric. Localized cleaning to remove stains and graffiti can lead to staining or bleaching of the stone surface.
- Use of inappropriate surface consolidants, water repellents, dirt inhibitors and graffiti barriers. The use of early 'protective' coatings, such as beeswax, paraffin, gums, fats and resins, during the nineteenth century with varying degrees of success.

## Bulging and displacement of cobbles, pebbles and flints

- Loss of bond between facing flints and backing. In Norfolk this outward movement of the facing is known as the wall 'becoming pregnant'. In certain cases a flint facing may not be positive-

ly bonded to the backing at all, relying instead on the restraint offered by dressings, quoins and mortar snots (Figure 9.1).
- Evaporation of moisture from within a

wall occurs mainly through the joints. Where dense mortars based on artificial cements are used, evaporation is forced to take place through the masonry. With dense masonry units, such as flint or granite, this evaporation is also restricted, and moisture can build up within the wall until hydrostatic pressure causes localized displacement.

- Displacement of gallets leading to loosening of flints.
- Entry of water behind the knapped flints used in flushwork can wash away the mortar causing them to become dislodged.
- Masonry bees: extensive burrowing in wide joints can loosen the material and cause localized displacement.

*Figure 9.8* Spalling and staining of stone after recent fire at Norwich Castle.

- Disintegration of flint surface caused by frost or fire.

- Displacement caused by pressure of inappropriate grouting techniques.

### Surface disintegration of terracotta and faience

- Inherent weaknesses, such as poor pressing, inadequate drying, inadequate firing, faults in glazing and defective fireskin.
- Frost damage: failure of, or damage to, the protective fireskin can expose the softer underbody to saturation and subsequent frost action and/or salt crystallization.

- Disruption to fireskin caused by salt formations from joints and backing.
- Differential movement between backing structure and terracotta block or faience cladding.
- Corrosion and expansion of embedded ironwork, including backing structure, armatures and cramps.
- Aggressive surface cleaning.

### Surface disintegration of chalk, clay and earth walls

- Rising damp: earth-based walls need a degree of moisture to retain their coherence, but an excess will cause the fabric to lose its constructional strength. Where the walls are built off a masonry plinth it may be possible to install a damp-proof course within this, but otherwise it is preferable to

keep the wall relatively dry by suitable external surface finishes and adequate ground-water drainage.
- Penetrating damp: traditional construction detailing would usually include wide overhanging eaves. These may have been cut back during reroofing.
- Frost damage.

*Figure 9.9* Cracking to faience cladding on Kirby & West building, Western Boulevard, Leicester.

- Localized erosion: rain splash from hard ground surfaces can cause erosion and damp penetration.
- Physical damage caused by animals, such as cow lick, and rat runs.
- Erosion caused by masonry bees.

- Failure of external protective finishes, such as limewash or coal tar, through lack of maintenance.
- Hard cement-based impervious renders: these restrict moisture evaporation, leading to a build-up of moisture

*Figure 9.10* Structural failure of shuttered-clay wall in north-east Norfolk, resulting from a combination of moisture penetration, rat runs within the thickness of the wall and surface erosion caused by masonry bees.

within the construction and subsequent decay. Often such renders are spread onto chicken-mesh, which corrodes and fails, causing the render to crack and let in moisture.

• Impervious finishes, such as certain modern paint systems, to internal and/or external surfaces causing moisture entrapment and eventual failure.

• Inappropriate repair materials and techniques, such as the use of blockwork in place of clay lump.

## Cracking and spalling of concrete

• Corrosion and expansion of reinforcement caused by direct moisture penetration, inadequate concrete cover, loss of protective alkalinity in concrete through carbonation, and the presence of aggressive chemicals introduced with the aggregate or to aid construction. This will lead to spalling of the concrete and further penetration of moisture.
  – Simple site tests include the use of phenolphthalein indicator for assessing the alkalinity of concrete and electromagnetic 'cover meters' for measuring the depth of cover over reinforcement.
  – Rust staining on the surface of the concrete may be an indication of corroding reinforcement, but can also be caused by stray pieces of wire, nails or crystals of iron pyrites within the aggregate. Early mesh reinforcement used for thin concrete sections is often inadequately covered.

• Surface cracking and detachment, caused by corrosion or impact damage. Cracking will increase the chance of moisture penetration and corrosion of reinforcement.

• Cracking due to an over-rich mix, shrinkage, expansion and contraction, or poor compaction.

• Frost damage: this can occur where moisture enters the body of the concrete through existing cracks and fissures, or other surface defects, and remains trapped by impervious surface finishes.

• Presence of calcium chloride used as an additive, or chlorides from sea spray and de-icing salts, both of which will increase the risk of reinforcement corrosion.

• Chemical reaction between the concrete and aggressive sulphates found in certain soil types.

• Alkali silicate reaction, or 'concrete cancer', occurs when alkalis within the concrete react with silicates in certain

*Figure 9.11* Recent fire damage to mass concrete maltings (c. 1857) in Newark, Nottinghamshire.

aggregates, causing the formation and subsequent expansion of a gel-like substance. Cracking, followed by further moisture-related damage, may occur.

- Thermal movement within restrained frame members.
- Spalling at edges of corbels and nibs, often as a result of inadequate cover or direct damage.

## Surface disintegration of mundic blocks

- Cracking and surface disintegration as a result of the reaction between iron pyrites ($FeS_2$), air and moisture, leading to the expansion and decay of the cementitious matrix.

## STRUCTURAL FRAMES AND INFILL PANELS

## Typical forms of construction

- **Timber-frame**: the earliest surviving timber-framed buildings date from the thirteenth century, although most date from the sixteenth, seventeenth and eighteenth centuries. Regional variations are particularly prevalent, and based on a broad highland/lowland division. In the lowland zone of the east and south-east of England close studding, crown posts, Wealden houses and aisled buildings are common, while square panels, decorative framing and crucks are common in the midlands, south and south-west area of the highland zone, and crucks and king posts in the northern highland zone. The two main forms of timber-framed building are the box frame and cruck:
  – Box-frame buildings have frames fabricated and jointed to form side walls, cross walls, floors and roofs, with trusses carried by posts and wall plates.
  – Cruck buildings have curved timbers or blades framed together in pairs rising from ground level, or part way up the wall, to the ridge. Cruck buildings appeared from the twelfth century and later for less important buildings, and are found in the north, south, west and midlands of England and Wales, but not in the lowland zone.
  – Bay divisions within timber-framed buildings relate to the use of the particular spaces, such as the hall, cross passage and smoke bay.
- The nature of the infill panels in timber-frame construction varies from area to area according to the available materials and local custom:
  – Wattle and daub: common form of infill to internal and external timber frames, with clay or lime-based daub applied onto pliable sticks woven around vertical staves.
  – Mud and stud: mud-based infill built up around wall studs in light timber-framed buildings erected in the Lincolnshire Wolds during the late seventeenth century and early eighteenth century.
  – Clam-staff and daub: clay-based infill built up around thin studs set between the wall plate and sill in cruck buildings on the Lancashire plain.
  – Brick nogging: used from the seventeenth century to replace defective wattle and daub panels, and later as a decorative infill using herring-bone pattern.
  – Solid infill: stone slabs, tiles or slates held in grooves to the sides of vertical studs as an alternative to wattle and daub.
- **Cast-iron frame**: the use of cast-iron framing started with the construction of fire-proof industrial buildings in the late eighteenth century. Early frames of beams and solid columns, such as Charles Bage's flax mill in Shrewsbury of 1796–97, were enclosed within load-bearing masonry, and supported floors constructed as segmental brick vaults or jack-arches. Tie rods were used to

resist the spread of these arches. Developments in the design of iron frames in the early nineteenth century led to the use of hollow columns, complex connections and composite construction, and the increased use of wrought iron for structural members in tension. Cast-iron columns remained in use until the early twentieth century.

- **Wrought-iron frame**: an increased knowledge of mathematics and engineering principles, together with improved techniques of fabrication, in the early nineteenth century led to an increase in the use of wrought iron for tension members in the construction of structural frames. Early wrought-iron members were limited in size due to the techniques of rolling and hammering, and larger members were fabricated from riveted angles, plates and sections. Framed buildings continued to be constructed using either timber or wrought-iron beams and cast-iron columns for much of the nineteenth century, although the need for better natural light in deep-plan buildings led to the early use of glazing and cladding in place of the traditional masonry envelope.
- **Mild-steel frame**: following improvements to the steel-making process by Henry Bessemer in the 1850s, steel production increased rapidly. In America,

steel members were being used for the construction of the new city skyscrapers in the 1880s. Approval for the use of steel in construction engineering came in Britain in 1877, and the first complete steel-framed building was erected in West Hartlepool in 1896.

- **Reinforced-concrete frame**: the introduction of reinforcement into concrete in an attempt to improve its tensile strength was first patented using wrought-iron bars in 1818. From that time many other forms of reinforcement, including iron mesh, wire rope and perforated iron bars, were used. The first reinforced-concrete framed building was erected in Swansea in 1897–98, with high-rise framed buildings appearing from the early twentieth century. Pre-stressed concrete was used from the 1920s.
- **Prefabrication and standardization**: the earliest prefabricated iron-framed structures appeared in the late eighteenth century and early nineteenth century for use in the building of mills and a small number of churches. Later prefabrication included iron frames, standard cast-iron cladding panels and the lightweight iron and glass structures such as the Crystal Palace of 1851. Standardized concrete detailing appeared from the late nineteenth century.

## Symptoms and diagnosis

### Deterioration of exposed timber frame

- Inadequate scantling: from the eighteenth century framing members had become smaller and spacings increased in response to a lack of suitable timbers.
- Excessive weathering: this may be prevalent to south and south-west elevations.
- Exposure and weathering of frame intended to be covered.
- Build-up of mosses and lichens to shaded north-facing surfaces.
- Beetle infestation: it is important to assess the extent of the damage with regard to the capacity of the remaining timber by careful probing and, where

necessary, opening up. Care should be taken to avoid damage to remaining mouldings and paint finishes, and the removal of the affected surface, or defrassing, should not be undertaken unless deemed necessary to assess the condition of remaining timber. Where possible, non-destructive techniques should be employed for this purpose.
- Fungal attack: decay is particularly common where water can penetrate the timber, such as at joints, the bottom of upright members such as studs and posts, and the cill beam.
- Presence of shakes, splits or knots near to joints or areas of maximum stress.

- Moisture penetration through shakes in external timbers.
- Stresses imposed by failure of a member.
- Failure of joints, either by loss of pegs or by use of resin repairs to pinned joints.
- Sections of timber treated with resins become stiff and impermeable, and so not subject to the usual moisture and thermal-related movements of adjacent timber.
- Failure of replacement timber due to incompatibility with original in terms of seasoning, species, method of conversion and grain.

## Displacement of wattle and daub panels

- Excessive deterioration: usually this results from the failure of an external protective coating such as limewash or coal tar. Internally damage may be caused by animals and vermin.
- Water penetration at open joints around panels. Shrinkage may be more noticeable on south-facing elevations.
- Cracking to panel, increasing the risk of water penetration, draughts and loss of thermal insulation.
- Fungal attack of staves, withies or laths.
- Beetle infestation of staves, withies or laths.

## Displacement of other infill materials

- Distortion of frame caused by weight of brick, stone or slate infill panels used to replace lightweight wattle and daub.
- Movement of brick panels.

*Figure 9.12* Exposed timber framing to late 16th-century cottage. Notice the incised assembly marks, different forms of internal and external covering, and the unusual use of cobbles as partial infill between the studs.

## Deterioration of cast-iron members

- The crystalline structure of cast iron causes it to be brittle, strong in compression, as with columns, but relatively weak in tension. Eccentric loading should therefore be avoided, as should applied loads to cast-iron beams. Cast iron has good resistance to corrosion, but a low strength to weight ratio.
- Casting flaws, such as uneven thicknesses of hollow sections, cooling cracks, surface pitting, blow holes, air voids and uneven cooling, setting up internal stresses and causing localized weaknesses.
- Corrosion causing fracture through expansion. Although cast iron is resistant to corrosion, it should be protected by an appropriate paint system.

- Corrosion at joints (locating, sub-assembly or principal connections) due to capillarity.
- Pressure of freezing water trapped inside columns, sometimes used as rainwater downpipes.
- Tensile failure due to additional or applied loads.
- Failure of lugs, eyes or cleats 'burnt on' to main casting.
- Impact damage, drastic changes in temperature, as with welding or fire fighting, and freezing water can cause fracture.
- Poor weld repairs causing re-crystallization and fracture due to thermal shock.
- Thermal shock from flame cleaning as preparation for redecoration.

## Deterioration of wrought-iron members

- The fibrous nature of wrought iron results from the processes of heating, hammering and rolling used to form structural members and decorative items. The iron is soft and malleable, yet tough and resistant to fatigue, and good at withstanding tension. Early wrought-iron members were, however, limited in size and length, necessitating the use of riveted plates and trusses to form larger beams.
- Lamination of the iron if poorly rolled.
- Delamination as a result of corrosion due to the presence of slag between the layers of almost pure iron.

- Corrosion causing distortion through expansion. Although wrought iron has a moderate resistance to corrosion, it should be protected by an appropriate paint system.
- Corrosion at joints due to capillarity.
- Deformation due to impact, temperature changes or freezing water.
- Yielding, fatigue or rivet failure.
- Damage caused by inappropriate abrasive cleaning techniques. Sandblasting and needle guns should not be used.
- Damage and reworking of surface caused by abrasive cleaning.

## Deterioration of mild-steel members

- The crystalline structure of mild steel is without the beneficial threads of slag found in wrought iron, and its resistance to corrosion and weldability is therefore inferior.

- Corrosion causing distortion through expansion.
- Corrosion at joints due to capillarity.
- Yielding or rivet failure.

## EXTERNAL WALL COVERINGS AND FINISHES

## Typical forms of covering and finish

- **Plaster**: used from the late sixteenth    century to cover external timber frames and often remaining infill panels, secured to laths nailed to frame.

- **Render**: durable external plaster based on lime or cement and aggregates. Also a term used to loosely describe plasters, stuccoes and other applied external finishes.
- **Clay render**: clay and sand plaster, reinforced with hair or chopped straw, and used in parts of East Anglia, Ireland and Scotland.
- **Stucco**: a form of external render in imitation of stone, based on either hydraulic lime or patented oil mastics and cements used particularly in the late eighteenth century and early nineteenth century. The term stucco was used in the eighteenth century to describe any form of external or internal plaster.
- **Patent stuccoes**: by far the most important of these patent materials was Parker's Roman Cement (patented 1796), based on clay-rich septaria, and used until the widespread acceptance of Joseph Aspdin's Portland cement in the late nineteenth century. Other patent stuccoes included Dehl's mastic (patented 1815) and Hamelin's mastic (patented 1817).
- **Coade stone**: used instead of stucco for decorative casts from the late eighteenth century.
- **Pargetting**: used from the late sixteenth century to mid-eighteenth century as either incised or raised plaster decoration, particularly in eastern counties, and later for buildings of the Domestic Revival and Arts and Crafts movement. Also known as parge-work.
- **Harling**: thick-coat thrown render, including graded aggregate, found particularly in Scotland and northern England.
- **Chalk slurry**: white chalk-based external coating, used particularly on buildings in chalk downlands.
- **Coal tar**: semi-porous external finish derived from coal in town-gas production. Applied neat or blinded with sand and limewashed while hot.
- **Tile hanging**: used from the late seventeenth century to clad the external faces of timber frames, using either plain or decorated tiles. Found particularly in the south-western counties.
- **Slate hanging**: used as a cladding to timber frames and exposed masonry walls, often with decorative banding. Found generally in the south-east, north Wales and the Lake District.
- **Mathematical tiles**: also known as mechanical or brick tiles. Introduced in the mid-eighteenth century to imitate brickwork, with shaped tiles hung on battens or nailed to boards or battens. Found particularly in Sussex and east Kent.
- **Weatherboarding**: used from the sixteenth century on agricultural buildings, and on domestic buildings from the eighteenth century. Usually fixed horizontally onto the frame or laths, but occasionally used vertically. Found particularly in the south-east and East Anglia. Also known as clapboarding.

## Symptoms and diagnosis

### Cracking and detachment of renders and stuccoes

- Incorrect materials and techniques, such as excessively thick coats, inappropriate mix strengths or overworking.
- Weak undercoat used with a dense, hard finishing coat.
- Failure of bond between render/stucco and underlying fabric, caused where there is inadequate key, the substrate is dense and has limited absorption, or where there is contamination of the surfaces. Timber laths or wire mesh were often used to provide a key for renders or pargetting over timber-frame members.
- Variations or discontinuity in underlying fabric.
- Water penetration behind render/stucco and into the underlying fabric, whether it be masonry or timber frame and infill, with the risk of frost damage, fungal attack, and

staining to internal finishes and decorations. This may be caused by incorrect or defective detailing where water is concentrated onto particular areas of the render. When a wall is subsequently rendered/stuccoed for reasons of protection or fashion, the drips on window cills may be concentrating water onto the render/stucco surface rather than throwing it off the wall.

- Surface cracking and crazing caused by the use of contaminated aggregates, rapid drying, inappropriate mixing or overworking, particularly when using steel floats. Where gypsum is added to a cement-based render the sulphate reaction will also cause cracking and spalling.
- Shrinkage cracking. Seen as a 'map-pattern' cracking associated with the drying shrinkage of cement-rich renders.
- Horizontal cracking patterns, caused by the expansion of the joints to the underlying masonry affected by sulphate attack or the corrosion of embedded ironwork. Where bricks hold high quantities of soluble salts these will react with the tricalcium aluminate in Portland cement to form a crystalline product that expands within the mortar joints and at the interface between masonry and render causing cracking and detachment. Salt deposits may be visible at these points. Such cracking is often seen on rendered chimney stacks due to high levels of exposure and sulphate-rich soot deposits.
- Sympathetic cracking in render in response to cracking or movement in the substrate.
- Cracking caused by movement within the substrate, as at changes in material, construction joints or structural elements such as timber lintels.
- Efflorescence: soluble salts in solution migrate to the surface where the liquid evaporates and salts crystallize out.
- Restricted evaporation of moisture caused by the application of impervious paints and coatings, or by cement-rich render coats.
- Vegetation growth, with roots and tendrils forcing the render/stucco off the substrate.
- Failure of paint finish: cracking or localized detachment may be limited to excessive thicknesses of paint applied to the stucco.
- Shrinkage of hard cement-based stucco.
- Corrosion of iron armatures forming features in stucco such as cornices.

## Slipped or displaced vertical tiling, mathematical tiling or slating

- Decay of timber peg fixings.
- Broken nibs to tiles.
- Absence or failure of tilting fillet at bottom edge of tiling.
- Corrosion of fixing nails, with subsequent damage to slates/tiles sometimes referred to as 'nail sickness'.
- Enlarged fixing holes to slates resulting from excessive movement.
- Broken, loose or decayed battens.
- Absence or failure of lead soakers and flashings at corners and junctions.
- Lack of ventilation behind tiling or slating, increasing the risk of fungal attack to battens and/or framing members.
- Wind uplift and storm damage.
- Displacement caused by window cleaners and workmen.
- Incorrect identification of mathematical tiling as brickwork.
- Open or defective mortar joints in mathematical tiling.

*Figure 9.13* Detachment of cementitious render to clay-lump building in central Norfolk. Although the render is now considered too hard for the substrate, it is original to the building as constructed in the 1920s, and has only failed in recent years. The building was incorrectly identified as a rendered brick building by the surveyor undertaking a mortgage valuation.

## Displacement of weatherboarding

- Direct moisture penetration or localized saturation, causing swelling of timber and increased risk of fungal attack.
- Failure of fixings, causing localized displacement and increased risk of moisture penetration.
- Fungal attack.
- Beetle infestation.
- Wind suction and storm damage.
- Displacement caused by window cleaners and workmen.
- Decay caused by presence of soil and vegetation to lower boards.

*Chapter Ten*

# Building element III: Ceilings, partitions and floors

## INTRODUCTION

Although ceilings, partitions and floors perform essentially functional roles they, nevertheless, have in the past formed broad canvases on which to explore decorative forms ranging from simple plain colour washing to geometrical plaster reliefs. Much of what is seen today results, therefore, from the changing tastes and fashions of generations, or else the influence of pattern-book designs and schools of craftsmen. This should be remembered when undertaking an inspection before condemning decayed panelling or a set of beetle-infested floorboards on first appearance.

## CEILINGS

### Typical forms of construction

- **Joists and floorboards**: the earliest ceilings came about with the insertion of upper floors, and were formed by leaving the underside of the floorboards exposed between the joists. The boards could be left bare, simply coloured or decorated with painted designs. Bridging beams and joists were often decorated with chamfers and stops, and the joists sometimes laid flat to increase the area for such decoration.

- **Plaster infill between joists**: from the sixteenth century to the late seventeenth century the underside of floorboards could be covered by a plaster finish secured onto reed or straw laid over or secured between the joists, and later onto timber laths fixed directly to the boards.
- **Plastered and painted ceilings**: from the sixteenth century great houses had ceilings fixed to the underside of the joists (sealed or underdrawn), often with decorative patterns formed by moulded ribs and the application of low-relief plaster motifs. More detailed plasterwork, together with a growing use of colour and decoration, was seen from the seventeenth century. Revival of earlier styles was popular in the eighteenth and nineteenth centuries.
- **Stuccoed ceilings**: used for a short time by continental craftsmen in great houses during the sixteenth century and late eighteenth century. Stucco differs from plaster in its use of marble dust and supporting armatures for tensile strength, rather than the inclusion of animal hair.
- **Cement ceilings**: patent fireproof cements became available from the early nineteenth century to replace plaster and stucco.
- **Pressed metal sheets**: at Erddig (Clwyd) the ceiling to the enlarged ground-floor saloon is made up of decorative plates added in the late nineteenth century as 'protection' against fire.[1]

## Symptoms and diagnosis

- Fracture of plaster key between timber laths caused by vibration or impact damage. Cracking and detachment is likely to be random. As an earlier remedy, defective lath and plaster ceilings may have been covered with plasterboard, thus increasing the thickness and weight of the ceiling.
- Cracking beneath beams, as there is limited key unless the laths are counter-battened.
- Cracking and localized detachment of plaster at the junction between ceiling and wall or partition, caused by movement of one or the other.
- Deflection of ceiling joists caused by the weight of the ceiling or additional loading to the floor or in the roof space above. Cracking may follow the lines of the joists.
- Movement of laths caused by beetle infestation, fungal attack or corrosion of fixing nails.
- Beetle and/or fungal attack in joists, particularly at end bearings.
- Pattern staining. As convection currents cause warm air to rise, dust is carried upwards where it adheres to the ceiling between the joists in a similar manner to the staining on a wall above a radiator.

## PARTITIONS

## Typical forms of construction

- **Wattle and daub**: used to form infill panels within medieval timber frames, continuing in use in rural areas to the mid-nineteenth century.
- **Plank and muntin**: used during the sixteenth and seventeenth centuries for polite houses, and continuing into the nineteenth century with softwoods for humble buildings.
- **Wood panelling**: simple undecorated vertical boarding and panelled wainscoting of oak used from the sixteenth century, with later decorated and moulded panelling of cedar and deal common in the seventeenth and eighteenth centuries. Early stiles and

rails were typically decorated with scratched beads, with the junction formed firstly as a butted mason's mitre and later as a true joiner's mitre. Panelling had reduced to a dado by the nineteenth century, often as simple matchboarding in smaller houses.

- **Screens**: decorative timber screens, as used to divide the medieval hall from service rooms, continued in use into the seventeenth century.
- **Stud partitions with brick nogging**: used during the eighteenth and nineteenth centuries.
- **Stud partitions with lath and plaster**: used pre-1930.
- **Board and canvas**: used as a light-weight lining, with or without plaster, on studwork or masonry during the nineteenth century.
- **Reinforced paper**: paper reinforced with loose-weave fabric was used as a lightweight lining during the nineteenth century, fixed onto studwork and painted. It was also used as a pallia-tive measure to hide problems of dampness in masonry walls.
- **Trussed partitions**: a rigid structural framework used from the late seventeenth century to form upper-floor divisions where there was no support beneath. Such partitions may also carry the roof or floor above, and support the floors and ceilings beneath. Increased use was made of wrought-iron tension rods and cast-iron shoes during the nineteenth century.
- **Brickwork**: supported on a lower wall, beam or joist. Poor-quality bricks were often used for party walls and partitions, often underburnt or containing high levels of ash.
- **Proprietary systems**: late nineteenth century systems using terracotta blocks with joggled joints, *in situ* coke breeze, reinforced coke breeze, breeze concrete slabs and dove-tailed corrugated steel. Patent fireproof lathing systems based on wire were available from the early twentieth century.[2]

## Symptoms and diagnosis

### Solid (loadbearing and non-loadbearing)

- Distortion resulting from movement in structural walls or frame. This may cause doors to stick, and cracking of plasterwork at the junction(s) with structural walls.
- Cracking at junction with outside walls. The wall may have bowed outwards due to a lack of lateral restraint.
- Inadequate support from walls below, particularly if local stress concentrations set up by inserted doorways.
- Inadequate support from joists.

### Lightweight (loadbearing and non-loadbearing)

- Distortion resulting from movement in structural walls or frame. This may cause doors to stick, and cracking of plasterwork at the junction(s) with structural walls.
- Inadequate support from wall or double joists beneath partition leading to cracking.
- Shrinkage or distortion of timber framework.
- Deflection of trussed partition caused by removal or modification of structural member and redistribution of loads, often to form new doorways.
- Failure of pegs to tension joints in trussed partitions.
- Long-term creep of trussed partition under load.
- Failure of lath and plaster finish, caused by vibration, impact damage, deflection or movement in laths.

## FLOORS

## Typical forms of construction

- **Bare and treated earth**: the earliest and most simple floors were formed by compacting the earth or an imported material, such as chalk or gravel, and covering it with rushes and herbs to reduce the amount of dust. Variations included the use of clays, ashes and dung.
- **Bricks and tiles**: tiles, such as pamments, and thin floor bricks were being manufactured and imported by the fourteenth century, with local variations and traditional decorative designs much in evidence in ecclesiastical buildings. Decorative tiles were either pressed and decorated with an inlaid clay of differing colour (encaustic tiles), or painted and sealed. Medieval patterns were revived in the nineteenth century.
- **Stone, marble and cobbles**: local durable stones used as slabs or smaller tiles for paving and ground floors, or in smaller pieces random laid or set upright to form the 'pitched' floors seen in the western counties and Wales. Contrasting or imported stones were used with plain stone to form decorative schemes in the seventeenth and eighteenth centuries, while coloured marbles were most sought after for fine polished floors. Cobbles were often used to form durable surfaces in out-buildings and yards.
- **Plaster**: availability of materials and local tradition have resulted in two related flooring materials, lime and gypsum, appearing in both lowly and elegant buildings from the sixteenth century to the nineteenth century. The plaster is supported on reeds, straw or timber laths secured over the joists for upper floors, or laid over rammed earth for ground floors. The inclusion of brick dust, animal blood, ash and other materials imparted durability, colour and finish.
- **Timber boards**: early boards, usually of oak, were used from the fifteenth century with the new or inserted upper rooms of large houses, and often formed the ceilings to the rooms below. They were often laid parallel to the closely spaced joists, either over or rebated into the top edges. By the sixteenth century softwoods from Baltic countries were being imported, and later, in the eighteenth century, boards or planks known as deals were widely used. Exotic woods, such as cedar and mahogany, were in use during the eighteenth century. Double or bridging floors were used from the eighteenth century to provide a stiffer floor under load. Pugging, of sand, sawdust, sea or nut shells, was used to reduce the direct transmission of noise. Eighteenth and nineteenth century floors were occasionally decorated with painted or stencilled decoration, or covered with painted floorcloths. Timber boards may also be used in solid-floor construction, fixed to joists or battens bedded into a concrete screed.
- **Wood blocks and parquetry**: used in decorative schemes with woods of differing colours from the seventeenth century to nineteenth century, with earlier floors based on pattern-book designs.
- **Terrazzo**: a hard polished *in situ* or precast flooring made up of white cement and marble aggregate.
- **Granolithic concrete**: a hard-wearing *in situ* flooring made up of cement, sand and granite aggregate.
- **Magnesium oxychloride**: a hard-wearing *in situ* flooring made up of calcined magnesite, various fillers and magnesium chloride. Also known as a magnesite floor.
- **Flitched beams**: composite construction incorporating an iron or steel plate, or hardwood strip, within a timber beam, used for long spans found in industrial buildings during the eighteenth and nineteenth centuries.
- **Brick or jack arch**: used during the nineteenth century for fire-proof

construction, with brick arches spanning between iron and later steel beams. Tie rods are used to resist the outward movement of the beams. A layer of pugging sand is sometimes incorporated beneath the floor finish to increase fire resistance, or else the floor is formed with clinker concrete.

• **Filler joist floor**: close-set steel joists infilled with unreinforced clinker concrete used during the late nineteenth century and early twentieth century.

• **Reinforced concrete**: used from the early twentieth century, either cast *in situ* or later as precast units.

• **Floor coverings**: during the eighteenth century painted canvas floorcloths formed ideal washable coverings in hallways and dining rooms, while imported carpet, and those manufactured in this country from the 1740s, were in use elsewhere. Rugs and carpets became increasingly common during the nineteenth century, with linoleum being popular as a washable covering after its patenting in America in 1860. Exposed timber boards were commonly polished or varnished.

## Symptoms and diagnosis

### Solid floor

• Chemical reaction between hardcore and concrete, causing hogging and cracking of slab.

• Compaction or settlement of hardcore, with hump over walls at doors.

• Absence or failure of damp-proof membrane. Reliance has, in the past, been placed on the adhesives used for securing certain floor finishes, which can deteriorate in persistent damp conditions.

• Absence or failure of link between damp-proof course and damp-proof membrane.

• Leakage from water, waste or heating pipes embedded in floor or screed.

• Rising damp, with risk of damage to, and deterioration of, floor finishes and coverings.

• Use of impervious floor finishes, such as linoleum, under which condensation forms.

• Fungal attack in wooden flooring. Floorboards fixed to timber battens or grounds set into a solid floor construction, or to joists infilled with concrete, are particularly susceptible to decay.

• Moisture-related expansion of wood blocks and parquetry can caused individual pieces, or whole areas of flooring, to lift. The absence or failure of perimeter expansion joints, often of cork, will prevent even minor movements being accommodated.

• Cracking and disintegration of plaster floors caused by movement in supporting material, impact damage, excessive heat or persistent dampness.

• Cracking and lifting of screeds due to inadequate thickness or because of failed bond with substrate.

• Cracking and disintegration of terrazzo caused by shrinkage, lack of expansion joints, and presence of excessive dust or small aggregate in mix.

• Dusting of unsealed granolithic concrete floors.

• Disintegration of magnesium oxychloride floors due to persistent dampness.

• Wear and tear, particularly on heavily-trafficked pavings and stairways, and damage to wood surfaces caused by sharp heels and heavy furniture.

### Suspended floor

• Lack of underfloor ventilation. Air bricks may be covered by earth, leaves, rubbish or later render finishes, obscured by vegetation, be inadequate in number, or inappropriately positioned. Sleeper walls may be of solid, rather than honeycomb, construction. Floor joists may be laid directly onto the ground, rather than suspended clear of the damp earth. Stagnant pockets of moist air provide ideal conditions for the germination of fungal spores.

- Fungal attack affecting bearings and strength of floor joists. This may be caused by rising or penetrating damp, leaks or a lack of underfloor ventilation. Floors above basements and cellars are particularly vulnerable as a result of dampness and limited ventilation.
- Fungal attack to boards where abutting damp walls, or subject to spillages or leaks from water or waste pipes. The surveyor should be cautious of recommending the wholesale removal of decayed floorboards that often confer a degree of rigidity and stiffness to the floor, and to the walls, through diaphragm action.
- Beetle infestation affecting bearings and strength of floor joists.
- Deflection in floor caused by inadequate sizing or overloading of floor joists; excessive notching and cutting of joists for service runs; splits and shakes; unsupported board ends at room perimeters; or settlement in sleeper walls. The surveyor should be aware of any special loading requirements that a client may have before undertaking an inspection.
- Localized settlement of floors resulting from movement in partitions. Trussed partitions often provided the load-bearing spine wall to eighteenth and nineteenth century terrace houses, and

can be seriously affected by the removal or modification of members for the insertion of doorways.

- Absence or failure of strutting, noggins and packing pieces that stiffen the floor and prevent the joists twisting. The struts are usually held tight with folding wedges, and these may drop out when the pressure is released with slight movement in the walls.
- Uneven floor surface causing problems with doors binding, furniture being unstable and, in severe cases, distress to occupant. Door leaves may be cut to clear uneven floor surfaces, floorboards levelled by wedges, and gaps beneath skirtings masked with secondary skirting boards or fillets.
- Raised section of floor. This may be caused by joists settling on either side of a supporting beam or wall over which the floorboards are laid.
- Inadequate fixing of boards to joists. This may cause localized movement and creaking.
- Localized deflection caused by inadequate trimming for openings.
- Cracking and disintegration of plaster floors caused by movement in supporting material, impact damage, excessive heat or persistent dampness.
- Chemical reaction between wetted clinker concrete and steel joists in filler joist floors, causing corrosion and expansion of steel, with subsequent cracking and spalling of breeze concrete.

*Chapter Eleven*

# Building element IV: Doors, windows and stairs

## INTRODUCTION

While the door, window and staircase are essentially practical elements of a building, they have often been used to display, through their nature, form and ornamentation, the fashions of the period, and the wealth and social standing of the owner. Such decoration may, however, obscure the true nature of their construction.

It is therefore important for the surveyor to appreciate not only such stylistic differences, but also to have a sound knowledge of typical construction details, an understanding of associated fixings, fastenings and furniture, and a regard for the high quality of home-grown and imported timbers available during previous centuries.

## DOORS

### Typical forms of construction

- **Early boarded doors**: door leaf made up of heavy timber boards or planks, either fixed to horizontal battens and harr-hung, or hung from the jamb with wrought-iron strap and hook hinges. Heavy boarded doors con-tinued in use for church buildings into the sixteenth century, often with ornate wrought-iron hinge plates.
- **Later boarded doors**: doors of lighter boards secured to horizontal ledges, often strengthened with diagonal braces

*Figure 11.1* Deterioration of 'Costesseyware' terracotta window to Hôtel de Paris (1895–96), situated in an exposed marine position in Cromer, Norfolk.

or full framing, and hung from simple strap hinges. Joints between the boards are either rebated or covered by vertical mouldings. Used in larger houses from the fifteenth to the seventeenth century, and continuing into the twentieth century for cottage doors.

- **Panelled doors**: used in high-status buildings with decorated panels and carved frames from the fifteenth century. Plain panelled doors, often with ornate door-cases, are seen in elegant domestic architecture from the mid-seventeenth century, while doors in lesser houses of the seventeenth century used smaller panels to match the wainscoting. Details of panels, mouldings and door furniture are important as a reference for the date and place of use. Sets of printed decorative papers for door panels were common from the late nineteenth century.
- **Steel doors**: popular from the 1920s and '30s, with principal manufacturers being Crittalls of Braintree and Thomas Hope of Birmingham.
- **Gib doors**: doors concealed or disguised by the wall finishes, panelling or tapestries of the room, often giving access to passages, dressing rooms or ante rooms. In libraries the door might be disguised with false book spines.
- **Interior door porches**: used in high-status houses during the sixteenth century both as a decorative feature and to reduce draughts.
- **Glazed panels**: plain, coloured, sand-blasted or acid-etched glass popular in doors or door surrounds from the nineteenth century.
- **Fanlights**: used from the early eighteenth century over an external door with glazing bars of timber, iron or lead. Lanterns were often hung close to, or let into, the fanlight to shed light onto the steps or path approaching the door. Internal fanlights were

used to give 'borrowed light' to rooms and passages without windows.
- **Associated ironmongery**: a variety of items, including hinges, locks, handles, knobs, knockers, bell pulls, boot scrapers, finger plates, door porters, curtain portières, keyhole escutcheons, house numerals and letter plates (after introduction of Penny Post in 1840), made of cast and wrought iron, polished brass, bronze or china.

## Symptoms and diagnosis

- Distortion of door frame caused by absence or failure of lintel(s).
- Distortion of frame caused by imposition of early loads.
- Increased moisture content causing swelling and distortion of timber, and breakdown of animal glues, with subsequent difficulties in use.
- Fungal attack: persistent dampness common at the base of the door and/or door frame, particularly where set below ground level as on a downward step. Also localised decay where surface protection has failed.
- Direct ingress of rainwater beneath a door due to an inadequate or missing weatherboard, over a defective water bar, through poorly sealed openings such as letter plates and catflaps, and through open joints to boarded doors.
- Corrosion or failure of small-section iron fixings due to tannic acid present in oak.
- Failure of hinges and other furniture, causing the door to drop and bind on the threshold, or become inoperative.
- Corrosion and distortion of steel doors. Early doors were not galvanized, but rather painted for protection.

## WINDOWS

## Typical forms of construction

- **Unglazed masonry windows**: narrow openings or loops cut through a wall with or without splayed reveals for light and ventilation from the eleventh to the thirteenth century.
- **Unglazed timber windows**: square-section oak mullions set diagonally into a surrounding frame, with internal horizontal sliding shutters, or hinged shutters set either internally or externally.
- **Traceried windows**: separate lights pierced through a masonry panel to form plate tracery in the thirteenth century, developing into bar tracery with moulded stone mullions and transoms from the thirteenth to the sixteenth century, and in later church architecture. Typically, used only in ecclesiastical buildings and larger houses of stone, and from the twelfth century carrying imported and later local plain, painted or coloured glass held in lead cames.
- **Mullion and transom cross windows**: mid- to late seventeenth century design using stone or timber members, often fitted with wrought-iron casements.
- **Wrought-iron lights**: rectangular or diamond-shaped glass quarries set in lead cames within wrought-iron casements or fixed lights. Used individually or with mullions and transoms from the mid-sixteenth century onwards.
- **Ferramenta**: iron framework or fittings used to provide a fixing for panels of glass within large openings.
- **Vertical sliding lights**: fixed upper light, with lower sliding light raised and lowered in channels and secured with pegs or stays, used during the mid-seventeenth century.

- **Vertical sliding sashes**: counterbalanced single or double-hung sliding sashes used from the late seventeenth century. Seventeenth century sashes held small panes of glass in thick glazing bars, with thinner bars used in the eighteenth century and holding larger panes of plate glass in the nineteenth century. Sashes used singly or in combination, as with three-light Venetian windows introduced in the early seventeenth century and used later in Palladian architecture of the eighteenth century.
- **Horizontal sliding sashes**: sashes running on horizontal runners used in Yorkshire in the eighteenth century, and elsewhere in the nineteenth century. Also called Yorkshire sliding sashes or cottage lights.
- **Timber casement window**: used from the eighteenth century to the present day as a practical alternative to tall sash windows. Tall casement windows opening on to a balcony or garden, now called French doors, were popular from the late eighteenth century.
- **Cast-iron windows**: used particularly in industrial buildings and for fanlights during the eighteenth century, and later for many fixed and casement lights.
- **Steel windows**: popular during the 1920s and '30s, with principal manufacturers being Crittalls of Braintree and Thomas Hope of Birmingham.
- **Oriel windows**: projecting from the face of a wall on upper storeys only, and used from the fifteenth century to give increased light and views along as well as away from the building.
- **Bay windows**: small canted bay windows used in the fourteenth century, but increasing in size as a statement of fashion and wealth during the fifteenth and sixteenth centuries. Curved bays used from the late eighteenth century.
- **Bow windows**: segmental bay windows popular in the late eighteenth century.
- **Top-lights**: roof lights and glazed domes popular from the early nineteenth century for use over a staircase hall or gallery, with framing of cast iron or timber.
- **Glass**: until the late sixteenth century most secular windows were either protected by shutters or carried transparent material such as oiled cloth or animal horn. Early glazing was limited to small diamond-shaped and later rectangular quarries of imported blown cylinder glass held in lead cames within an iron or timber frame. Local cylinder glass was produced from the mid-sixteenth century, and crown glass was introduced during the late seventeenth century. Plate glass became available from the late eighteenth century. Methods of producing larger sheets of cylinder glass, also called broad or sheet glass, were developed during the early nineteenth century.
  – Hand-blown coloured and painted glass was imported from the ninth century or earlier, and available from local workshops from the eleventh century. White, coloured or painted glass was used almost exclusively for church windows and decorative panels in large houses. Competition from foreign craftsmen and increased use of enamel stains led to a decline in the traditional practice of cutting and leading in the early sixteenth century. Revival of production and use of stained glass in the nineteenth century. Frosted or acid-etched glass was popular in the late nineteenth century.
  – The care and treatment of historic painted, stained or plain glass is an extremely specialized craft, and work should only be undertaken by a skilled conservator. Equally, the inspection and assessment of historic glass requires knowledge of the materials and techniques used, how glass responds to various environmental conditions, typical defects and the appropriate courses of action. For this reason it is often preferable to employ a conservator to inspect and report on both glass and glazing.
- **Shutters**: early internal or external shutters were used to increase security and retain heat, while later boxed or vertical shutters were also used to reduce light levels.
- **Curtains**: early curtains were used principally to reduce draughts, rather than for privacy, with a fashion for decorative curtaining commencing in the mid-seventeenth century. Various

types of material became available from the eighteenth century to reduce light levels within the room, used with or without separate sun or sub-curtains.
- **Blinds**: simple painted cloth blinds first used in the seventeenth century, with spring-loaded blinds or 'spring curtains' developed from the early eighteenth century. Venetian blinds based on laths of deal were available from the late eighteenth century. Half-height 'snob screens' were commonly used during the eighteenth and nineteenth centuries to restrict the view into a room from pavement or road.
- **Associated ironmongery**: a variety of hinges, catches, locks, lever or screw-bolt sash fasteners, and upper sash handles were available to suit all forms of window.

## Symptoms and diagnosis

- Increased moisture content causing swelling and distortion of timber, and breakdown of animal glues, with subsequent difficulties in use.
- Moisture penetration, often seen at defective putties; failed mortar fillets to junction between frame and reveal, or render to reveal; as a result of inadequate drips to cills causing water to run back onto the wall and into the masonry joints; due to inadequate weathering of cill surfaces; or via open joints and exposed end grains.
- Fungal attack: suitable conditions may arise with a failure of surface protection, within inadequately ventilated shutter boxes, or with condensation forming on the inside face of glass, with a subsequent risk of failure of back-filled putties.
- Absence or failure of lintel(s) imposing load onto frame.
- Decay of timber lintels: additional loads imposed on masonry arch or lintel may lead to cracking and localized distortion.
- Crushing or failure under load of timber bressumer over wide opening such as a shop front.
- Distortion of frame caused by imposition of early loads.
- Removal of load-bearing mullion(s), often on the introduction of larger panes of glass in the late seventeenth and eighteenth centuries, causing the overloading and deflection of the lintel(s).
- Failure of relieving arch, imposing load onto lintel or bressumer.
- Disruption caused by corrosion and expansion of iron fixings and ferramenta.
- Distortion of leaded lights, caused by wind pressure, thermal movement, failure of soldered cames or lack of supporting saddle bars.
- Entry of wind-blown rain through joints between glass quarries and lead cames due to failure of tallow or later bedding compounds, or at junctions with timber or stone surrounds.
- Corrosion of wrought-iron glazing bars, sometimes used in combination with moulded timber fillets in large sashes of the late eighteenth century.
- Corrosion of metal sprigs or pins for glazing, leading to cracking of glass.
- Corrosion or failure of small-section iron fixings due to tannic acid present in oak.
- Inoperative casement windows caused by corrosion and breakage of wrought-iron hinges and fasteners; absence or failure of associated furniture, such as fasteners and stays; or misalignment and binding in frame.
- Inoperative sashes caused by broken sash cords, fouled pulleys, jammed counterweights, inadequate weights or misaligned parting beads.
- Loose or failed beads causing sashes to rattle, and rain to be blown in.
- Removal of glazing bars causing increased loading on bottom rail, resulting in deflection and breaking of joint between stile and rail.
- Strain put on sash joints where glazing bars are used to open and close sashes instead of handles. This can cause joints to open, with subsequent moisture penetration, and putties to fail.
- Movement of bay or bow windows due to lack of adequate foundation or differential settlement.
- Spread of bay and bow windows due

to corrosion of iron tie straps and subsequent loss of restraint.
- Corrosion of steel windows causing distortion and cracking to glass. Early windows were not galvanized, but rather painted for protection.
- Breakage and/or misalignment of mechanical window controls, and loss of fasteners and stays.

- Inoperative shutters caused by excessive paint thicknesses, misalignment or failure of mechanisms for vertical shutters.
- Defective mechanisms to spring-loaded blinds or vertical chain-operated shutters.
- Defects to associated features, such as curtain cranes and curtain poles.

## STAIRS

## Typical forms of construction

- **Timber ladder**: formed with rungs fixed either through a single pole or between split poles.
- **Newel stair**: used from the eleventh century to the early sixteenth century, formed either with timber treads framed into a vertical timber newel post, or as stone or solid timber steps rising one above the other about the newel formed by the integral circular bosses of the steps. Such stairs took up little space and were often located within the thickness of a wall, beside a chimney stack or in a corner turret.
- **Ladder stair**: triangular timber baulks fixed onto a pair of raking beams used in medieval houses, and also in rural housing, into the eighteenth century.
- **Framed staircase**: made up of individual treads and risers framed into strings, with handrails fixed to walls or supported by balustrading.
  – Straight flights used in larger houses

from the sixteenth century, with dog-legs and flights around a solid core from the late sixteenth century, and open-well staircases from the mid-seventeenth century.
  – Late sixteenth century and seventeenth century staircases tended to use closed strings, heavy oak newels and flat or turned balusters. Pierced wooden panels were used instead of balusters in the seventeenth century, and wrought-iron balustrading was popular from the late seventeenth century.
  – Open strings with plain balusters and panelled spandrels were common from the early eighteenth century, with a return to decorative newels and balusters of timber or cast iron from the early nineteenth century.
- **Geometric stairs**: used from the eighteenth century, formed from individual stone steps 'cantilevered' out from the walls of an open well.

## Symptoms and diagnosis

- Movement caused by inadequate support to staircase, beetle infestation, fungal attack, breakdown of glues, inadequate fixings, or movement of supporting wall(s).
- Movement within a geometric stair causing individual steps to act in cantilever, rather than bearing on the steps below. Although sometimes called a cantilever or hanging stair, it is neither, and relies in practice on tor-

sion at the point where it is built into the wall.[1]
- Squeaks and creaks caused by loose fixing blocks under treads, or loose wedges where treads are housed into strings.
- Localized wear to nosings.
- Movement or opening up of joints to handrail, caused by defective balusters or loose handrail bolt connecting separate lengths.

*Chapter Twelve*

# Building element V: Finishes, fixtures and fittings

## INTRODUCTION

It is essential to provide here at least a brief summary of those historical forms of decoration or finish that provide, at times, the only evidence on which to base conclusions on the condition of the fabric beneath. The presence and quality of finishes may also suggest the relative importance of a room and how it was intended to have been used.

In terms of definition, finishes are generally understood to be the final surface to the primary and secondary elements of construction, applied during manufacture, prior to inclusion, or on completion; whereas fixtures are those items that are built in to complete the building. Fittings are usually considered to be furniture that is fixed rather than loose, and used for the particular activities accommodated within the building.

The finishes, fixtures and fittings of a historic building, together with the furnishings and chattels of the owner or occupier, may, therefore, form an important social record or represent part of a unified architectural composition, in which the control of environmental and other external factors is essential to their well-being. It is therefore suggested that the advice of a trained conservator is sought when a surveyor is required to comment on the condition of certain decorative finishes and fittings as part of a larger survey.[1, 2]

## PLASTERED WALLS AND CEILINGS

### Typical forms of finish

• **Plaster**: plasters of lime and sand were used from the thirteenth century to form a thin protective coating directly onto masonry. Moulded plaster, for both walls and ceilings, was developed from the fourteenth century, and applied to laths nailed to wall studs or ceiling joists, decorated with applied ornamentation, and usually finished with whitewash. Thick plasters were being reinforced with hair by the sixteenth century.
  – Early plaster ceilings were divided up by moulded plaster or carved timber ribs, each compartment containing repetitive moulded ornaments secured to the plaster surface. Decorative motifs were typically copied from emblem-books, continental treatises and illustrated versions of the Bible. Seventeenth century plasterwork continued with shallow interlocking ribs, low-relief ornament and plaster pendants.
  – The influence of Continental European craftsmen was seen in the finer and less rigid schemes following the return of the monarch in 1660. Pattern-book architecture of the eighteenth and nineteenth centuries brought about a return to earlier forms of decoration, with plaster, stucco, composition or papier mâché used for embellishments.
• **Gypsum plaster**: used for fine work from the thirteenth century, particularly over fireplaces as it withstood heat better than lime plaster. It was later extensively used to form moulded decorations as quicker setting than lime.

*Figure 12.1* Fine naturalistic plaster ceiling (c. 1687) at Melton Constable Hall, Norfolk.

- **Patent plasters**: high-strength plasters, based on gypsum and Plaster of Paris, were available from the early nineteenth century, and included Martin's Cement (patented 1834), Keen(e)'s Cement (patented 1838) and Parian Cement (patented 1846). These were used for finishing and mouldings.
- **Stucco**: used for a short time by Continental European craftsmen in the great houses during the sixteenth century and late eighteenth century. Stucco differs from plaster in its use of marble dust and supporting armatures for tensile strength, rather than the inclusion of animal hair.
- **Composition**: a mix of glue, linseed oil and natural resins used to form

*Figure 12.2*  Remaining plaster overmantle (c. 1591–92) depicting Gog and Magog in the Hill Great Chamber to Hardwick Old Hall, Derbyshire.

moulded enrichments for plaster cornices from the late eighteenth century.
• **Fibrous plaster**: used from the mid-nineteenth century as plaster units cast in moulds and reinforced with fibres.

## Symptoms and diagnosis

• Fracture of plaster key between timber laths caused by vibration or impact damage. Bomb blasts during the wars caused many such ceilings to collapse as a result of vibration.
• Inadequate key or bonding to underlying fabric.
• Failure of plaster key caused by inappropriate spacing of laths.
• Movement of laths, battens or counterbattens, caused by fungal attack, beetle infestation or corrosion of fixing nails.
• Movement of underlying fabric. This may occur as a result of structural movement or where the plaster covers different materials that react to changes in moisture content and temperature, such as across a timber lintel within a masonry wall. Later plaster may, however, hide earlier defects within a wall.
• Movement in supporting structure, such as deflection in joists, distortion of studs or decay of fixing grounds.
• Corrosion of metal fixings, causing staining to plaster.
• Excess moisture, whether as a result of rising or penetrating damp, condensation, spillage or leakage, causing disruption to decorations and deterioration of wall hangings and pictures.
• Where moisture is trapped by impervious external paints or renders, evaporation is likely to take place through internal surfaces. Where this is denied by the use of dense plasters or impervious paint systems, the moisture level will increase within the wall. The growth of salt crystals beneath the surface will cause localized detachment or failure of the plaster. In addition, the moisture may rise up within the wall and evaporate out at a higher level causing further damage.
• Hygroscopic salts, often retained in original plaster after the insertion of a damp-proof course, or carried into inappropriate new plaster, will attract moisture to the wall surface.
• Beetle infestation to decorative carved wood mouldings, cornices and ornamentation.
• Splits or tears in canvas, hessian or boarded lining used in poor-quality housing as a base for plaster or direct decoration.

## WALL PANELLING

### Typical forms of panelling

• **Wood panelling**: simple boarded panelling developed into more elaborate forms of wainscot, such as linenfold, from the fifteenth century. Early boards of Norway fir were often painted, but later carved panels were usually left undecorated to show the attractive graining of the wood. The use of painted wainscot continued until the early nineteenth century.

### Symptoms and diagnosis

• Unventilated voids between the panelling and outside wall may lead to an increase in humidity and risk of fungal infection. Inspection of such voids is greatly helped by the use of fibre-optic surveying techniques.

- Fungal attack, beetle infestation or impact damage to dado rails, skirtings and cornices.
- Warping, twisting and splitting of panelling caused by high temperatures and low humidities, particularly where panels are fixed and unable to move.

## APPLIED AND SURFACE DECORATION

### Typical forms of decoration

- **Traditional paints and coatings**: naturally-derived finishes include those that can be thinned with water, such as whiting or whitewash, pigmented washes, limewash, and soft or oil-bound distempers; those that are thinned with turpentine, such as oil and lead-based gloss paints, varnishes and stains; and those that are thinned with spirit, such as shellacs and French polishes.[3]
- **Painted decoration**: white and colour washes have been applied either directly to masonry or plaster as a means of decoration since the eleventh century and probably earlier. Some of the earliest forms of painted decoration were the red masonry joints and repetitive details, such as flowers, that were popular in the twelfth and thirteenth centuries. Decorative techniques, such as stencilling and marbling, were also used from this time. Later painted decoration was much influenced by pattern books and published treatises of the eighteenth and nineteenth centuries. Trompe-l'oeil decoration was popular from the seventeenth century.
- **Wall paintings**: ecclesiastical paintings survive from the thirteenth to the nineteenth century, but with much damage sustained during the Reformation. Secular painting, particularly of religious themes during the early years, is seen from the fourteenth century, with an increase in use for smaller houses during the sixteenth and seventeenth centuries, where often seen as conversation pieces.
- **Fresco paintings**: medieval practice of applying paint to wet plaster to form a combined paint/plaster finish. Rarely found in the United Kingdom.
- **Applied paintings**: painted schemes applied to canvas, paper or wood, and secured to either a ceiling or wall.
- **Colour**: up to the mid-seventeenth century coloured paints were formed by tinting white lead with earth pigments, often being applied as a uniform finish to softwood panelling. With the introduction of stucco in the eighteenth century colours were increasingly used to pick out details, often in imitation of stone, with oil paints available from the middle of the century. Stronger colours were also becoming popular for walls and ceilings by the mid-eighteenth century, and used in contrast to white sculpture and plasterwork. By the latter part of the century there was a reaction to such excesses of colour, and a greater use made of complementary and modulating colours, including those introduced in the curtains and furnishings of a room. Graining, marbling and the imitation of metals were also popular by the end of the eighteenth century.
  - In order to appreciate the effects of a particular colour it must be remembered that those now seen may well have faded under the influence of natural and artificial light. It is often worthwhile looking at the unfaded colour of a wall behind a picture or mirror, or else referring to earlier paintings which may give at least an idea of how an interior once looked.
  - Aside from the use of simple decorative colouring, it is also important to appreciate that colours might also be introduced by differing materials, particularly in the polychromatic schemes of the seventeenth, eighteenth and nineteenth centuries, and used for architectural emphasis or as an hierarchical statement.

- **Applied ornamentation**: decorative wooden mouldings, cornices and rails were used from the sixteenth century, with the carved ornamentation of the seventeenth and eighteenth centuries typified by the work of Grinling Gibbons (1648–1721). Chimney-pieces became important features of a room from the early sixteenth century, with elaborate carved examples in stone, marble and wood seen up until the mid-eighteenth century, when concern became more for efficient heating of the house.
- **Sgraffitto**: an early form of decoration, scratched into plaster, revived during the nineteenth century.
- **Scagliola**: a mixture of plaster, marble aggregate and pigments applied to a suitable background, polished and oiled in imitation of marble. Used from the sixteenth century, but particularly popular in the nineteenth century and early twentieth century.
- **Marezzo marble**: a mixture of plaster and pigments used, as scagliola, to provide a polished finish in imitation of marble.
- **Papier mâché**: internal applied moulded ornamentation used during the seventeenth and eighteenth centuries. Also used to construct items of furniture and fittings.
- **Carton-pierre**: a mixture of pulped paper, glue size and whiting used during the eighteenth and nineteenth centuries to form applied moulded architectural decoration and small fittings.
- **Gesso**: a mixture of linseed oil, glue and whiting used to form hand-carved ornaments as enrichments for plasterwork, and as the basis for gilding.
- **Gilding**: although there is little architectural gold-leaf gilding in the United Kingdom as compared with the rest of Europe, it is important to appreciate its significance with regard to furniture and fittings. Oil gilding is more commonly used on architectural forms, over gesso and bole, whereas the more expensive water gilding is usually limited to fine furniture, mirror and picture frames.
- **Wallpaper**: early European paper was produced from the sixteenth century, with Chinese papers imported by the East India Company from the mid-seventeenth. Early papers were hand painted, stencilled or printed with wood blocks, sometimes in imitation of expensive woven fabrics. Flock papers, giving the effect of a cut pile, were popular from the mid-seventeenth century to eighteenth century, while lustre papers and relief papers, using papier-mâché to imitate carved plasterwork, were available from the mid-eighteenth century. Machine-printed papers of various sorts became common from the mid-nineteenth century, and also embossed and patterned papers such as Lincrusta and Anaglypta. Papers were either attached directly to the surface of a wall, or applied to a stretched canvas attached to the wall by means of a wooden framework.
- **Tapestries**: hung on the walls by means of hooks and rails, often over panelling, from medieval times up until the mid-seventeenth century, with a revival in the late nineteenth century. The growth of picture collecting in the eighteenth century led to a decline in the use of tapestries in principal rooms.
- **Wall hangings**: decorative tooled leather hangings, often decorated with paint or gilding, were popular from the seventeenth century. Waxed cloth hangings of linen or canvas were used in the eighteenth century.
- **Tiles**: aside from the decorative tiling associated with the medieval monasteries and great houses, domestic tiles only became common after the seventeenth century. Plain quarry tiles were widely used, with hand-painted Dutch tiles available during the eighteenth century. Local tile works became established during the nineteenth century to cater for the increased use of tiles to provide decorative, hygienic and easy-to-clean surfaces. A wide range of tiles were produced, including encaustic, geometric, glazed, relief and transfer-printed tiles, and used for floors, pavements, walls and fire surrounds.

## Symptoms and diagnosis

- The removal of original paint finishes, often as part of the preparation required by modern synthetic coatings or treatments, can destroy important historical information. De-frassing of timber beams as a prelude to a detailed inspection should only be undertaken once satisfied that mouldings and decoration are not present. The nature and purpose of early coatings should also be understood before being dismissed. The regular application of grease on to Purbeck columns in Norwich Cathedral prior to the

*Figure 12.3* Remains of 18th-century hand-painted wallpaper exposed on removal of later partitions.

Reformation, for instance, is viewed by some as having had beneficial effects on a stone that is now suffering from decay.

• Defective limewash due to carbonation embrittlement, abrasion, reduction in binding qualities as a result of excess pigment, powdery finish if made from hydrated lime, and reduction in per-

meability with addition of linseed oil and tallow.

• Damage to wall paintings. Deterioration can occur due to the effects of excess moisture, salts, pollution, biodeterioration, light, differential thermal movement in the backing, structural movement or inappropriate interventions. With the current

*Figure 12.4* Moisture trapped by modern impervious paint finish, causing surface flaking and blistering. Notice the cracked and detached plaster, and displacement of the skirting board, as a result of differential subsidence.

concern about the presence of bats within churches it is also important to remember that wall paintings can easily and irreparably be damaged, unless adequately protected, by the oils, fats and fungal spores carried in the faeces, and high salt concentrations of the urine.

• Many modern external paint systems are designed to be impervious and so prevent the ingress of moisture into a wall. Moisture that inevitably enters through cracks and other defects cannot therefore evaporate, and will either pass out through internal surfaces or remain trapped and so cause further damage to the surface finishes.

• Clogging of detail due to successive re-decoration.

• Staining, wear and tear caused by inappropriate handling and abrasion, particularly close to doors and windows, and in corridors and passages.

• Ultraviolet degradation of paint systems, as often seen on the exposed faces of timber window shutters.

• Damage to scagliola caused by dampness and inappropriate polishes.

## FURNISHINGS AND CHATTELS

### Typical furnishings and chattels

• Books and documents.
• Ceramics.
• Clocks and watches.
• Furniture.
• Glass.
• Metalwork.
• Musical instruments.
• Natural history collections.
• Photographs.
• Pictures.
• Sculpture.
• Textiles.

### Symptoms and diagnosis

• Fungal attack.
• Beetle infestation.
• Changing humidities, particularly caused by central heating, create cycles of dryness and lead to the flaking of veneers and painted surfaces.
• Warping, twisting and splitting of wood panelling caused by high temperatures and low humidities.
• Corrosion of iron hinges, catches and mechanisms.
• Aggressive micro-climates, particularly within small enclosures, setting up levels of temperature, humidity and acidity that can cause damage to the contents.
• Damage to papers and fabrics caused by mice, silverfish and moths.
• Damage to textiles, such as tapestries and wall hangings, from the effects of light, humidity, temperature, insect attack, pollution, and general wear and tear.

• Damage caused to joinery during redecoration by burning off or aggressive use of scrapers.
• Damage caused to the joints and delicate sections of furniture by faulty hinges and fasteners, and by inappropriate handling.
• Failure of joinery repairs caused by the use of unseasoned timber moving differentially to the original material.
• Damage to marble statuary, furniture and balustrading caused by impact damage; discoloration from smoke, rust and moulds; corrosion of iron cramps, rods and dowels; and surface deterioration.
• Damage to soluble, non-porous alabaster caused by inappropriate cleaning and condensation.
• Failure of protective coatings, caused by inappropriate handling and by the presence of acids, grease and dirt from human hands.

*Figure 12.5* Damage to tapestry over gib door, particularly around the hinges and latch, at Sausmarez Manor, St Martin, Guernsey. The tapestries are of late 17th-century date, possibly of English Mortlake origin, with designs based on Ovid's *Metamorphoses*. Courtesy of Peter de Sausmarez and the National Trust Textile Conservation Studio.

*Chapter Thirteen*

# Building element VI: Services

## INTRODUCTION

Services are obviously only found in properties constructed since their invention and acceptance, or installed at a later date in earlier surrounds. Services in the earlier periods were confined to security and basic comfort; considerations of health came later.

Servants were an obvious asset, and in the larger houses indispensable. Making old buildings habitable without such assistance may be seen in the future as one of the main achievements of twentieth-century technology.

Standardization and mass production were important factors in the servicing of nineteenth-century houses. Mirrors, for example, were made in standard sizes so as to fit exactly over standard fireplaces. Catalogues and brochures illustrating household conveniences and labour-saving devices make interesting reading, and can often be found in museums and book fairs.

It was in the late nineteenth century and early twentieth century that services, as we know them today, began to be installed in earnest. Their introduction was not, however, without complication. At Baslow Hall in Derbyshire, built in 1907 in imitation of the seventeenth century vernacular, its second owner, the electrical engineer and inventor Sebastian Ziani De Ferranti, supplied electrical light and power to the house with a 25 hp oil engine up until 1923. Heating was provided by radiators within the ceilings, but this was interrupted by frequent power failures. A hot-air system was also given a short trial. Electrical labour-saving devices abounded, most of which seemed to have worked for most of the time.

An early experiment in battery farming, however, led to a large number of chickens being inadvertently electrocuted.[1]

The purpose of this chapter is to outline the nature of these services, rather than to consider the symptoms and diagnosis of defects that affected such archaic installations and the shortcomings of associated fittings. Modern considerations, such as foul and rainwater disposal, water supply and heating are, however, considered in more detail.

## WATER SUPPLY

### Typical methods of water supply

Perhaps the most important consideration in the siting of a new property before the age of pumped supplies was a reliable source of good water. Where a gravity feed was not possible the water was often carried by servants up to storage cisterns located in the roof space or on high ground to provide a piped supply. Such conduits were typically of stone, lead or wood.

- Hand pumps were commonly used, both inside and out, to raise water by suction from the ground. Larger horse- or donkey-powered pumps, treadwheels and steam engines were also used. By the mid-nineteenth century hydraulic rams were being used for lifting and transporting water over greater distances.
- The source of this water could be springs, wells, boreholes, rivers, streams, lakes or, later, reservoirs, with the supply pipe to the property being either lead or galvanized iron.

- Hot water for laundry and bathroom use was originally provided from coppers and small boilers, both heated by a small fire set beneath the container. Plumbed baths became common during the nineteenth century, as did the early pillar showers seen in houses such as Erddig (Clwyd) and Calke Abbey (Derbyshire). Cold plunge baths, either indoors or outside in a garden building or grotto, were popular during the eighteenth century primarily for reasons of health, rather than cleanliness.

### Symptoms and diagnosis

#### Water supply

- All water to be used for cooking or drinking that is not from a mains supply should be chemically analysed before use.
- Health considerations with regard to lead pipes, connections and cisterns.
- Bimetallic corrosion where there is contact between different metals in water. Copper, and alloys of bronze and brass, in contact with zinc (as gal-

vanizing) or aluminium will form a galvanic cell in the presence of an electrolyte. The rates of corrosion will depend on the respective potentials of the metals.
- Corrosion of copper pipes in contact with concrete or cement screed.
- Frost damage. Where pipes and cisterns are located in ventilated roof spaces it is prudent to increase

*Figure 13.1* Stone well head at Hardwick Old Hall, Derbyshire. The water for this, and the later hall, was pumped by hand from the well into a lead cistern by the remaining arched stone canopy, and then fed by a lead conduit to two storage cisterns inside the hall.[2]

standards of insulation and consider the use of heating tapes connected to a froststat.

•  Leaking joints caused by thermal expansion of firmly fixed pipes, thermal contraction, poor workmanship, bimetallic corrosion or chemical action of fluxes within the joints.

•  Water hammer or knocking caused by defective washers, different diameter pipework, inappropriate float valve or inadequate supports to pipes.

•  Check for proper support of cistern(s), provision of cover(s) to avoid contamination, operation of stopcocks, electrical cross bonding, overflow pipes(s) and adequate means of draining down.

### Hot water

•  Check solid fuel, oil, gas or electrical boilers for leakage, corrosion, adequate ventilation for combustion air (unless sealed unit), adequate and appropriate flue, and history of regular and competent servicing.

•  Check for proper support of cylinder, operation of stopcocks and gate-valves, and adequate means of draining down.

•  Check fuel storage facilities (if appropriate).

## DRAINAGE AND WASTE DISPOSAL

### Sanitary convenience

The collection and removal of human waste was, until the nineteenth century, more a matter of convenience rather than necessity, despite the risk of diseases. Medieval monastic rere-dorters were usually equipped with latrines discharging into flowing water downstream from where water was collected for drinking and washing, while the larger houses made use of gardrobe chute(s), discharging either into a receptacle or water course for disposal. Internal gardrobes usually discharged into culverts with running water.

- Individual rooms and lesser houses relied on close stools, also known as night stools or stools of ease, and other containers, this continuing into the present century with privies, earth closets and chemical toilets. Pots, either loose or contained within a commode, were common in all households, and often, for convenience, in the dining rooms of the eighteenth and nineteenth centuries.
- Toilets or water closets, as we know them, were first seen in the designs of Sir John Harington in 1596, and later with Joseph Bramah's valve closet in 1778, but did not appear in any number until the nineteenth century. By the middle of that century flushing cisterns were available, and there was great rivalry between manufacturers to produce ornate and decorated bowls and cisterns of vitreous china. Water traps were seen on early closets, such as the Cummings Closet of 1775, and low-level cisterns starting to appear at the end of the nineteenth century.
- The water supply for these early water closets was either pumped from a convenient water course or collected as rainwater in cisterns within the roof space. Pipework was typically of cast iron, lead and, later, copper for above ground use, and glazed earthenware below ground.

## Foul-water disposal

The disposal of collected waste was rarely a problem in rural areas, with earth or ashes used to reduce unpleasant odours. In the urban areas, however, disposal was an increasing problem, and use was increasingly made in the eighteenth century of water to carry the waste a suitable distance from the house.

- Salt-glazed pipes were introduced by the middle of the eighteenth century, either of an oval section and butt jointed, or tapered. By the beginning of the present century circular glazed and vitrified pipes were in use, with spigot and socket joints made up with hemp or mortar. Other materials that have been used include concrete, asbestos and grey iron for rigid pipes, and pitch fibre and plastic for flexible pipes.
- Early foul-water drains would often discharge into convenient rivers or water courses, but later, in the nineteenth century, more organized forms of disposal were being considered. Around 1899 a pumped sewerage system using compressed air was installed beneath the streets of Norwich to replace an earlier system dating from the middle of the nineteenth century. The remaining New Mills pumping station is also the site of a mid-seventeenth century pumped water system supplying water to a cistern in the tower of a city church, with gravity feed to public taps.[3]
- The disposal of foul water, whether from sanitary conveniences, cooking or washing, has more recently relied on a system of above- and below-ground drainage connecting to a suitable outflow, such as a public or private foul sewer, septic tank, cess pit or settlement tank. Requirements are that the foul water is conveyed to a suitable

outfall, there is little risk of leakage or blockage, there are adequate falls to ensure self-cleansing velocity, foul air is prevented from entering the building, the system is ventilated and accessible for clearing blockages.

- During the first half of the present century it was common to use separate systems to dispose of foul water from sanitary conveniences and from baths, basins and sinks, but problems of siphonage, back pressure and loss of seal led to the use of vent pipes for both systems. Such excesses of pipework led to the introduction and acceptance of the vented single-stack system in the 1950s, which has continued in use to the present day.

## Symptoms and diagnosis

### Below-ground drainage

- Fracture of pipes caused by ground movement, excessive loading such as heavy vehicular traffic, impact damage, tree roots and freezing of blocked water in shallow or exposed pipes.
- Fracture of rigid mortar pipe connections.
- Failure of connections with cast-iron or pitch-fibre pipes.
- Damage to joints as a result of excessive pressure used with water jetting for clearing blockages or as a water test.
- Tree-root entry through cracks and failed joints.
- Distortion of pitch-fibre pipes caused by very hot water.

- Damage to pitch-fibre pipes caused by rats.
- Localized settlement causing drain in dip.
- Drains laid to inadequate gradients.
- Lack of access points for inspection and cleansing.
- Failure of pumps used to push or raise sewage in drains or sewers.
- Inappropriate drain route. This can be checked by the use of CCTV, video or drain dye.
- Blocked outflow.
- Blocked and/or cracked gullies.
- Inadequate or defective pointing behind gullies.

### Inspection chambers

- Settlement of chamber.
- Defective brick walls.
- Cracked or detached render.
- Cracked, corroded or distorted covers and frames.
- Cracked or rough benching.
- Loose, broken or corroded step irons.
- Blockage/detritus in invert.
- Backing up with material on benching and sides.
- Branches joining against the flow.

- Branches joining opposite each other.
- Blockage or damage to interceptor trap, including missing stopper or chain.
- Absence of, or damage to, fresh air inlet (FAI) serving interceptor trap. Such inlets are positioned at the lowest part of the drain within the curtilage, and often set discreetly against a boundary wall.

### Septic tank

- Defects to brick walls of tank.
- Failure of impervious finish to internal walls.
- Corrosion or damage to tank covers.
- Cracking or damage to roof of

tank, often caused by heavy vehicular traffic.
- Absence or failure of filters.
- Clogging of filter material.
- Entry of inappropriate material, such

as foul water discharging from a kitchen sink without a grease trap.
- Inadequate ventilation.
- Inadequate capacity for foul-water load.
- Damage to working of tank (anaerobic and aerobic bacteria) caused by biological washing powders and excess water. Effluent should be periodically tested to ensure satisfactory treatment.

- Accumulation of sludge. There must be adequate vehicular access to allow for pumping out.
- Proximity of springs or wells used for water supply.
- Adequate legal arrangements to allow for continued usage where the tank is sited on the land of another party.

## Cess pit

- Defects to brick walls of tank.
- Failure of impervious finish to internal walls, causing leakage.
- Inadequate capacity for foul-water load.
- Inadequate vehicular access for pumping out.

- Presence of outlets, such as an overflow pipe into a ditch or onto neighbouring land.
- Absence or failure of seals allowing escape of noxious gases.

## Rainwater disposal

Rainwater has, for centuries, been collected and used for various purposes, and it is unlikely that much thought was given to disposal until the eighteenth or nineteenth centuries. The disposal of rainwater from roofs or hard surfaces is today reliant on a system of drains connecting to either a combined or separate rainwater sewer, soakaway, water course or ditch. Requirements are that water is conveyed to a suitable outfall, there is little risk of leakage or blockage and the system is accessible for clearing blockages.

## Symptoms and diagnosis

### Blockage or overflow of eaves guttering

- Loose material from roof, such as moss, bedding mortar, broken slates or tiles; and leaves, birds' nests, plastic bags or tennis balls, causing blockages. Often the wire or plastic balloons fitted in the gutter outlets capture this material and form a restriction to flow.
- Build-up of snow.
- Inadequate or impaired falls caused by

structural movement of building, corrosion of metal gutter brackets, decay of supporting fascia boards or rafter feet, or damage by ladders.
- Inadequate capacity of gutter for area and pitch of roof.
- Insufficient number of downpipes.
- Overflow of rainwater causing saturation of underlying wall.

### Failure of eaves guttering

- Corrosion of cast-iron guttering. Ogee and other styles of gutter with flat sections that lie tight against fasciae and

corbels make the painting of outside surfaces almost impossible.
- Corrosion of cast-iron or aluminium

guttering due to rainwater run-off from copper-covered roof.

- Absence or failure of stop ends. Wooden stop ends are sometimes found with cast-iron guttering.
- Distortion and leakage from timber or stone gutters with lead or bituminous linings.
- Fungal attack to timber gutters.
- Movement and displacement of uPVC guttering. Temperature-related expansion and contraction of excessive gutter lengths can lead to failure of joints. The ladders of window cleaners and workmen can also disrupt gutter joints and falls.
- Distortion of uPVC guttering can result from localized sources of heat, such as balanced flues.
- Failed joints between gutter lengths. Such leaks sometimes show as a line of discoloration on the underside of cast-iron gutters, as staining on paved surfaces below or as localized erosion to soil of flower beds.

## Blockage or failure of parapet and valley gutters

- Blockage caused by mosses, leaves and nesting material, often trapped by duckboards set too low to the gutter. Where access is difficult for inspection and maintenance, it is suggested that alternative routes are investigated, and provision made for emergency discharge spouts to give early warning of problems.
- Blockage of narrow spouts and gargoyles, typically with leaves, nesting material and dead birds.
- Defects to parapet box gutters, including restricted width, inadequate falls and drips, blockage of sumps, inaccessible leaks, inadequate size and number of outlets, and failed connections to downpipes.
- Inappropriate fixing of valley gutter linings so preventing thermal movement.
- Thermal movement of sheet metal box and tapered gutter linings. Where drips cannot be formed to allow for thermal movement it is possible to insert proprietary expansion joints (T-Pren™).
- Inappropriate valley detailing. Plain tile and slate valleys can be swept, laced or mitred. Single-lap tiles require open valley gutters with linings.
- Moisture penetration at drips and rolls. After a heavy fall of snow, meltwater often cannot flow to a point of discharge because of frozen blockages in sumps, outlets and downpipes. The level of water will rise and cover the joints. Snowboards and trace heating tapes should be recommended for keeping gutters free from snow and ice.
- Localized corrosion of lead, particularly gutter linings, caused by acidic run-off of rainwater over mosses and lichens. Sacrificial lead flashings should be used if the mosses and lichens are not to be removed.
- Concentration of discharge, particularly onto a lower roof slope, leading to localized saturation or penetration.
- Failure of internal lead-lined timber troughs serving a central flat roof to deep-plan houses or central valley(s) to M-shaped and multi-pitch roofs.
- Failure of the underlying timber boarding, bearers or rafter feet, through beetle or fungal attack, causing gutter lining to distort.

## Blockage or overflow of rainwater downpipes

- Blockage caused by loose material from roof, leaves, silt or nesting material.
- Products of corrosion from unprotected inside surfaces of cast-iron guttering.
- Build-up of snow, especially in hopper heads.
- Blockage of hopper heads.
- Blockage of gullies.
- Back-surge resulting from restricted flow in storm conditions, such as silt traps and defective surface-water/combined drains.
- Concentration of discharge leading to localized saturation or penetration.

With inaccessible hopper-heads and other collection points it is advisable to consider the provision of overflow pipes or chutes that discharge away from the fabric of the building and warn of a blockage.
• Inadequate capacity of downpipe for area and pitch of roof, and size of gutter or hopper.

• Excessive number of angles and offsets in downpipe, particularly with lead pipes shaped over projecting features.
• Inadequate brackets.
• Failure of downpipe collars and joints.
• Splitting of downpipe as a result of retained water freezing and expanding.
• Mechanical damage to lead downpipes restricting flow.

## Failure of downpipes

• Concentration of discharge, particularly via a shoe onto a lower roof slope, leading to localized saturation and penetration, or erosion of roof covering. Discharge over a sacrificial slate may reduce these problems.
• Corrosion of cast-iron downpipes. When downpipes are fixed directly to a wall there is no space to allow for the backs of the pipes to be ventilated or painted. It is advisable for such pipes to be fixed off the wall using spacers or holder-bats to allow for un-

restricted air flow and decoration.
• Distortion of uPVC downpipes can result from localized sources of heat, such as balanced flues, or pressure from ladders and stored items.
• Fatigue in lead pipes caused by insertion of branch pipes.
• Localized dampness due to leaks from downpipes set into chases or within the wall thickness.
• Inappropriate route for downpipe, such as running through roof space from front to back of property.

## Ineffective surface-water disposal

• Cracking of perimeter drainage channels.
• Vegetation growth in french drains.
• Blocked underground pipes.

• Fractured underground pipes.
• Concentrated ground saturation leading to risk of localized settlement.

## Soakaway

• Situated too close to a building, with risk of subsidence.
• Improper construction.
• Level of water table too high.

• Clogging of material.
• Compaction of material.
• Impermeability of ground.

## HEATING AND VENTILATION

### Typical forms of heating and ventilation

The earliest forms of heating came from the burning of wood, peat and other combustible materials on an open hearth, in a wall fireplace or in a container such as a brazier. Smoke would find its way out through roof vents or gaps within the covering. With the demand for increased levels of comfort in the early sixteenth century open hearths gave way to an increased use of fireplaces, with associated flues and chimney stacks. By the end of the sixteenth century sea coal was seen as an alternative to wood, requiring the use of fire baskets instead of firedogs or andirons.

- Elaborate brick chimney stacks and decorative chimney-pieces surrounding the fireplaces became symbols of wealth and important elements in the architectural design of late sixteenth-century houses. Coal had become the principal fuel by the seventeenth century, with grates developing from simple wrought-iron baskets to elaborate hob grates, and later in the nineteenth century to mass-produced cast-iron register grates. The efficiency of open fires and stoves was greatly improved by the work of Count Rumford in the late eighteenth century.

- Requirements for artificial ventilation increased in response to demands for improved levels of comfort in the large public buildings of the late eighteenth and early nineteenth centuries, and developed alongside systems of central heating using warm air, hot water and steam.[4]
- Modern methods of heating have moved away from the burning of solid fuels within the room, and now rely on alternative fuels such as oil, gas and electricity. Delivery of heat can be by direct radiation or convection, typically using a system of water-filled radiators, ducted warm air or storage heaters.

## Symptoms and diagnosis

### Defects to chimney stack

- Excessive weathering. Chimney stacks are particularly exposed and can suffer from the effects of weathering, frost action and atmospheric pollution leading to rapid fabric deterioration and eventual loss of stability.
- Expansion of cement-based mortar joints on exposed north side of stack under influence of sulphates from masonry. Condensation forming within an unused or unventilated flue, or due to the use of an unlined flue with gas or oil-fired appliances, will allow sulphates within the tars and gases to be carried into the mortar causing localized expansion.
- Failure of protective render covering, caused by cracking, moisture penetration or sulphate attack.
- Corrosion and expansion of iron fixings or embedded ironwork, such as television aerial fixings.
- Instability and eccentric loading following the removal of supporting chimney breast(s).
- Instability due to increased slenderness arising from failure of flue dividers (also known as withes and mid-feathers).
- Water penetration around stack caused by absence or failure of flashings or damp-proof course, and blockage of associated gutters.

### Defects to flues

- Absence or failure of flue dividers (also known as withes or mid-feathers) within chimney breast or stack, causing gases to escape into neighbouring flues, with the risk of entry into accommodation.
- Absence or failure of bonding between flue dividers and chimney stack. The surveyor should be aware that snapped headers might have been used to maintain the brick bond, thereby giving the appearance of adequate bonding.
- Absence or failure of parging to flue walls, with risk of fire from sparks and hot gases penetrating roof space.

- Moisture penetration. Rainwater entering the flue will collect on the internal surface and penetrate into the surrounding masonry unless the flue is adequately ventilated, regularly used or lined.
- Dampness and staining caused by faulty flashings, fillets and defective brickwork to chimney stack.
- Condensation: moisture in the flue gases, particularly from burning wet wood, will condense out on cooler flue surfaces unless the flue is kept sufficiently warm or the flue gases mixed with cooler air. Moisture within a flue will pick up tars and soluble salts, and carry them into the surrounding masonry causing discoloration and contamination of plaster by sulphates, particularly to chimney breasts. Condensation will

also form in blocked or disused flues unless adequately ventilated at both top and bottom.
- Absence or failure of ventilated capping, air bricks or grilles to redundant flue(s).
- Build up of soots within flue, particularly with wood burning, causing risk of fire developing within flue.
- Blockage of flue caused by birds' nests and other material.
- Broken or unstable chimney pot(s), together with associated cowls and covers, caused by failed flaunchings, corrosion of iron fixings or supports, careless flue sweeping, excessive weathering or inappropriate fixing of spark arresters.
- Fire risk to thatch roof coverings from build-up of soot deposits on spark arresters.

## Defects to fireplaces

- Inadequate throating or gather causing smoke to escape into accommodation.
- Inadequate supply of air for combustion.
- Where upper-floor hearths are formed

on brick trimmer arches, spanning away from the stack onto timber trimmer joists, timber shrinkage and movement may cause the half-arches to move and deform.

## Defects to radiators

- Corrosion and leakage at joints and valves.
- Inadequate fixings for pipe drops allowing movement at joints.
- Damage to unprotected pipe drops located within wall construction, or pipe

runs within screed, caused by restraint to thermal movement.
- Air trapped in radiator.
- Inadequate amount of water within system.

## COOKING

### Typical methods of cooking

Open or raised hearths, portable loam ovens, table-top stoves, ranges and ovens have all been used to cook food. Each had its own tools and utensils, including fire backs, pot hooks, spits, spit dogs, jacks and grates. The two main considerations with all such early methods were control of fire and smoke disposal.

*Figure 13.2* Copper and fireplace to early 20th-century outbuilding.

## LIGHTING

### Typical forms of lighting

Rushlights, tapers, candles and simple lanterns provided the earliest forms of illumination, using animal fat, tallow or the more expensive beeswax. Latterly, in the eighteenth and nineteenth centuries, decorative candlesticks, candelabras, wall sconces and elaborate counterbalanced

*Figure 13.3* Addition of an oven to the side of the main stack serving a 16th-century cottage in Leicestershire. Notice the use of local sandstone for the walls and Swithland slates for the roof of the oven.

chandeliers were used to hold the candles, often with mirrors positioned to reflect the light around the room.

Gilbert White, writing in the late eighteenth century, provides an interesting study in Letter XXVI of *The Natural History of Selborne* on the preparation and use of rushes for lighting instead of candles.[5] A good rush, of two feet four and a half inches in length, was timed to have given a good clear light for 57 minutes, and a poor family shown to be able to enjoy five and a half hours of such light for a farthing.

During the late eighteenth century oil lamps became increasingly common, and burnt either whale oil or vegetable oils, such as Colza oil derived from oil seed rape. Later, in the 1860s, a cheaper, cleaner and more controllable light was possible with the introduction of refined paraffin. Glass 'smoke eaters' were often suspended from the ceiling above a lamp to reduce the amount of surface staining.

Domestic gas lighting, based on coal gas, was first used in 1787, and public lighting introduced into London in 1803. The gas mantle, developed in the 1890s, provided a strong incandescent glow, and carried the use of gas lighting into the twentieth century. Early internal fittings were typically fed by flexible lead piping, and vitiated air vented through ceiling roses to air bricks in the outside walls.

The first electrical lights seen at the end of the nineteenth century were thought too bright in contrast to the familiar gas lighting, and were therefore restricted to outside uses. The first private house to be lit by electricity was Cragside (Northumbria) in 1880, using a hydro-electric system fed by man-made lakes and underground piping. By the 1930s cheaper electricity led to an increase in demand and the growth of electrical fittings sometimes still seen today.

## ELECTRICAL SUPPLY AND FITTINGS

### Typical forms of installation

- **Gas generators**: during the late nineteenth century, and before the availability of commercially-generated electricity in the early twentieth century, a number of larger houses were provided with power and light from small petrol-driven gas generators set up within the property.
- **Vulcanized rubber cable**: formed with cotton braid and used between 1900–20, usually surface installed behind a ribbed wooden cover. Switches and sockets have brass cover plates. This form of installation should be condemned.
- **Lead sheathed cable**: used between 1910–39, and typically run on the surface. Switches and sockets again have brass cover plates. Such an installation is likely to be faulty and will need to be replaced.
- **Tough rubber insulated cable**: used between 1925–35, usually two wires in round insulation fixed on the surface. Absence of an earth system in this, and the above two, means that they will fail modern standards.

- **Vulcanized India rubber cable**: used between 1928–39, often run in screwed conduits on wall surfaces. Movement will cause failure in insulation and absence of earth wire on lighting circuits will fail modern standards. Switches and sockets have brass or brown plastic cover plates.
- **Tough rubber sheathed cable**: used between 1925–60, usually run through walls and floors, and with round pin sockets.
- **PVC insulated cable**: used from 1950 onwards, with square pin sockets. Since 1967 all outlets, switches and ceiling roses have had separated earthed cables.
- **Light fittings**: the earliest light fittings were based on simple electroliers or pendants, with later standardized lamp designs catering for oil, gas and electricity. In the early twentieth century many candle, oil and gas fittings were adapted for electricity in an attempt to retain a traditional appearance. In the 1930s an enormous range of fittings were produced to meet the demand brought about by cheaper electricity.

## COMMUNICATIONS

### Typical forms of communication

In a house with servants a system of bells and indicators was often used to summon staff to various parts of the building. Simple handbells were replaced by pulls connected to remote bells and bell-boards from the early eighteenth century. The complexity of such arrangements of copper wires running within tin tubes and over wheels meant that bell-hangers were considered as an important member of the building team.

Direct person-to-person communication was possible using speaking tubes between rooms and floors, and later by telephone after its invention by Alexander Graham Bell in 1876.

## MECHANICAL CONVEYANCE

### Typical forms of conveyance

The earliest form of mechanical conveyance was Elisha Otis' safety elevator (a form of hydraulic lift), used to give easy access to the upper floors of the new skyscrapers in New York and Chicago during the mid-nineteenth century.

Personnel lifts were also in use from the mid-nineteenth century, the first being installed in the Haughwout and Company department store on Broadway, New York, in 1857. Early lift cars are often things of great comfort and beauty, with leather, mirror glass, fine ironwork and polished wood much in evidence.

Manual or mechanical dumb waiters were also used to transport food and goods between floors.

## Modern considerations

If the lift is still in use it is suggested that an appropriate maintenance contract be let, which will allow for regular inspection for the purposes of insurance, and responsibilities under health and safety legislation.

FIREFIGHTING

## Typical methods of firefighting

The earliest and most simple form of firefighting inside the house was by the use of water-filled buckets, often made of leather. Small hand-pumped fire engines were also available for the larger house. Glass containers charged with water, known as 'fire grenades', could also be thrown into a fire with sufficient force to scatter the contents.

Outside, hand-pulled or horse-drawn engines, either manually or steam pumped, provided a basic service, often directly in the employment of certain insurance companies.

## Modern considerations

The protection of today's historic buildings and their contents from fire, and the damage inflicted by heat, smoke, water and dirt, has progressed, in part, from lessons learnt with the much-publicized disasters at York Minster in 1984, Hampton Court Palace in 1986, Uppark in 1989 and, more recently, Windsor Castle in 1992.

Factors that were found to have contributed to the outbreak and spread of fire at such historic buildings related, in part, to the nature of the structure and its fabric, and to how the buildings were used. Exposed flammable materials, interconnected voids, penetrations through fire-resistant constructions, the age and condition of electrical services, the provision of fire detection and firefighting systems, means of escape, management of multi-occupancy or public properties, and a need to avoid damaging and visible alterations, should be carefully considered when assessing the condition of a building.

For more detailed commentary, including risk assessments, contingency planning and fire management advice, the surveyor should seek the employment of suitable fire consultants, and discuss details with the local fire service.

## SECURITY

### Typical forms of security

Historically the security of person and property was assured by means of bailiffs, watchmen and a hierarchy of house staff, providing a continual presence and deterrent to all but the most determined or desperate. The law often lay with, or was taken up by, the landowners themselves, and punishment could be severe. Humphrey Repton wrote of two forms of mantrap in his *Encyclopaedia of Gardening* (1827) that were used in suburban gardens, while gamekeepers on the rural estates were often feared and respected.

### Modern considerations

The quality of today's security precautions in and around the home is an aspect of a building's services that most surveyors are not qualified to deal with. The surveyor is therefore advised to commission an inspection and report from a security adviser or approved company if required to assess the security of a property on a change of ownership or in the light of internal reorganization.

Although many owners decide to install an intruder detection system only after experiencing an actual break-in or hearing of a theft from the home of a neighbour or friend, a surveyor should be able to advise on the need for security measures in the report to his client. The regulatory body for the installation of intruder detection systems is the National Approval Council for Security Systems (NACOSS), who should be consulted for details of local approved companies.

In considering an existing system, or discussing the installation of a new system with the suppliers, the surveyor should give consideration to the cost or rental charge of equipment; the costs of the installation, maintenance or service charges; equipment guarantees; call-out charges; requirements for central-station monitoring and remote signalling; and the need for insurance to cover rented equipment. Monitoring stations should be advised of all changes to telephone numbers and national dialling codes as soon as they are known.

Additional internal security measures to be considered include locks, latches, restrainers, letterboxes and optical viewers to external doors; locks and latches to windows; the security of leaded lights; the condition of window shutters; protection to pantry or larder windows that are often only covered with a flyscreen; the position and protection of individual items of value; identification marking; and the preparation of an inventory of contents including measurements, descriptions and photographs.

External features that should be carefully considered include flat roofs, downpipes, trellising, screening close to doors and windows, recessed doorways, vehicular and pedestrian access, paths, steps, gates, and boundaries. Further details concerning security of the site are given in Chapter Fourteen.

The surveyor should also be aware of services that are available to owners of antiques and other items of value. *Thesaurus* searches and maintains a database of British, and increasingly Continental and North American, auction-house catalogues for descriptions of stolen items reported by its subscribers, while *Trace* magazine provides details of stolen works of art and antiques.

The *Stately Homes Hotline* collects and collates reports, descriptions and movements of suspicious persons, and offers advice on the protection of historic houses and gardens, for use by its participants who open their houses or gardens to the public.

*Salvo* promotes the legitimate salvage of architectural goods and reclaimed building materials, and operates a system of theft alerts through the regular publication of its magazine *SalvoNews*.

Finally, organizations such as *Control Risks Group Limited* are able to offer advice on the recording of art and antiques, risk assessments with regard to fire, theft and personal safety, and crisis management.

*Chapter Fourteen*

# Site and environment

## INTRODUCTION

The natural and man-made features used and enjoyed within the curtilage of a historic building, and those features of the immediate environment that have a bearing on the use and performance of the building, should be considered by the surveyor. It is often these interrelationships between building, monument, place and landscape that make the difference between a mere building and true architecture.

As with the previous chapter it is not intended to consider in detail all aspects of a site and its environment, but rather to give an indication of what might be encountered, and what may require further consideration. Certain features or conditions may lie outside the experience of the surveyor, and require the skills of a particular specialist.

## SITE

### Aspect

The direction in which certain parts of a building are orientated, with regard to sunlight and the prevailing winds, can have a significant effect through thermal movement of materials, solar gain to internal spaces, driving rain, and the build-up of mosses and lichens to cooler shaded parts. This is of particular concern in marine locations. In built-up areas consideration must also be given to potential noise and pollution from roads, industry and neighbouring land uses.

Climatic phenomena such as frosts and dew may have had an effect on earlier works of repair and maintenance. For example, at Denver cornmill in Norfolk (Figure 14.2) the redecoration of the rendered brick tower was

*Figure 14.1* Bishop Bonner's Cottage, an early 16th-century property in East Dereham, Norfolk. Heavy road traffic was responsible for earlier structural problems. Notice the tile-hanging to the gable and decorative pargetting to the front façade.

found to have been spoiled when dew dripped off the cap and sails onto the fresh paint. Despite being mid-morning, the condensed moisture had remained unnoticed on the sheltered white-painted woodwork longer than other, darker coloured, surfaces.

## Prospect

The views from a house, either into a garden or towards features outside the site, were often intended when the building was constructed or the garden laid out. It is important that these vistas, and any features or eye-catchers that form part of such a scheme, are considered as part of the property, and comment made, as appropriate, to ensure their protection.

Such schemes were, however, often devised with a particular range of planting and height of tree in mind, and the prospect now enjoyed may not be as intended by its creator. Reference to drawings, paintings, planting schedules and contemporary correspondence may be of use to those charged with managing such gardens and landscapes.

## Access and circulation

The way in which a site is entered, seen, used and departed from, is often as important as how one uses a building. Consideration should therefore

*Figure 14.2* Denver cornmill, Norfolk (c. 1835). Working until the 1940s, the mill is now managed by the Norfolk Windmills Trust.

be given to how people move about within a site; how garden machinery, such as lawnmowers, are moved from one place to another; and how these could affect factors such as maintenance and security.

Careful consideration should also be given to those sites or gardens that are opened to the public or through which there are public rights of way. The presence of gates in hedges and fences may provide an indication of such public routes.

## Flora and fauna

The gardens or natural surroundings of a building will attract and sustain plants and animals, and while not usually part of a survey brief should, nevertheless, be considered when commenting on other site features such as ponds, moats, outbuildings and garden structures.

In urban situations flocks of feral pigeons (*Columba livia var*) can congregate at certain locations for nesting, preening and feeding, and cause problems by displacing roof coverings, blocking rainwater disposal systems, defacing buildings, fouling access ways, and causing nuisance by their droppings, noise, fleas, parasites, and carried diseases.

## Pollution

The identification and measurement of atmospheric pollutants, and particularly their effects on built fabric, has been of concern to conservationists for many years. Continued studies of how stone and other materials react to changing levels and types of pollution remains an important area for research, together with the related subjects of cleaning and surface consolidation.

Monitoring of pollution and related material degradation has been undertaken by the Building Research Establishment at various sites for a number of years, while the Joint Working Party between the Cathedrals Fabric Commission for England, National Power and PowerGen have been particularly concerned with the effects of pollution on the fabric of our cathedrals since its formation in 1985.

In recent times attention has also turned towards the legacy of pollution inherited from earlier generations. The great quantities of carbon and sulphur dioxides put into the atmosphere in urban locations from domestic coal fires and industries, such as town-gas production, should not be forgotten in assessing the condition of exposed fabric, nor when attempting to date earlier repairs and insertions.

## GROUND AND SITE CONDITIONS

Although the ground and site conditions that might affect the siting, design and construction of a new building are unlikely to have a direct effect on an existing property, it may be important to consider certain factors in relation to proposed alterations, extensions or changes of use.

Features to be borne in mind include gradients, slope angles, soil type, the presence of geological faults, height of water table, land drainage, vegetation growth, the size and number of living and felled trees, previous land usage, made ground and back-fill, buried services and structures, former mine shafts and quarry edges, water courses, old moats and ponds, underground streams, risks of flooding and deposit of materials from adjacent land, mineral deposits, ground contamination, radon-bearing rock formations, buried waste, and the risks of gas transmission and leachate movement.

Environmental protection standards with regard to visual impact, noise and vibration, smoke, dust and fumes, traffic, waste disposal, water resources, archaeology and nature conservation are enforced by the local authority in relation to mining, quarrying and extraction.

### Flooding

A location close to a river, water course or sea can pose a risk of flooding, arising due to the low-lying nature of the site, alterations to existing water courses, or failed site drainage. Changes to the width, gradient or construction of adjacent roads might also affect a designed or natural system of surface and ground-water drainage, with serious implications for the well-being of adjacent properties.

At Thurton Lodges (Figure 3.11) alterations to the highway increased ground-water levels with subsequent problems suffered by the buildings, while at Whittlingham Lane Farm works associated with the construction of the Norwich southern bypass caused surface water to undermine the gable wall of the barn.

## SITE FEATURES

### Boundaries

Whether formed as a wall, railing, hedge, fence, ditch or ha-ha, it is important to confirm with the client prior to carrying out a survey of a property the position of legal boundaries and the responsibilities for

*Figure 14.3* Collapsed bank to the rear of Oulton Chapel (1728–31), Norfolk. The natural fall of the higher land, together with the direction in which the root crop had been planted, contributed to the extent of the problem. Photograph by David Watt, courtesy of the Norfolk Historic Buildings Trust.

maintenance and upkeep. Where unknown, it may be necessary to inspect title deeds or enter into discussion with adjacent landowners.

Other boundaries that may need to be established are those of curtilage for buildings or structures listed as being of special architectural or historical interest, conservation areas, scheduled sites, national parks, sites of special scientific interest (SSSI) and areas of outstanding natural beauty (AONB).

## Boundary and site walls

Freestanding masonry walls require careful inspection and consideration with regard to material deterioration, stability and safety.

Points to note include the form of construction, the height in relation to thickness, plan form with regard to thermal movement, verticality, cracking, degree of exposure, the nature and extent of tree and vegetation growth, surcharge by soil or other materials, condition of pointing or rendering, design and condition of copings, and condition of gates and railings.

## Retaining walls

Retaining walls, in particular, require careful inspection with regard to the form of construction, material deterioration, the presence of adequate drainage behind and through the wall, the risk of overturning due to increased or imposed loadings, and the potential problems of tree growth, land slippage and adjacent excavation such as service trenches.

*Figure 14.4* Rendered walls to Villa Le Balze, Tuscany. Notice the damage to the render and stone edging caused by watering, while there is none to the wall beyond where the box hedging is not watered.

## Hard and soft landscaping

The many and varied hard landscape features that may need to be considered within a survey preclude detailed commentary, but might include footpaths, paving, steps, ramps, drives, hardstandings, car-parking areas, balustrading and garden furniture.

Soft landscape features usually lie outside the scope of a building survey, although certain items may require consideration with regard to the well-being of the property. Such considerations might include the

*Figure 14.5* Retaining wall and terracing to the Villa Le Balze, Tuscany. Notice the outlets taking rainwater from the upper level.

species, size and proximity of trees; potential risks from decayed and overhanging branches; and the extent of shading affecting both light and ventilation. Specialized advice would normally be required for the identification of trees and shrubs, and an assessment of their condition.

Where tree growth is threatening the stability or survival of buildings or standing ruins it is possible to use traditional woodland techniques of coppicing and pollarding to reduce the risk of damage, and avoid the equally damaging removal of the whole tree.

*Figure 14.6* Damage to stone balustrading caused by corroded dowels and contour scaling of sandstone.

*Figure 14.7* Nineteenth-century Gothic fountain constructed of moulded brick and flint in the Plantation Garden, Norwich. Photograph by David Watt, courtesy of the Plantation Garden Preservation Trust.

It should be noted that a single tree, groups of trees or an area of woodland may be protected by a Tree Preservation Order (TPO), which will prohibit unauthorized felling, topping, lopping, damage or destruction. Trees within designated Conservation Areas are similarly protected.

Water features, such as lakes, ponds, pools, moats, fountains and cascades, are, again, a subject that will usually require the advice of an ecologist, engineer or landscape archaeologist.

## Garden buildings and structures

The history and design of the various buildings and structures set up within a garden or landscape setting are a fascinating topic in themselves, and the subject for many detailed publications. Here are simply listed the more common types for future reference. An assessment of condition will depend on the individual form of construction, choice of material, location and current usage.

The buildings and structures associated with a garden or landscape might include conservatories, verandahs, summer-houses, tree-houses, bath-houses, cistern or water towers, follies, grottoes, viewing towers, artificial mounds, lakes, ponds, pools, moats, fountains and cascades.

*Figure 14.8* Mid-19th-century glasshouse, with later addition. Corrosion of the pierced cast-iron rafters has caused a partial collapse.

A large house or estate might also include dovecotes, ice-houses, wells, stables, coach-houses, garages, glasshouses, dairies, brew-houses, smoke-houses, various sheds and stores, brick kilns, lime kilns, saw pits and fish ponds.

## Statuary and ornamentation

Garden statuary, whether of bronze, copper, lead or stone, requires specialized skills in order to accurately locate and diagnose defects. Typical problems include casting defects, metal fatigue, corrosion of supporting internal armatures, instability, impact damage, loss of finish, staining, and vegetation encroachment. Cisterns and urns, when used as planters, should be provided with suitable liners and have positive drainage.

## Services

The presence and location of above- and below-ground services will need to be confirmed with regard to accessibility, appropriateness, compatibility with new installations and conflict with proposed alterations.

*Figure 14.9* Erosion of stone statuary. Notice the surface deposit beneath the chin where the stone is not washed by rainwater.

Points to consider include the location of incoming services, the position and age of meters and switchgear, overhead cables, storage tanks, irrigation equipment, traps and gullies.

A check should be made to ascertain the existence of adopted sewers passing across the site, which serve other properties and over which the local water authority may have certain rights. A check should also be made of the responsibilities that an owner may have for shared drains or sewers.

Culverts or tunnel drains that carry water beneath roads and buildings should be identified and inspected as part of the survey of the property.

Remote CCTV or video can provide a quick and relatively inexpensive method of inspection and tracking, preferable to crawling through in wet mud.

## SECURITY

The incidence of furniture, ornaments and rare plants being stolen from parks and gardens is an increasing problem that has to be considered when assessing a site and its environment. Basic precautions given by Scotland Yard's Arts and Antiques Squad to representatives of the National Gardens Scheme include taking good general colour photographs of individual items, together with close-ups of distinguishing features and damage; recording measurements; and preparing written descriptions.

In gardens open to the public, stewards and gardeners can be used to provide overall security, with signs indicating specific routes and areas that are out of bounds to visitors. Photography in the garden should be considered as it is within a house, and restrictions imposed as necessary.

The security of sheds and outbuildings should also be considered by the surveyor, as these can offer shelter for intruders and provide the means of entry with steps and ladders. Garden tools and machinery should be kept locked away when not in use, and each item recorded by way of serial numbers, descriptions and photographs. Items of value should be clearly marked with identification tags.

Security of individual items of value, such as statues, urns and cisterns, should be considered in collaboration with the local crime prevention officer, and may include additional permanent fixings or the provision of outdoor alarms. These may take the form of movement sensors cabled to remote analysers, radio frequency transmitters signalling to a central monitoring station or transponders detected by scanning equipment.

Overall site security may require movement detectors linked to sirens and floodlights, monitoring cameras, patrols, or simply the suggested presence of a dog.

*Chapter Fifteen*

# Industrial monuments and sites

## INTRODUCTION

The relics of our industrial past offer a very real challenge to those required to inspect and prepare an assessment of their condition.

Setting aside the difficulties of interpretation, the surveyor must consider not only the remaining buildings and structures, but also ancillary parts and features in the landscape. Extraction, processing or manufacture may only have taken up part of the site, with related administration, storage, distribution and sales often requiring separate accommodation and facilities.

A surveyor asked to assess the condition of an industrial monument or site will have to think carefully about whether he or she has the necessary experience and understanding to tackle the many and varied problems that can be found.

The following sections highlight some of the more important issues to be addressed when inspecting an industrial monument, ancillary buildings and its site.

## STATUS

The importance and status of the buildings, structures or site features that make up the monument, whether seen individually or collectively, will need to be established in order to confirm how they should be treated and what assistance might be available. The surveyor should check to see whether the monument is listed as of special architectural or historic

*Figure 15.1*  King's Mill Viaduct, a pre-locomotive viaduct (dated 1817) in Mansfield, Nottingham-shire. Notice the distortion of the parapet caused by tree roots and corroding wrought-iron cramps, and the later iron ties and pattress plates.

interest, scheduled as an ancient monument, or located within a conser-vation area, national park, site of special scientific interest (SSSI) or area of outstanding natural beauty (AONB).

The acknowledgement of architectural, historical or archaeological importance, and the level of protection that comes with listing or sched-uling, has, until recently, been absent from many industrial monuments and sites. Although in recent times a growing awareness of the diversity and merit of our industrial heritage has highlighted the need for recog-nition, it remains the case that many monuments are being lost without adequate research and recording.

## Importance

At the present time the Monuments Protection Programme (MPP) aims to reassess many categories and classes of monument and structure for scheduling, in a similar manner to the resurvey for listed buildings during the 1970s and '80s. Whether for reasons of commonality, or as a deliberate attempt to avoid opening the floodgates to sites considered to be too recent or mundane, there will, undoubtedly, remain certain industrial monuments and sites without adequate protection against change and neglect.

## Ownership

A further difficulty particularly encountered when carrying out a sample survey of a particular type of monument, is ascertaining the correct identity of the owner. Often, industrial monuments that are no longer in use pass with the land to new parties, who neglect the decaying building or machinery and are ignorant of the interest that they might attract. Sites may lie forgotten for many years before being discovered by chance or careful research.

Such a case was that of Cadge's Mill, a derelict, but listed, drainage mill on the Reedham Marshes in Norfolk (Figure 15.2). Despite lengthy searching the legal owner could not be found and so the County Council was forced to serve a repairs notice in order to establish that ownership was unknown. The mill was compulsorily purchased, and is now in the care of the Norfolk Windmills Trust.

A further, though more complex, example of the difficulties in establishing ownership is demonstrated by the concrete road bridge at Homersfield (Norfolk) of 1869, considered to be the earliest of its kind in

*Figure 15.2* Cadge's Mill on Reedham Marshes, Norfolk. Notice the one-piece cast-iron windshaft, brake wheel and canister in the foreground, and two further redundant drainage mills in the background. As is often the case, the mill had several names: Batchie's Mill and Stimpson's Mill.

England. The bridge crosses the river boundary between two counties, lies within two districts and three parishes, and was purported to be in the ownership of one individual while lying on land in the ownership of two others (Figure 15.3). Following agreement between all parties a repairs notice was served under delegated powers by one county council, the structure compulsorily purchased, and its ownership passed to the Norfolk Historic Buildings Trust.

Sites made up of various buildings or structures can often appear derelict and unused, but remain partly in use for related or separate activities. Again there may be difficulties in establishing ownership and rights of access with separate, and often unknown, parties.

## DOCUMENTATION

In assessing the condition of an industrial monument, ancillary buildings or an entire site, the surveyor must be sufficiently prepared to be able to understand the purpose of each building, structure or site feature; the

*Figure 15.3*  Homersfield Bridge, Norfolk.

relationships between disparate parts; and the influence that locality, techniques of construction and working practices may have on the well-being of the fabric.

Much of this information, if not already available to the surveyor through acquired knowledge or personal interest, will come from research undertaken in advance of preparing a quotation, tendering in the case of fee bidding or commencing the inspection, depending on the nature of the commission and the relationship of the surveyor to the client and site.

Reference material of use to the surveyor will include previous survey reports; written histories relating to the site or industry; geological maps; early Ordnance Survey maps showing relevant site features such as spoil tips, containers or water courses; aerial photographs; and records made by local or national industrial archaeological bodies.

Often the surveyor will find the name, emblem or mark of the manufacturer on machinery, sometimes discretely located or otherwise emblazoned for all to see. Such information can be used to trace the date and place of manufacture, a chain of owners, and even the existence of patterns or availability of replacement parts.

## Local records

Useful archive material, often held at the local library or museum, may include site and production records, accounts, service documents, trade directories, sale catalogues and patterns. Illustrations showing the site prior to alterations or redundancy can be particularly useful in identifying earlier uses of materials and forms of construction.

The workings of a site may also survive in the memories of local inhabitants, and it is therefore worth enquiring in pubs, libraries and churches, as well as approaching individuals.

The recorded oral tradition can give much valuable information, and flesh out the bones of an otherwise lifeless site. This was the case when researching fen drainage in Norfolk, where it had been recorded by a local mill enthusiast that at Betty or Big Betty Mill in Nordelph, demolished sometime before 1945, '. . . the marshman and his family had their living and sleeping in two tiny rooms in the body of the mill. The smoke from their fire escaped into the mill and found its way out as best it could. In gusty weather the family would move . . . to the adjoining engine-house to escape the smoke blown back into the room'.[1]

Local industrial archaeological groups can also provide much useful information, collected through documentary research, interviews, surveys and comparative knowledge.

## Interpretation

In order to understand the pattern of activities and movement of goods on a site, it is worth spending some time preparing a simple flow chart that identifies key buildings or machinery; routes for incoming raw materials and fuel; routes for outgoing completed goods, waste and by-products; and links with distant and off-site facilities. Such simple site interpretation will often assist in the comprehension of complex sites, such as breweries and foundries, and may be extended to cover the often essential associations of one industry with another.

## PHYSICAL CONDITION

## Design and construction

Before a surveyor is able to assess accurately the condition of an industrial monument a crucial first step is to understand the purpose of the buildings or structures, and appreciate the reasons behind their location, siting and construction. It is particularly important to realize the influences of the use, or process, on the actual choice of materials or methods of construction.

The builders of the Broadland drainage mills in Norfolk, for instance, appreciated the poor loadbearing qualities of the land, and sometimes adopted the practice of building the brick towers in stages to allow for gradual settlement. It is understood that at Brograve Mill the lower part of the tower was built and allowed to settle over a period of two years before further work was undertaken. Further sections were added in this manner, with cut bricks and tapering joints used to level the brickwork for the next section (Figure 15.4).

## Local variations

It is also important that the surveyor understands the subject building(s) of the survey in the context of other such monuments, and the degree to which national, regional and even local variations can make direct comparison worthless. Lime and brick kilns situated in Norfolk are, for instance, different in form and thus operation from those in neighbouring counties, and indeed from one part of the county to another. Without such knowledge, or guidance given by an appropriate adviser, mistakes can be made in seeing, or not seeing, a particular element as a defect.

## Inherent defects

An understanding, or appreciation, of how industrial monuments were constructed and used will guide the surveyor in the correct diagnosis of

*Figure 15.4* Brograve Mill at Sea Palling, Norfolk. Redundant drainage mill dated 1771. Notice the profile of the mill, and the use of iron bands to restrain outward movement.

defects. Often materials had a short life as a result of the processes that took place around them, and regular rebuilding or reassembly was required. Retort settings and kilns were dismantled and rebuilt in this manner.

It is possible, also, to link certain defects or failures with a particular type of industrial monument, manner of operation or form of construction, giving the surveyor advance warning of potential problems. Windmills can, as an example, survive being tailwinded, but should the sails be turned backwards the brake band around the brake wheel is likely to slip, the friction generating sufficient heat to risk a fire.

## Continued occupation

When reporting on the condition of an industrial site, either as a condition of its continuance in use or as a prelude to it recommencing operation, it is important that the surveyor understands all the processes, and their effects on the built fabric. This is particularly so when considering the refiring of kilns or boilers.

At the Heritage Brewery Museum in Burton-on-Trent (Staffordshire), which operated as both a commercial brewery and working museum from 1985 to 1992, certain changes were forced on the former in response to the latter. Wear patterns on the floors and stairs, stemming from years of brewery activity, were lost to the countless feet of visitors or works required to conform to health and safety requirements, while working practices had to be modified to take account of visitor access and circulation. Safety requirements, including the use of accompanying guides, had also to be met to take account of the risks inherent in certain of the processes, such as the boiling of the wort in the copper and carbon dioxide given off from the fermenting vessels.

## Assessment criteria

Finally, there are certain considerations that the surveyor should bear in mind when assessing the physical condition of an industrial monument:

- Are temporary works present or considered necessary?
- Are physical interventions needed or proposed?
- Are there ancillary buildings remaining?
- Is there plant and/or machinery on the site?
- Does the machinery appear to be in working order?
- Are there related site features to consider, such as waste heaps, tailings, ponds, settling lagoons or slag?
- Are there ground contaminants?
- Are there buried or otherwise hidden

hazards, such as stored chemicals, flammable or volatile substances, or contained noxious gases?

- What maintenance has been carried out, when and by whom?
- Are there above-ground voids present, such as flues, shafts, containers, ovens, chambers, furnaces or kilns?
- Are there below-ground voids present, such as sumps, tanks, pits, tunnels or shafts?
- Are there detached items, such as machinery, available in store or as museum exhibits that can be viewed and possibly returned?
- Is there any risk of theft of valuable items for scrap, such as lead jointing, cast iron or phosphor-bronze bearings?
- Is there potential for the site to be brought back into operation, either commercially or as a working museum?
- Are standard assessments of condition required, such as buildings at risk classifications?

## ARCHITECTURAL AND ARCHAEOLOGICAL FEATURES

Industrial monuments and sites are, like others types of property, able to present their story through the visible patterns of alterations and adaptations made by successive generations of employers and employees. By reading such patterns the surveyor is able to deduce how, and sometimes why, changes were made.

The surveyor should be alert for features that might explain the nature or purpose of a particular building or site feature. Engine beds and holding-down bolts are obvious, but the rings for an airship three-point mooring system are less so.

Industrial monuments are themselves rarely devoid of architectural interest, and the surveyor may be surprised at the variety and extent of embellishments. The reasons behind the nature of such work can call for an awareness of social, political and cultural values.

Features that are common in many types of property may be less so in others, and thus point towards a particular pattern of occupation or usage. Fireplaces inside the drainage mills of the Norfolk Broadland are rare, but where found suggest a conscious attempt at comfort for the marshman who might have to grease machinery as many as four times in a single stormy night. Living accommodation inside such mills is similarly rare, but proven by the presence of architectural features such as fireplaces, ceilings and simple partitions.

## SITE AND ENVIRONMENT

The siting of an industrial monument, and its later successes or failings, may be directly related to its location, particularly with regard to natural

*Figure 15.5* Reedham Marsh steam-engine house, Norfolk, dated JWP 1880. The building is suffering from severe subsidence, but ownership is, at present, unknown.

or man-made features such as rivers, woods and quarries. Subsequently the monument may, itself, become part of the landscape as its presence becomes accepted.

The surveyor should, therefore, consider such wider implications during his survey, and consider the following points:

- Is the presence of the monument important in the landscape?
- Is the setting of the monument significant, as with a windmill or chimney?
- Is there public access to the monument, and therefore a potential conflict between access and safety?
- Are facilities available for visitors?
- Is the monument subject to vandalism?
- Is the monument exposed to wind erosion?
- Is the site contaminated by past processes?
- Are there surface or underground water courses present?

The flora and fauna of the site may also deserve attention. Cattle, and to a lesser extent sheep, can cause indirect damage to below-ground remains through grazing, as well as direct damage to upstanding masonry. The surveyor may also need to consider the presence of certain lichens, plants and mammals, and note whether the monument provides nesting or roost sites for bats and birds.

## SPECIALISTS AND SPECIALIZED EQUIPMENT

In assessing the condition of an industrial monument it may be necessary to consider the use of specialists and/or specialized equipment. The following questions may need to be asked:

- Is monitoring of structural movement and/or environmental conditions necessary?
- Are geophysical surveys necessary to indicate underground features?
- Are specialized skills required to understand the monument and/or site, such as those of an industrial archaeologist, environmental archaeologist,
- landscape archaeologist or social historian?
- Can machinery be brought back into working order?
- Is high-level access required, using ladders, hoists or platforms?
- Are non-destructive surveying techniques appropriate?

## THREATS

### Redundancy

When an industrial building or site passes out of use, perhaps the two most serious threats to its continued well-being are misunderstanding and abuse. Another significant, yet insidious, threat is the loss of knowledge and experience for the specific operations and processes held by the men and women who worked at the site. Without this insight, staff, advisers and contractors have to guard against inadvertent damage and loss of misunderstood features. The surveyor should have no hesitation in asking for the advice of a specialist when working in such circumstances.

Where an industrial monument or site remains in occupation it is sometimes found to have been split into separate units, perhaps with different ownerships. This can cause difficulties for the surveyor in trying to assess the condition as a whole, and in many cases it is found that where one party has a genuine interest, another can be at best indifferent and at worst alerted to the potential salvage value of plant and machinery.

It is not unknown in certain instances for plant and machinery to be deliberately broken up or disposed of under the misapprehension that present activities may be challenged or curtailed due to the importance of the site.

## Restoration

One of the best ways of preserving a redundant industrial monument is to put it back to use, either commercially as with corn and watermills, or as a working demonstration of past processes. Industrial sites can also be run as working museums, operating as a commercial venture, educational resource or recreational facility. Finding regular operators or volunteers can be difficult, and careful tuition and supervision are essential. In this respect operations manuals may be particularly useful (Figure 15.6).

Where partial or complete restoration of the building or structure has been carried out, or is anticipated, care must be taken to ensure that regular maintenance is undertaken by a reliable local contact. Where, for instance, a windmill is allowed to wind, greasing of the fantail bearings will need to be carried out on a regular basis, while stocks and sails, if fitted, will need to be turned, say, a quarter revolution to avoid continual exposure to sun and rain.

## Lack of knowledge and experience

A lack of appropriate knowledge or training with professional advisers can, in itself, pose a very real threat to a monument, even if what is proposed is done with the best of intentions. The SPAB Wind and Watermill Section and its millwrighting members have, for instance, become concerned at the number of schemes brought to their attention for mill restorations that have been inadequately prepared by such advisers without experience of mill work.[2]

## Lack of materials

As well as a lack of appropriate knowledge and experience, there is often also a lack of appropriate materials. As an example, timber has always been used to form the stocks on English corn and drainage mills, firstly using oak and chestnut, and later, from the mid-nineteenth century, imported pines such as North American pitch pine and memel fir from Russia. Steel stocks were first used in England in the early 1960s, following the use of wrought iron and steel that had grown up in Holland since the latter part of the nineteenth century.

In Norfolk there are many mills that are no longer worked, the sails being left in a static position that increases the rate of deterioration through exposure to sunlight and rain. The need to provide such a mill with stocks, often of a greater length than found in other counties, has reduced the choice of material to that of steel or laminated timber. While the former will usually outlast the latter, the question remains as to whether an alien material should be used if a craft tradition of centuries is to be continued.

| | | | | |
|---|---|---|---|---|
| 1 - No 1 Waterwheel | 8 - Adjustable Frame | 15 - Flywheel | 22 - Feed Mechanism Clutch | 29 - Fixed Bed & Rails |
| 2 - No 2 Waterwheel | 9 - Drum | 16 - Saw Frame | 23 - Feed Mechanism Wheel | 30 - No 1 Flat Belt |
| 3 - Shutter for Waterwheel 1 | 10 - No 2 Flat Belt | 17 - Blade Guides | 24 - Handles | 31 - Pulley |
| 4 - Shutter Opening Arm | 11 - Push Rod | 18 - Frame Guides | 25 - Carriage Retaining Roller | 32 - Pinion |
| 5 - Shutter Control Rope | 12 - Eccentric Slider | 19 - Saw Blade | 26 - Lashing Hook | 33 - No 1 Layshaft |
| 6 - Jockey Roller | 13 - Drive Pulley | 20 - Support Rollers | 27 - Jockey Control Rope | 34 - Pitwheel |
| 7 - Intermediate Pulley | 14 - Crankshaft | 21 - Feed Mechanism Brake | 28 - Timber Carriage | 35 - No 1 Waterwheel Shaft |

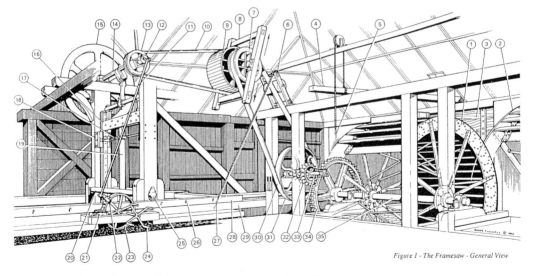

Figure 1 - The Framesaw - General View

*Figure 15.6* General view of the frame-saw at the early 19th-century water-powered sawmill at Gunton Park, Norfolk. Reproduced from Gunton Park Sawmill: *Operating Manual. An Easy-to-Read Guide for Trainee Operators and a Good Read for Armchair Sawyers,* credited to Barré Funnell.

## Salvage and theft

Where no use is found, both the machinery and associated buildings can be at risk. Redundant industrial sites are often shunned by people, and can thus be particularly susceptible to vandalism, theft and arson. Simple and selective measures should be recommended to safeguard the buildings and machinery in the event of redundancy.

Illegal salvage can pose an equal problem, particularly if the site is of archaeological or historic interest. The removal of material for use as hardcore, and crude excavation to release buried or bedded objects, can cause disruption to below-ground features as well as reducing contextual information at ground level.

## Conversion

While conversion to another use is often seen as a suitable solution for redundant buildings and structures, in the case of industrial monuments this can be particularly difficult and damaging. Many people imagine that they would like to live in a wind or watermill, but for such a conversion to be successful, in terms of space planning alone, the character and appearance of the structure will be compromised. The presence of machinery makes the chances of a successful conversion all the more difficult.

## Location

Often the location of a site places particular stress on the continued well-being of a redundant monument. Brick works and lime kilns were often sited in or near woods from which to obtain timber. In time these sites can become overgrown, with tree roots causing irreversible damage to rigid features. The Suffolk-type kiln at Rougham brick works has suffered from such tree growth (Figure 15.7), while the flooded clay pits, pug mill, wash pit and settling beds remain only as indistinct landscape features.

Other sites can suffer from the effects of livestock, ploughing or increased exposure to wind and rain brought about by changes in use. Gradual erosion can, in time, lead to collapse and irreversible decay.

An isolated location, or one with difficult access, can also be a cause for neglect. Many of the drainage mills and engine houses situated on the marshes and fens of the eastern counties can only be approached by land during dry weather or by boat. Where such a structure passes with the land on sale from an Internal Drainage Board to a farmer its historical parentage is broken and, with no obvious use, is likely to be left to decay.

## Old age

Finally, certain types, parts or products of industrial monuments are, by their nature, ephemeral, and cannot be realistically preserved without treating them as a museum exhibit. Features such as tunnels, culverts, tanks and pits formed in the ground are likely to fill with vegetation, become overgrown, and are destined to eventually be lost to sight and mind.

In time a natural balance is struck between being recognizable as part of our industrial past and as part of the landscape. Both are important. The surveyor should respect this in his or her work, and endeavour to make this distinction to the client so that both are protected and preserved.

*Figure 15.7* Extensive damage to late 19th-century brick kiln at Rougham in Norfolk, caused by the action of tree roots and other vegetation growth.

*Chapter Sixteen*

# Standing ruins

## INTRODUCTION

A standing ruin is above-ground evidence of a building type or complex stripped and exposed to its bones. In assessing its condition, different criteria are needed from those referred to in earlier chapters. By its very nature a ruin is in a ruinous condition, and if deterioration continues it remains a ruin. This gradual slide through degrees of ruination has been well described by Sir Osbert Lancaster:[1]

> Architecture, unlike painting and to a certain extent sculpture, does, save in the absolute sense, exist in time. It suffers the effects of wind and weather, and the additions and alterations of man. It may be 'frozen music', but it melts. This process is by no means invariably a disadvantage, and its operation should always be foreseen by architects; for at a certain point in time even the greatest architecture ceases to be completely architecture and becomes partially landscape. It follows logically, therefore, that any attempt to arrest this process is to go against the natural order, and that preservation should aim at doing no more than maintaining a building in a state in which it is still capable of being subject to this long transformation.

It is important, therefore, to acknowledge that the assessment of a ruin's condition must be based on its level of deterioration in relation to present and future expectations.

An inspection and assessment must take into account not only the ruin, but also its site, and their combined importance in the landscape. Ruins can be emotive subjects, romantic in character and offering an open book on the past. Their importance is, to an extent, based on that of their former owners, and associations with events or periods in history. Public awareness and understanding of this local or national history may be heightened or diminished by the way in which a ruin is preserved and presented.

Considered and accepted philosophies for the treatment of standing ruins have undergone changes to a greater extent than for other forms of building, and have themselves changed from that of previous generations. There is today a greater emphasis on detailed analysis and evaluation of the upstanding remains, rather than on formal excavation in order to seek an understanding of the site. The approach to repair has also changed, with a greater understanding of how materials respond to exposure and decay.

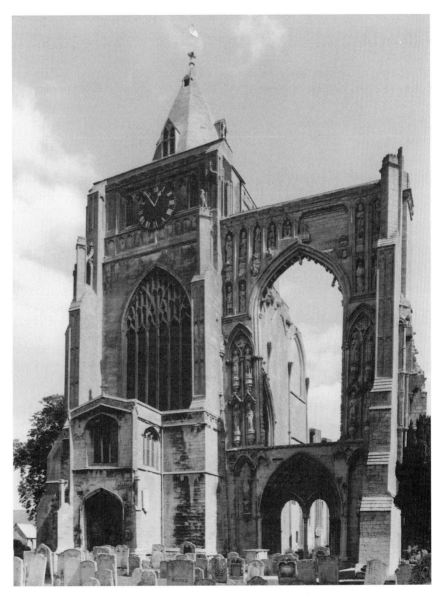

*Figure 16.1* Remains of the Abbey of Our Lady, St Bartholomew and St Guthlac in Crowland, Lincolnshire. The choir, transepts, central tower and monastic buildings were all demolished at the time of the Dissolution, leaving only the nave and aisles in use. Collapse of the nave roof in 1720, and dismantling of the south aisle in 1743, left only the north aisle which remains in use today as the parish church.

A surveyor is thus in a unique position to be able to inspect and study a ruin, to attempt to understand earlier forms of construction, to consider the ways in which the building was used, and ultimately to influence how the remaining physical evidence for all this is to be preserved. An assessment of the condition of the remaining fabric, an understanding of present and future threats, and an opportunity to attempt an understanding of the former life of the site are the essentials of working with standing ruins.

Criteria and considerations for the inspection and assessment of standing ruins are covered below.

## STATUS

It is important to establish at an early stage whether the ruin is listed as of special architectural or historic interest, scheduled as an ancient monument, or within a conservation area, national park, site of special scientific interest (SSSI) or area of outstanding natural beauty (AONB). Each will require consideration to be given to the necessary approvals

*Figure 16.2* Ruined church of All Saints at Oxwick, Norfolk. Services ceased in the early 1940s, and the church has since fallen into disrepair. Notice the outward leaning walls and remaining ivy which is allowed to die naturally over a twelve-month period before removal as part of the contract works.

and consents, availability of grant aid and technical advice when reporting on condition.

An important consideration in the well-being of a standing ruin is the attitude of present and past owners. Many people who profess an interest in historic buildings are, however, disinterested in ruins, often to the extent of wilful neglect.

Establishing the legal owner of an individual monument can itself be difficult. Wayside crosses, in particular, may be thought to be in the ownership of the Parish Council, Parochial Church Council, highway authority or private individual, and in certain cases, such as boundary markers, in joint ownership. Listed or scheduled status may not be a guarantee of documented ownership.

Certain buildings, while in a ruinous state, are nonetheless deemed to remain in use. Ruined churches, although having been functionally redundant for many years, may remain consecrated and the responsibility of the Parochial Church Council (Figure 16.2). Faculty jurisdiction must be acknowledged unless the church has been formally declared redundant.

## DOCUMENTATION

It is essential that documentary information is collected and collated for both the ruin and its site in order to provide background information on which to base an inspection. Understanding the history of the site, as well as local and national history, can assist in explaining the reasons for the location of the building and its eventual demise.

The deliberate stripping of stones for salvage or slighting for political gain are, in this respect, considered to have been more of a mechanism for ruination than simple neglect, and documentation relating to the dissolution of the monasteries, reformation and civil war may well help to piece together the early lives of buildings before they became ruins.

National and local sources of information, including written descriptions and possible drawings or photographs, may be able to indicate what the structure was like prior to ruination. This can assist in understanding the reasons for deterioration and failure.

Many sites have been the subject of early archaeological excavation and investigation, and written up in specific texts or journals. Published material, while often extremely useful, can, however, prove to be selective, vague or even factually incorrect, and should be treated with caution.

Interpretation of a site, as part of earlier works or undertaken as a separate exercise, will help in the understanding building phases and how changes in use or intensity have been accommodated (Figure 16.3). Features such as blocked openings, straight joints, scars of previous roof pitches, coloration of stone as a result of fire damage, changes in joint size

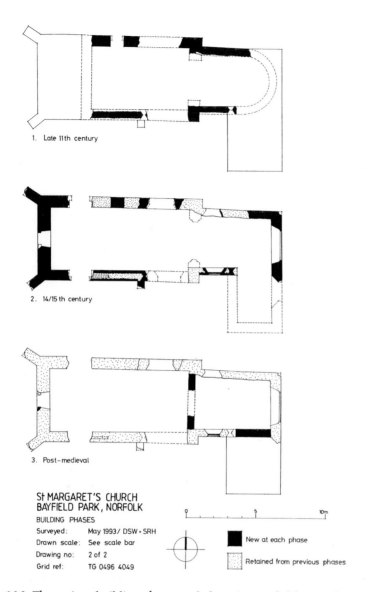

1. Late 11th century

2. 14/15 th century

3. Post-medieval

St MARGARET'S CHURCH
BAYFIELD PARK, NORFOLK

BUILDING PHASES

| | |
|---|---|
| Surveyed: | May 1993/ DSW•SRH |
| Drawn scale: | See scale bar |
| Drawing no: | 2 of 2 |
| Grid ref: | TG 0496 4049 |

0       5       10m

New at each phase

Retained from previous phases

*Figure 16.3* The various building phases and alterations at St Margaret's Church at Bayfield, Norfolk.

and mortar composition, differences in tooling to stones, changes in material resulting from refacing, as well as stylistic and iconographic significances, will all help to build up a picture of usage and change.

Technical reports and survey information, from past or present owners, will be an invaluable aid to understanding how the site has been treated in more recent years. Much of the damage seen today may, for instance, have been a direct result of earlier attempts at preservation, including the use of hard cements in mortars, and insertion of iron cramps and dowels.

## PHYSICAL CONDITION

When assessing the condition of a standing ruin the following questions should be asked.

- Has the ruin been repaired and consolidated in the past?
- Are temporary works present or considered necessary?
- Are physical interventions needed or proposed?
- Has the structural equilibrium of the ruin been altered by recent works or collapses?
- Is wind loading likely to present problems to unsupported walls?
- Have arches adequate counter-thrust?
- Are there unsupported sections of masonry visible?
- Are there obvious areas where water is standing?
- Do ivy, trees, shrubs or undergrowth obscure areas of masonry and pose a threat to stability?
- Has the amount of ventilation been reduced by vegetation or blocking of openings, increasing the risk of fungal growth?
- Have the facings and/or dressings been robbed?
- What is the condition of broken wall faces and heads?
- Is the corework exposed and what condition is it in? Core that contains poor weathering material, such as chalk and decayed lime mortar, will decay rapidly causing settlement and failure.
- What is the number and distribution of fallen stones and masonry?
- Is there detached fabric available in store or as museum exhibits that can be viewed and possibly returned?
- Are there above-ground voids present, such as flues, shafts or mural passages?
- Are there below-ground voids present, such as vaults or crypts?
- Are standard assessments of condition required, such as buildings at risk classifications or English Heritage field warden reports?

## ARCHITECTURAL AND ARCHAEOLOGICAL FEATURES

When inspecting and assessing the condition of a standing ruin it is important to be aware of any significant elements or forms of construction that are visible, or have come to light, as a result of further investigation. The presence of blocked openings, embedded timber members or changes in the style of masonry can all point to significant events in the life of the building, whereas construction details can aid interpretation of how the building was erected.

Lift lines, often seen clearly in flintwork, show the extent of building in relation to the seasons or longer periods of delay, with timber, tile or mortar used to level the lift in readiness for the next. The presence or imprint of formwork used in the formation of structural openings may also be seen. At Castle Rising (Norfolk), for instance, visible evidence remains within the twelfth century keep for how the vaulting was constructed using wicker formwork.

*Figure 16.4* Interior of the medieval gatehouse to Pentney Priory, Norfolk. Notice the remaining stone springer for the vaulting, pockets for first-floor construction and damage to stone tracery of upper window.

It is important also to be aware of the possibility of finding surviving features such as floor tiles, glass, ferramenta, plasters, renders, wall painting or other forms of decoration. Historical reuse and abandonment of materials is another source of interesting finds. At Waxham Great Barn (Norfolk), a terracotta putto was found inside a decayed buttress that was identical to the figures on the fine Bedingfeld monument of about 1525 in the Church of St John the Evangelist at Oxborough, over 50 miles (80 km) to the west (Figure 16.5).

*Figure 16.5* Archaeological drawing of terracotta putto found at Waxham Great Barn, Norfolk. The reconstruction drawing is based on the Bedingfeld monument. Courtesy of Steven Ashley, Norwich.

## SITE AND ENVIRONMENT

The location and setting of a ruin may have a great impact on the landscape, standing out as a prominent landmark or being the object of local pride. The surroundings to the ruin may also be of importance, as with many of the ruined churches in Norfolk that are the only above-ground evidence for deserted medieval villages (DMVs).

### Education and recreation

Public access to a ruin and its site may, in itself, be a consideration, requiring fencing, warning signs or temporary works. It may also suggest likely patterns of ground or masonry erosion, and the likelihood of vandalism or graffiti. Erosion of the individual stones that make up the late Bronze age Nine Ladies circle at Stanton-in-the-Peak in Derbyshire has, for instance, been found to have been caused by the swinging heels of persons sitting on the stones.

Visitor facilities, such as parking areas, interpretation boards, litter bins and toilets, can have an effect on the setting of the ruin, and be the cause of ground erosion and disturbance.

## Local conditions

The location of the ruin with regard to topography, and exposure to wind, rain and atmospheric pollution, can be of particular concern with regard to levels of erosion and material degradation. The sandstone of Whitby Abbey, for instance, standing high up on the east coast in North Yorkshire, suffers visibly from the effects of its coastal location and almost constant scouring by wind-borne grits and sands.

Erosion can also occur when the wind is channelled through openings, forming vortices that can pick up and carry grit to scour inside surfaces (Figure 16.6). Careful thought has to be given when considering the provision of a temporary roof structure over a ruin in order to avoid creating a problem or making an existing one worse.

Other features of the site, including the level of the water table, position of water courses, and the presence of rabbits and moles, may all have an effect on the well-being of the ruin. Livestock can play a significant part

*Figure 16.6* Eroded brickwork at door opening at Limpenhoe drainage mill, Norfolk. Notice the number of exposed stones within the soft red bricks.

in the erosion of a ruin with, for example, cattle dislodging stones as they rub against the walls. The feet of grazing cattle can also cause damage to below-ground features, particularly in wet conditions, and therefore sheep rather than cattle are often encouraged in site management agreements.

## Flora and fauna

Sites may also be important in terms of their flora and fauna, with the ruins being host to lichens, plants and mammals. Many ruins provide roost and nest sites for various bats and birds.

The strict removal of all vegetation from the masonry of standing ruins has recently given way to a less harsh approach that reflects the importance of an often ideal natural environment. At Jervaulx Abbey (North Yorkshire) and various other sites, English Heritage has used a technique of soft capping to retain grass and other plants on wall tops.[2] Such material can offer protection to the underlying masonry by reducing extremes of temperature and reducing risks of frost damage.

## SPECIALISTS AND SPECIALIZED EQUIPMENT

In assessing the condition of a standing ruin it may be necessary to consider the use of specialists and/or specialized equipment. The following questions may need to be asked:

*Figure 16.7* Controlled vegetation growth to remains of 15th-century castle at Claxton, Norfolk.

- Is monitoring of structural movement and/or environmental conditions necessary?
- Are geophysical surveys necessary to indicate underground features?
- Is mortar analysis necessary to provide evidence for repair and/or interpretation?
- Are specialized skills required to understand the structure and/or site? These may include architectural historians, environmental archaeologists, landscape archaeologists and social historians.

- Is high-level access required, such as ladders, hoists and platforms? (Figure 16.8).
- Is high-level recording necessary?
- Is accurate recording required, such as stereo photogrammetry, computer-aided mono-photogrammetry or rectified photography?
- Are non-destructive surveying techniques appropriate? This might be appropriate for detecting voids inside walls or piers of masonry.

## THREATS

### Public access

Aside from natural rates of deterioration and decay a ruin is also likely to suffer from damage caused by visitors. While deliberate acts of vandalism, including incised and sprayed graffiti, have an immediate effect on the appearance of the masonry, unintentional damage can also be caused by well-meaning visitors walking and climbing on wall tops and sections of unconsolidated corework. Although most managed sites attempt to avoid a clutter of barriers and notices, it remains a threat that needs to be considered both when assessing overall condition and presentation.

Where public access is present, or being considered to a site, there may also be conflict between the need to provide facilities and the preservation of the remains. Drainage runs and the provision of underground cables for spotlights will often need to be carefully considered in conjunction with an archaeologist. Public events within the proximity of standing ruins, such as open-air concerts and fairs, will require the provision of certain amenities, and careful planning of car parking and access routes.

### Lack of knowledge and experience

The skills required in repairing standing ruins, and presenting the monument and its site to the public, are specialized in nature and as such not widely available. It is essential that all personnel involved with a ruin, including staff, advisers and contractors, are suitably experienced and adequately supervised. The loss of material will mean nothing if it is not

*Figure 16.8* Mobile hoist in use at the Church of St Margaret, Pudding Norton, Norfolk.

understood, and for this reason careful recording is essential both as a site record and management tool.

Loss or damage to below-ground features, which may be relevant to an understanding of the standing ruin, can occur through ploughing, grazing, vegetation clearance, public access or changes in the conditions of the ground. With regard to the last of these points changes in ground-water drainage or the introduction of water extraction can upset the finely-balanced environment of the surrounding soil.

## Theft

Theft of worked stones from certain ruins can pose a particularly difficult problem. Unless a stone or artifact is of sufficient merit to warrant its removal to a museum it is usually preferable to keep such things on-site. Dispersal will, in time, reduce the importance of the site and be a potential cause of confusion in later years. In response to this, fonts and memorial stones found at ruined churches may, for instance, be buried on-site following careful recording and archaeological approval.

Where long work contracts are envisaged, or temporary works are in place, the adviser and contractor should be aware of, and make provision for, the increasing risk of scaffolding being stolen from sites. The national Crimestoppers scheme, in conjunction with the National Association of Scaffolding Contractors, operates to give advice, increase awareness of potential risks and encourage liaison with local police.

## The risk of ruination

The most obvious threat to a building is that of becoming a ruin itself. Although outside the scope of this book it cannot be stressed enough that regular and diligent maintenance, whether of an occupied building or a standing ruin, is critical for its future. Where temporary or permanent redundancy is the final outcome for a building in use, planned protection and mothballing are essential.

*Figure 16.9* Late 16th-century cottage at Ratcliffe-on-the-Wreake, Leicestershire. Notice the condition of the roof covering, open windows and exposed timber frame.

# PART
# THREE

*Chapter Seventeen*

# A look to the future

## INTRODUCTION

This final chapter reviews the challenges faced by property professionals when employed to survey historic buildings, puts forward suggestions, and attempts a look into the future. This will inevitably be a personal view and much may therefore be open to debate.

## TECHNIQUES OF SURVEYING

Although the basic skills of today's surveyors are little different from those of earlier generations, the need has risen for more detailed information to be provided to an increasingly well-informed client, in a clear and often prescribed format, and with a growing emphasis on professional competence.

There has also been a corresponding increase in litigation for actual and claimed professional negligence, forcing surveyors to adopt an often defensive form of reporting, including the frequently excessive use of disclaimers and exclusion clauses.

Many of the problems that end in legal action result from the surveyor being ill-prepared to face the demands of a historic building, whether from a lack of appropriate training or site experience. Education has a part to play, but there must also be an acceptance within the property professions that the demands of surveying a historic building are not the same as those required for dealing with modern structures. Inexperienced surveyors, using inappropriate general forms of inspection, cannot be expected to provide an adequate service.

## Holistic approach

Increasingly buildings are being viewed as living entities, each element, component or material reacting and interreacting with another. This has brought about a new way of looking at buildings and their defects, with an emphasis on the whole rather than the part. Such a holistic approach to understanding symptoms and defects is perhaps best seen in the radically different way in which dry rot is now being monitored and contained, rather than being subject to often damaging elimination.

As more needs to be known about a building, the skills of many disciplines will be required to ask the right questions and proffer the often elusive answers. At present such an approach is only, and rightly, used with large and important buildings, but increasingly answers are being required for lesser buildings undergoing adaptation, refurbishment or repair.

In this context the Historic Structure Report, from America, has much to offer. Such a report requires the interdisciplinary skills of the architect and surveyor, archaeologist and engineer, historian and scientist, to be brought together in what has, until now, been seen as an unlikely combination of professions. In this country such an approach could, at present, only be offered by the handful of consultancy units, typically operating from academic institutions, who are able to bring together such diverse talents. This should not, however, be used as an excuse for avoiding the issue, and bodies such as English Heritage should take the initiative in requiring such detailed reports and making their preparation grant eligible.

## The importance of planned maintenance

Much of the deterioration and disrepair diagnosed in surveys comes as a direct result of a lack of routine maintenance. While the property professions are aware of the benefits of planned preventive maintenance, owners and occupiers seem to see it as something either beyond their means or beneath their dignity.

It is, therefore, the opinion of the authors that all nationally important buildings, perhaps those that are scheduled or listed as Grade I and II*, should be regularly and competently inspected in order to point the way towards a realistic management of our historical legacy. The costs of such quadrennial or quinquennial inspections should be met, at least in part, by the owners, but with incentives from central government. The abolition of VAT on the repair and maintenance of listed buildings would be a long overdue step in the right direction.

The idea of regular inspections is not new. In the Netherlands building owners are able, under 'Monumentenwacht', to pay a small fee to secure the services of a travelling team of craftsmen who report on the condition of a building and carry out minor repairs.[1, 2] Such a scheme could operate in this country, regardless of listed status, and make the difference between survival and decline.

The rapidly developing field of facilities management brings together a wide range of property- and user-related functions and co-ordinates their management. Thus facilities such as buildings, utilities, grounds and equipment are managed collectively rather than as separate entities. In respect of historic properties there is much to commend a co-ordinated facilities management approach that not only monitors the condition of the fabric and responds appropriately, but also assists an organization to fulfil its mission and achieve its strategic objectives.

## Computerization

The growth in the use of computers for the survey and assessment of buildings has come largely from the need to record large amounts of site data in a form that is accessible and useful. Many organizations now make use of field computers and data loggers for recording qualitative and quantitative information, particularly when dealing with large numbers of similar properties, or to assist in the preparation of maintenance strategies. Such survey systems can be designed to offer prompts to the surveyor either on an elemental or material basis.

The next generation of survey computerization would appear to be the introduction of expert systems, which possess detailed specialist knowledge. Fault questionnaires and prompts for on-site diagnosis would enable the surveyor to leave the site with sufficient information on which to prepare schedules of costed repairs. This information could, in turn, be linked to measured surveys prepared in a similar manner.

A further development of traditional surveying practice is in the monitoring of defects. Where once glass telltales were used, now movement can be measured and recorded using discrete sensors and data loggers for later computer analysis and visualization. Such sophisticated monitoring is also suited to regulating environmental conditions and supplying data to building management and automation systems.

The need for greater data storage and retrieval facilities has also prompted an increase in the use of computers. The RCHME national database for England's architectural and archaeological heritage, MONARCH (MONuments and ARCHives), provides a single point of entry into the National Monuments Records (NMR), while the current Heritage Programme aims to computerize all listed building records. Industrial sites in England are, at present, being recorded for IRIS (Index Record for Industrial Sites). Property management and geographical information systems (GISs) are also in use within organizations such as the National Trust.

These developments are, without doubt, a step forward in the assessment and management of buildings, but it must be remembered that no system can take the place of an experienced and knowledgeable surveyor, practising the skills of observation and diagnosis with a feel for the building and its surroundings.


## RECENT SURVEY CONSIDERATIONS

Recently there have been several issues that have required revised procedures, or separate assessments, to be made with regard to the condition of a property. These have usually been based on environmental considerations arising from the imposition of European standards and directives. Many of these considerations become apparent when a change of use is being contemplated for a building, and as such can affect historic buildings.


### Health and safety

Although a traditionally constructed building is unlikely to hold obvious risks to the health of its occupants, it is possible that later works, the insertion of modern materials, or the provision of facilities as part of a change of use, may give rise for concern. While sick building syndrome (SBS) and legionnaires' disease have both received attention in the general press and professional journals, there is a growing awareness of the relationship between the structure and materials of a building, and its environments, occupants and contents. It is, therefore, incumbent on a surveyor to be alert to such potential hazards, and to be familiar with the growing body of information being produced by the emerging discipline of building pathology.

The presence of lead, for example, in paints or as part of the water supply system in a building must be reported on in the light of recent research that has shown occupants, particularly children, of properties built before 1945 with higher, and potentially damaging, cumulative concentrations of lead in their blood than those living in modern dwellings.[3]

A ban on the supply and use of lead carbonate or lead sulphate in paints was imposed by the Environmental Protection (Control of Injurious Substances) Regulations 1991. Its use is, however, allowed for the restoration and maintenance of certain historic buildings and works of art, but only with the express consent of the competent authority, be it English Heritage, Historic Scotland, Cadw or the Conservation Unit.

COSHH (Control of Substances Hazardous to Health), and other health and safety requirements, will need to be met when dealing with existing lead-based paints as well as other materials that might pose a risk. There may also be a ban on solvent-based paints in the future to bring us in line with European and North American standards and regulations.

The Construction (Design and Management) Regulations 1994 will require greater consideration to be given to the management of health and safety during construction work, which will include future maintenance of the building and its services, and necessitate the collection of information for the health and safety plan and file.

The presence of unsuitable and deleterious materials may come to light during works, or be affected by otherwise harmless activities. The use of asbestos as an insulant or as reinforcement in rigid components can have important implications for the later refurbishment of a building. More recent problems have arisen with the premature failure of cavity-wall ties, the risks associated with the presence of biocide residues,[4] and the rapid deterioration of mundic blocks in the south-west. How do we know whether modern building materials and practices will not come back to haunt us in 20 or 30 years time?

Building and fire regulations, when applied to historic buildings, have long been sources of consternation and debate. Often without justification, many people see such requirements as infringements of their personal liberty and freedom of choice. The ability to satisfy such regulations in the context of historic fabric is, without doubt, one of the essential skills of a professional adviser, and these skills must also be applied when reporting on the condition of a property in respect of planned or possible works.

Access for disabled people into historic buildings and their settings is also having to be carefully assessed and consideration given recent guidance documents and changing legislation.[5, 6, 7]

Following fires at York Minster, Hampton Court Palace, Uppark and Windsor Castle a great amount of research has been undertaken to attempt an understanding of how historic buildings react to extremes of heat and smoke. Advice on fire prevention and appropriate precautions in historic buildings can be obtained from divisional fire prevention officers or private consultants, and may include risk assessments, staff awareness training, technical detailing, detection, extinguishers and appropriate methods of salvage.

Health and safety requirements, introduced in line with European directives, can have a significant effect on the fabric and use of historic properties. The Health and Safety Executive (HSE) 'six-pack' of regulations introduced in 1993 may have important implications for how historic buildings are used as places of work, and their associated running costs.[8]

Where a building is used for the preparation and handling of food for public consumption there are stringent food hygiene regulations that have to be satisfied. The fact that the building is of historic value, and could not be satisfactorily adapted, will provide no defence in the event of legal action.

## Energy efficiency

Energy efficiency is rightly a significant consideration in assessing the quality of a property, but it is questionable whether modern standards should be imposed on historic fabric. The provision of insulation in roof spaces has been the cause of many outbreaks of fungal attack as natural ventilation routes are blocked and the risk of condensation increases.

Energy appraisals are increasingly being undertaken by surveyors as part of their standard inspections. Consideration should always be given to the particular plan form and spatial arrangements of a historic building when putting forward ideas for improvements to avoid potentially damaging alterations.

## Changes in standards of living

Changes in standards of living, and how we choose to spend our time, may also be reflected in how older properties respond to our needs and aspirations. The naturally-occurring radioactive gas, radon, for instance, is unlikely to pose a significant risk to the health of the occupants in a traditional property unless the air changes inherent with open flues and loose-fitting traditional joinery are reduced by often well-meaning improvements. Improved heating, lighting, sanitation and drainage may also have implications for a property built in a less service-orientated age.

Particular problems can arise where a building is divided into multi-occupancies. Arrangements for shared or separate access, servicing, sound insulation, fire stopping, means of escape, privacy and security are some of the issues that may have to be addressed in the context of a historic building.

The sale and division of country houses has, in particular, caused concern in recent years. While conversion to hotels, leisure centres and other commercial uses may offer new life for an otherwise unwanted building, sensitivity in the handling of the work has, in certain cases, been missing. What is also perhaps at risk is the associated and somewhat archaic way of life that the new owners of these houses cannot emulate.

## Archaeological and architectural importance

Where recommendations are made on alterations within a survey report, it may be necessary for the surveyor to make the client aware of possible requirements for archaeological and architectural evaluation and recording. Government guidance on archaeology and planning makes it clear that management is essential for the survival of important remains,[9] while more recent recommendations on the historic environment stress the importance of protecting and preserving buildings and areas of economic and social value.[10]

The recent vogue, however, for 'fully-analytical surveys' of above-ground fabric, taken up by commercialized archaeological units and others, may require consideration to be given to condition as well as dimension, whether for a programme of works to an occupied house or a standing ruin. It is therefore all the more important that, in our enlightened age of commerce and equality, assessments of condition are made by persons possessing appropriate levels of knowledge and experience. Decay might be easily identified, but correct diagnosis and informed prognosis may prove lacking.

## Wildlife

The well-being of a building's other occupants deserves particular attention. Under section 9 of the Wildlife and Countryside Act 1981 it is an offence for any person to intentionally damage, destroy and obstruct access to places used for shelter or protection by scheduled wild animals, or to disturb such an animal while occupying this place.

All 14 species of British bat and their roosts are protected by the 1981 Act. Information concerning bats, both general and with regard to buildings, may be obtained from the Statutory Nature Conservation Organization (English Nature, Scottish Natural Heritage or the Countryside Council for Wales), the Vincent Wildlife Trust or the Bat Conservation Trust. Badgers and their setts are protected under the Badgers Act 1991.

An increasing awareness and promotion of wildlife conservation in Europe also appears to have important implications for those responsible for buildings and their sites. The European Directive for Habitat and Species,[11] together with our own regulations,[12, 13] will introduce new European areas to be known as Special Protection Areas (SPAs). Their designation may need to be carefully considered with regard to how buildings may be used and maintained.

## Atmospheric pollution

Atmospheric pollution is a significant factor in the preservation of historic fabric. The findings of the Joint Working Party between the Cathedrals Fabric Commission for England, National Power and PowerGen have indicated that sulphur dioxide is the principal man-made pollutant contributing to stone decay, with sea salts having a significant effect at coastal sites.[14]

## Traditional materials and methods of construction

The drop in demand for certain traditional materials following the introduction of replacement products after the Second World War has left us with an industry unable to satisfy the growing demand for materials to be used in the repair and conservation of historic buildings. Salvage is becoming increasingly common, often with inappropriate usage of scarce materials to satisfy fashion or a misplaced desire for an 'olde worlde' look. A dealers' code of practice is, however, being prepared for the architectural salvage trade by the Council for the Prevention of Art Theft (CoPAT).[15]

Sources of materials have also become depleted or lost through greed or neglect of traditional husbandry skills. The provision of new sails to Old Buckenham cornmill, reputed to be, at over 19 feet (six metres) in diameter at the curb, the widest mill in the country, was complicated by the lack of suitable timber for the 60 feet (18 metres) long stocks. The availability and quality of appropriate timbers, such as pitch pine, was brought into question, and laminated timber or welded steel stocks considered to give the only realistic solution. The construction of the cap, however, used almost all traditional materials (Figure 17.1).

Traditional methods of construction, developed in response to the needs of the times, and with an understanding of the suitability, qualities and limitations of materials and techniques, gained through apprenticeships and experience, have been replaced by fast-track construction techniques with prefabricated components and standard detailing. Skills have to be relearned, and the opportunity given for craft training.

## Disposal of specialized properties

The current break-up and disposal of property estates, and rationalization of existing facilities, has brought about an increase in the number of specialized properties being purchased or protected. The adaptation of prisons, schools and hospitals; the closure of churches; the sale of surplus

*Figure 17.1* Construction of cap for Old Buckenham cornmill, Norfolk, using oak for the framing, elm for the ribs, Douglas fir for the internal braces and cedar for the boarding. Photograph by David Watt, courtesy of the Norfolk Windmills Trust.

military buildings by the Ministry of Defence; and the fate of buildings on retained or sensitive land, could prove to be either a blessing or a burden. It is up to the various property professions to ensure that such opportunities are not squandered.

## Modern architecture

Growing anxiety over the potential loss or mutilation of leading examples of twentieth century architecture, and the conservation problems raised by the innovative use of modern materials and construction practices, is stimulating discussion and debate. In the vanguard of raising the awareness and understanding of such issues are the Twentieth Century Society and DOCOMOMO-UK.

Recently, consultations regarding listing of modern architecture, the *Modern Matters* conference organized by English Heritage[16] and the publication of key papers[17] have helped to draw attention to the plight of many influential buildings and the need for a change in the attitudes of owners, occupiers and professional advisors.

## Security

Assessing the condition of a building damaged by a bomb blast, or commenting on the implications to historic fabric of introducing measures designed to reduce the risk of injury to occupants, is something that the majority of practising surveyors are unlikely to face. It is, however, a reflection of our times that property and persons are threatened by such action in London and other principal cities, and that thought must be given to providing sound advice based on appropriate training and experience.

Although the remains of the medieval church of St Ethelburga, damaged by the terrorist bombing of Bishopsgate in April 1993, are to be saved (Figure 17.2), there will be instances where a detailed assessment will be required for a building that has sustained less destructive damage to both fabric and contents. A programme of work will have to be put in hand on a scale not dissimilar to that undertaken after a fire, and to which a surveyor may be required to contribute.

Finally, theft of antiques and architectural features is on the increase. Architectural salvage is big business and unfortunately there are some who are not content to simply search demolition sites with the consent of the owners.

*Figure 17.2* Extent of bomb damage to Church of St Ethelburga, in Bishopsgate, London. Courtesy of the Society for the Protection of Ancient Buildings.

It is important that all movable or particularly valuable items are photographed and described in an inventory, and advice taken on providing identification marks. In empty properties chimney pieces, staircases, doors, balustrading and floorboards are all at risk. External items such as statues, urns, railings, balconies and architectural details, including door surrounds and lead downpipes, may also be stolen.

Advice with regard to crime prevention in historic buildings can be obtained from either the local crime prevention or architectural liaison officers, or private consultants, on matters such as risk assessments, technical details, detection, warning and insurance.

## WHAT IS CONSERVATION?

'Conservation' has a range of meanings from static preservation to dynamic change, in both the built and natural environments. When relating to historic buildings, monuments or structures, conservation is generally viewed as signifying positive action in response to negative circumstances. It therefore can embrace many of the activities described in Chapter One that require assessments of condition.

Architectural conservation, however, suffers from a reputation of being, on the one hand, an elitist crusade fought on behalf of a small minority of buildings and monuments, and on the other, a stifling bureaucracy incapable of any reasonable degree of flexibility. Both have – and may remain – closer to the truth than many would wish to admit. There is, however, a growing acceptance that the commonplace is as important as the unique, either in isolation or in the larger context of the community or landscape. This includes common vernacular buildings, industrial monuments and standing remains.

Architectural conservation is about buildings, whether occupied or empty, standing or ruined. Buildings do not evolve in isolation; they are documents of social change, having important links with the people and the place. Each building is a product of its own time, having to pay its way in a later, different, world. Many of the questions and dilemmas being faced today are those brought about by trying to justify the importance of the past in the present and for the future.

As the need increases for more information to support the decision-making processes, the arts and the sciences are coming together to create a new generation of conservationists. Their needs, and those of their clients and of the public at large, must now be addressed through education and training.

## EDUCATION AND TRAINING

### Training in architectural conservation

Education in architectural conservation has, until recently, been primarily at postgraduate level, aimed typically at architects, planners and surveyors. A small, but growing, number of other disciplines and craftspersons are now being represented on the various courses approved by the Conference on Training in Architectural Conservation (COTAC).

Recently, however, a trend towards more general 'heritage' courses has emerged, taught at undergraduate level, and aiming at providing a basic knowledge and awareness of issues concerning both the built and natural environments. This move comes at a time when the existing courses are

*Figure 17.3* Archive photograph of 1861 showing the exposed remains of a 12th-century undercroft in Guildhall Lane, Leicester, following demolition of a 16th-century house. The photograph provides an important record of the structure prior to being vaulted over by the present building, and of contemporary street life. Recent excavations have also confirmed the presence of a Roman crossroads at a lower level. Courtesy of Leicestershire Museums, Arts and Records Service.

having to contend with modularization and the inevitable 'pick and choose' approach to higher education.

Specific craft training is also on the increase, attempting to counter the loss of skills and talents to retirement and a lack of demand.

Whatever way is chosen, specific training is, without doubt, needed if conservation is to prosper as a credible discipline. In his inaugural address the then current (1994) president of the Royal Institution of Chartered Surveyors questioned whether there was adequate recognition for 'the importance and potential of the historic environment to the national economic well-being of the United Kingdom', with emphasis on the interdependence of tourism and heritage.[18] With this was seen an opportunity 'for academic institutions and others to answer an important need of the industry to provide training'.

Within this period of growth it must, however, be recognized that there is a finite demand for such professional skills, and overprovision is a waste of resources. The skills required to work in the field of architectural conservation must, therefore, not be gained at the expense of stifling creative design talent. Training must clearly address the needs of today's advisers and contractors if conservation is to go forward as anything other than an academic exercise.

## Educating the public

Education must also extend to the public, as well as to owners and occupiers of historic properties. The work of national campaigns, such as English Heritage's 'Framing Opinions', and that of amenity societies, educational trusts and local authority conservation officers, can raise an awareness about conservation and help to encourage a sense of local identity. Education must also address some of the wider issues, such as fundamental conservation philosophies and priorities. In this respect events such as the Heritage Open Days, organized by the Civic Trust, and the regional exhibitions and seminars proposed for the end of the millennium, encouraging the nation to face up to fundamental cultural, economic and political questions, should be applauded.

There must also be a drive for a greater understanding of appropriate professional and practical services, and an awareness of where to obtain specialized advice. The present confusion over the nature and extent of general forms of building survey points to a lack of public understanding, and an absence of clear direction from within the relevant property professions. At a time of rapid change, both nationally and with respect to closer European practices, it is critically important that owners and occupiers are able to respect, and have confidence in, their own advisers.

# APPENDICES

## APPENDIX A
## ENGLISH HERITAGE BUILDINGS AT RISK SURVEY FORM

SURVEY FORM FOR BUILDINGS AT RISK REGISTER (COMPUTER VERSION)

```
| 1.IDENTIFICATION                                                              |
|                                                                               |
|COUNTY      :_____    DISTRICT :_____    PARISH   :_____ |
|                                                                               |
|NGR         :_____   PRIME   '(Greenback No) _____ |
|                                                 REF NO                        |
|LOCALITY    :_____        (List Entry No)____/____/__|
|                                                                               |
|St No       :_____   St Name  :_____ |
|                                                                               |
|Bldg Name   :_____  |
|_____|
| 2.ARCHITECTURAL OR HISTORIC INTEREST                                          |
|          Grade           : I           ____       No of CA        ____        |
|                          : II*         |    |     (If not in      |    |      |
|                          : II          |____|     CA = 0)         |____|      |
|          Unlisted        : UL                                                 |
|_____|
| 3.BUILDING USE AND TYPE                                                       |
|                    Broad Function   Detailed Building Type (See Wordlist)     |
|                                                                               |
|          ORIGINAL        :_____    :_____  |
|                                                                               |
|          CURRENT/LAST    :_____    :_____  |
|          Upper Floors                                                         |
|          (Optional)      :_____                                            |
|                                                                               |
|AG  Barn           CL  Residential over  HW  Hospital       RC  Museum         |
|    Farm Building          shop              Workhouse          Theatre        |
|AY  Outbuilding    CO  Monument          IE                 RL  Church         |
|    Wall           DM  Terrace House     IT  Institute          Chapel         |
|CI  Hall               Cottage          LW  Courthouse      RS  Hotel          |
|    Townhall           Lodge                 Prison         ST  Warehouse      |
|    Government Office   Farmhouse        MP  Brewery        SF  Street Furniture|
|CL  Bank               Manor House           Maltings       TR  Bridge         |
|    Exchange           Country House         Industrial Mill    Railway Bridge |
|    Office             House             MT  Fortification      Station        |
|    Post Office        Flats             PO  Watermill          Canal Building  |
|    Public House   ED  Library               Windmill       UT  Utility        |
|    Shop               School                Plant          VA  Repairs        |
|    Retail Warehouse GL Garden Building  RC  Cinema                            |
|_____|
| 4.      CONDITION                            OCCUPANCY                         |
|                                                                               |
|Very Bad  : 1      ____       Not Applicable      : 0      ____    RISK CATEGORY|
|Poor      : 2    |    |       Vacant              : 1    |    |     CALCULATED  |
|Fair      : 3    |____|       Partially Occupied  : 2    |____|     BY COMPUTER |
|Good      : 4                 Occupied            : 3                           |
|_____|
| 9.    REPORTER'S NAME                       | Private           : 1  5.OWNERSHIP TYPE |
|                                             | Religious/Charity : 2  ____             |
|                                             | Company           : 3 |    |            |
|       DATE                                  | Local Authority   : 4 |____|            |
|_____| Statutory Undertaker: 5                 |
|XXXXXXXXXXXXXXXXXXXXXXXXXXXXXXXXXXXXXXXXXXXXXX| Crown             : 6                   |
|                                             |                                         |
|       SECTIONS BELOW TO BE FILLED IN ONLY FOR|                        6.MARKET STATUS |
|       RISK CATEGORIES 1 - 3   All Buildings in Condition 1 | For Sale    : Y  ____     |
|                               Buildings in Condition 2 and | Not For Sale : N |   |    |
|                               Occupancy 1                  |                  |___|   |
|       or Other Buildings of Concern         .              |                          |
|XXXXXXXXXXXXXXXXXXXXXXXXXXXXXXXXXXXXXXXXXXXXXXXXXXXXXXXXXXXXXXXXXXXXXXXXXXXXXXXXXXXXXXXXX|
|7.     OWNERSHIP                             |                         8.MARKET DETAILS |
|                  Details of Owner/Agent     |                                          |
|       Name                                  | Asking Price     :                       |
|       Address                               | As At (Date)     :                       |
|                                             | Floor Area       :                       |
|                                             |     Sq M  : M    :                       |
|                                             |     Sq Ft : F                            |
|_____|_____|
|10.REASON BUILDING IS AT RISK                | 11.PREFERRED USES                        |
|                                             |                                          |
|                                             |                                          |
|                                             |                                          |
|                                             |                                          |
|                                             |                                          |
|                                             |                                          |
|_____|_____|
|12.ACTION                                                                      |
|                                                                               |
|                                                                               |
|                                                                               |
|                                                                               |
|_____|
```

APPENDIX B
PLANNED MAINTENANCE INSPECTION CHECKLIST FOR
DRAINAGE MILLS

Title: Polkey's Mill.                        File Number: Env. WP. 51
Parish/Address: Reedham.                      Date of Inspection: 05.02.96
Date of last inspection: 04.05.95.           Inspected by: D&W
Keys/access: NMPT key.                       Weather conditions: fine and windy.
Owner: NMPT.                                 Photographic record: colour slide.

```
------------------------------------------------------------------
Condition of Element:  C1=Good; C2=Fair; C3=Poor; C4=Very bad
Priority of Work:  P1=Desirable; P2=Essential; P3=Urgent
N/A = Not Applicable (do not leave blank if relevant)
F/I = Further Investigation (detailed examination of element/defect required)
A/I = Additional information (notes/sketches on separate sheets)
------------------------------------------------------------------
```

**GENERAL BUILDING FABRIC**  C = 14 / P = 11

*** **Exterior**

| 1.0 GENERAL STRUCTURE | C1 | C2 | C3 | C4 | P1 | P2 | P3 | N/A | F/I | A/I |
|---|---|---|---|---|---|---|---|---|---|---|
| 1.1 Settlement, cracking, movement or loss of stability | X | | | | | X | | | | |
| 1.2 Failure of structural members | | X | | | | X | | | | |
| 1.3 Excessive deterioration of fabric | X | | | | | X | | | | |
| 1.4 Damp penetration | | X | | | | X | | | | |
| 1.5 **General condition** | | X | | | | X | | | | |
| 1.6 Additional information | | | | | | | | | | |

Ivy growth to both sides of entrance door to east
side. Open joint and cracking noted on last inspection
is part now jointed. Vegetation and elders growing
up around tower and in channel.

| 2.0 ROOF COVERING/CAP | C1 | C2 | C3 | C4 | P1 | P2 | P3 | N/A | F/I | A/I |
|---|---|---|---|---|---|---|---|---|---|---|
| 2.1 Main finish | X | | | | X | | | | | |
| 2.2 Flashings/mortar fillets | | | | | | | | X | | |
| 2.3 Ridges/hips/eaves/verges | | | | | | | | X | | |
| 2.4 Moss/lichens/vegetation | | | | | | | | X | | |
| 2.5 **General condition** | X | | | | X | | | | | |
| 2.6 Additional information | | | | | | | | | | |

Aluminium temporary cap in place ✓ appearing satisfactory.

| 3.0 RAINWATER DISPOSAL | C1 | C2 | C3 | C4 | P1 | P2 | P3 | N/A | F/I | A/I |
|---|---|---|---|---|---|---|---|---|---|---|
| 3.1 Gutters | | | | | | | | X | | |
| 3.2 Downpipes | | | | | | | | X | | |
| 3.3 Blockages/debris | | | | | | | | X | | |
| 3.4 Adequacy | | | | | | | | X | | |
| 3.5 **General condition** | | | | | | | | X | | |
| 3.6 Additional information | | | | | | | | | | |

| 4.0 EXTERNAL WALLS | C1 | C2 | C3 | C4 | P1 | P2 | P3 | N/A | F/I | A/I |
|---|---|---|---|---|---|---|---|---|---|---|
| 4.1 Gables | | | | | | | | X | | |
| 4.2 Chimney stacks | | | | | | | | X | | |
| 4.3 Pointing | | X | | | | X | | | | |
| 4.4 Damp courses/ventilation | | | | | | | | X | | |

| 4.5 | Debris | C1 | C2 | C3 | C4 | P1 | P2 | P3 | N/A | F/I | A/I |
|---|---|---|---|---|---|---|---|---|---|---|---|
| 4.5 | Debris | X | | | | X | | | X | | |
| 4.6 | Rough racking | | | | | | | | | | X |
| 4.7 | Decoration | | X | | | | | X | | | |
| 4.8 | **General condition** | X | | | | | | X | | | |
| 4.9 | Additional information | | | | | | | | | | |

4.9 Additional information

Ivy growth to east, with grass and vegetation to base of tower. Open joints in brickwork and spalling to upper courses. Tar finish deteriorating. Loose brick to segmental arch over Door D1. Repaired segmental arch over Door D2.

| 5.0 | EXTERNAL DOORS AND WINDOWS | C1 | C2 | C3 | C4 | P1 | P2 | P3 | N/A | F/I | A/I |
|---|---|---|---|---|---|---|---|---|---|---|---|
| 5.1 | Ease of use | X | | | | X | | | | | |
| 5.2 | Glazing beads/putty | | | | | | | | X | | |
| 5.3 | Broken/missing glass | | | | | | | | X | | |
| 5.4 | Paintwork/protection | X | | | | X | | | | | |
| 5.5 | Fungal attack | | | | | | | | X | | |
| 5.6 | Beetle infestation | | | | | | | | X | | |
| 5.7 | **General condition** | X | | | | | | X | | | |
| 5.8 | Additional information | | | | | | | | | | |

5.8 Additional information

Door (D1) to ground floor of painted timber boards, the paint now starting to peel. Door (D2) blocked with corr. iron sheeting over. Window (W1) to first floor blocked with aluminium sheeting over.

| 6.0 | EXTERNAL FITTINGS | C1 | C2 | C3 | C4 | P1 | P2 | P3 | N/A | F/I | A/I |
|---|---|---|---|---|---|---|---|---|---|---|---|
| 6.1 | Cap | X | | | | X | | | | | |
| 6.2 | Gallery | | | | | | | | X | | |
| 6.3 | Petticoat/curb/rack | | | | | | | | X | | |
| 6.4 | Fantail/carriage | | | | | | | | X | | |
| 6.5 | Sheers | | | | | | | | X | | |
| 6.6 | Y wheel/tailpole | | | | | | | | X | | |
| 6.7 | **General condition** | X | | | | | | X | | | |
| 6.8 | Additional information | | | | | | | | | | |

*** **Interior**

| 7.0 | INTERNAL ROOF STRUCTURE/CEILING | C1 | C2 | C3 | C4 | P1 | P2 | P3 | N/A | F/I | A/I |
|---|---|---|---|---|---|---|---|---|---|---|---|
| 7.1 | Sizing of timbers | | | | | | | | X | | |
| 7.2 | Damp penetration/staining | | | | | | | | X | | |
| 7.3 | Fungal attack | | | | | | | | X | | |
| 7.4 | Beetle infestation | | | | | | | | X | | |
| 7.5 | Insulation | | | | | | | | X | | |
| 7.6 | Chimney flues | | | | | | | | X | | |
| 7.7 | **General condition** | | | | | | | | X | | |
| 7.8 | Additional information | | | | | | | | | | |

| 8.0 | INTERNAL PARTITIONS/CEILINGS/ WALLS/DOORS | C1 | C2 | C3 | C4 | P1 | P2 | P3 | N/A | F/I | A/I |
|---|---|---|---|---|---|---|---|---|---|---|---|
| 8.1 | Physical damage | | | | | | | | X | | |
| 8.2 | Fungal attack | | | | | | | | | X | |
| 8.3 | Beetle infestation | | | | | | | | | X | |

8.4  **General condition** ———————————— |☒| | | | |☒| | || || ||
8.5  Additional information

*Ground floor walls show remains of limewash, with vertical cracking present. Two cross beams remain with a small number of boards. Two cross beams remain to first and second floors, and to third floor beneath cap.*

| 9.0 FLOORS (ground and upper) | C1 | C2 | C3 | C4 | | P1 | P2 | P3 | | N/A | | F/I | | A/I |
|---|---|---|---|---|---|---|---|---|---|---|---|---|---|---|
| 9.1 Deflection/stability | | | ☒ | | | | ☒ | | | | | ☒ | | |
| 9.2 Fungal attack | | | | | | | | | | | | ☒ | | |
| 9.3 Beetle infestation | | | | | | | | | | | | ☒ | | |
| 9.4 Finishes | | | | | | | | | | ☒ | | | | |
| 9.5 **General condition** | | ☒ | | | | | ☒ | | | | | | | |
| 9.6 Additional information | | | | | | | | | | | | | | |

*No floors remain, only cross beams.*

| 10.0 STAIRWAYS/GALLERIES/ BALCONIES/PLATFORMS | C1 | C2 | C3 | C4 | | P1 | P2 | P3 | | N/A | | F/I | | A/I |
|---|---|---|---|---|---|---|---|---|---|---|---|---|---|---|
| 10.1 Deflection/stability | | | | | | | | | | ☒ | | | | |
| 10.2 Fungal attack | | | | | | | | | | ☒ | | | | |
| 10.3 Beetle infestation | | | | | | | | | | ☒ | | | | |
| 10.4 **General condition** | | | | | | | | | | ☒ | | | | |
| 10.5 Additional information | | | | | | | | | | | | | | |

*Fixed ladder in place to cap.*

| 11.0 INTERNAL DECORATIONS/FINISHES | C1 | C2 | C3 | C4 | | P1 | P2 | P3 | | N/A | | F/I | | A/I |
|---|---|---|---|---|---|---|---|---|---|---|---|---|---|---|
| 11.1 Woodwork | | | | | | | | | | ☒ | | | | |
| 11.2 Plasterwork | | | | | | | | | | ☒ | | | | |
| 11.3 Paints/stains | | | | | | | | | | ☒ | | | | |
| 11.4 **General condition** | | | | | | | | | | ☒ | | | | |
| 11.5 Additional information | | | | | | | | | | | | | | |

| 12.0 FIXTURES AND FITTINGS | C1 | C2 | C3 | C4 | | P1 | P2 | P3 | | N/A | | F/I | | A/I |
|---|---|---|---|---|---|---|---|---|---|---|---|---|---|---|
| 12.1 Fireplaces | | | | | | | | | | ☒ | | | | |
| 12.2 Fixed furniture | | | | | | | | | | ☒ | | | | |
| 12.3 **General condition** | | | | | | | | | | ☒ | | | | |
| 12.4 Additional information | | | | | | | | | | | | | | |

| | C1 | C2 | C3 | C4 | P1 | P2 | P3 | N/A | F/I | A/I |
|---|---|---|---|---|---|---|---|---|---|---|
| 14.0 MILL/PUMP MACHINERY | | | | | | | | | | |
| 14.1 Sails/stocks/canister | | | X | | | X | | | | |
| 14.2 Windshaft | | | | | | | | | X | |
| 14.3 Brakewheel | | | | | | | | | X | |
| 14.4 Wallower | | | | | | | | | X | |
| 14.5 Upright shaft | | | | | | | | | X | |
| 14.6 Crown wheel | | | | | | | | X | | |
| 14.7 Pit wheel | | | | | | | | X | | |
| 14.8 Drive shaft | | | | | | | | | X | |
| 14.9 Scoop wheel/housing | | | | | | | | | X | |
| 14.10 **General condition** | | | X | | | X | | | | |
| 14.11 Additional information | | | | | | | | | | |

Stones covered with algae, and showing narrow splits and open joints.

Machinery not inspected in detail.

Much debris remains to ground floor with some over drive shaft. Y-wheel, fantail, etc inside, but should be sorted and cleaned for labelling.

Brick channel (lower) deteriorating with much debris, ivy growth and tree-root action. Collapse to be expected. Scoop wheel is part covered with brambles.

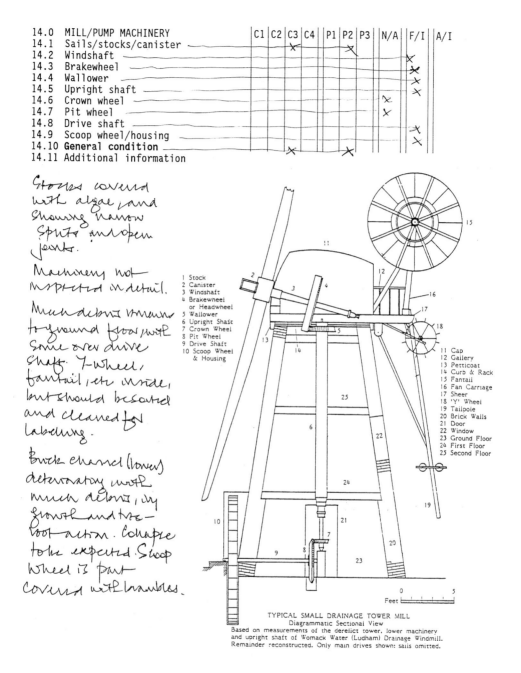

1 Stock
2 Canister
3 Windshaft
4 Brakewheel or Headwheel
5 Wallower
6 Upright Shaft
7 Crown Wheel
8 Pit Wheel
9 Drive Shaft
10 Scoop Wheel & Housing

11 Cap
12 Gallery
13 Petticoat
14 Curb & Rack
15 Fantail
16 Fan Carriage
17 Sheer
18 'Y' Wheel
19 Tailpole
20 Brick Walls
21 Door
22 Window
23 Ground Floor
24 First Floor
25 Second Floor

TYPICAL SMALL DRAINAGE TOWER MILL
Diagrammatic Sectional View
Based on measurements of the derelict tower, lower machinery and upright shaft of Womack Water (Ludham) Drainage Windmill. Remainder reconstructed. Only main drives shown; sails omitted.

## BUILDING SERVICES   $C \geq 1 / P \leq 1$

| | C1 | C2 | C3 | C4 | | P1 | P2 | P3 | | N/A | | F/I | | A/I |
|---|---|---|---|---|---|---|---|---|---|---|---|---|---|---|
| 1.0 ELECTRICAL INSTALLATION | | | | | | | | | | | | | | |
| 1.1 **General condition** | | | | | | | | | | X | | | | |
| 1.2 Additional information | | | | | | | | | | | | | | |

| | C1 | C2 | C3 | C4 | | P1 | P2 | P3 | | N/A | | F/I | | A/I |
|---|---|---|---|---|---|---|---|---|---|---|---|---|---|---|
| 2.0 DRAINAGE | | | | | | | | | | | | | | |
| 2.1 **General condition** | | | | | | | | | | X | | | | |
| 2.2 Additional information | | | | | | | | | | | | | | |

| | C1 | C2 | C3 | C4 | | P1 | P2 | P3 | | N/A | | F/I | | A/I |
|---|---|---|---|---|---|---|---|---|---|---|---|---|---|---|
| 3.0 PLUMBING | | | | | | | | | | | | | | |
| 3.1 **General condition** | | | | | | | | | | X | | | | |
| 3.2 Additional information | | | | | | | | | | | | | | |

| | C1 | C2 | C3 | C4 | | P1 | P2 | P3 | | N/A | | F/I | | A/I |
|---|---|---|---|---|---|---|---|---|---|---|---|---|---|---|
| 4.0 HEATING | | | | | | | | | | | | | | |
| 4.1 **General condition** | | | | | | | | | | X | | | | |
| 4.2 Additional information | | | | | | | | | | | | | | |

| | C1 | C2 | C3 | C4 | | P1 | P2 | P3 | | N/A | | F/I | | A/I |
|---|---|---|---|---|---|---|---|---|---|---|---|---|---|---|
| 5.0 SECURITY AND FIRE PRECAUTIONS | | | | | | | | | | | | | | |
| 5.1 Fire extinguishers | X | | | | | X | | | | | | | | |
| 5.2 **General conditions** | X | | | | | X | | | | | | | | |
| 5.3 Additional information | | | | | | | | | | | | | | |

**SITE AND ENVIRONMENT**   C = 8 / P = 7

| | | C1 | C2 | C3 | C4 | | P1 | P2 | P3 | | N/A | | F/I | | A/I |
|---|---|---|---|---|---|---|---|---|---|---|---|---|---|---|---|
| 1.0 | OTHER STRUCTURES ON SITE | | | | | | | | | | | | | | |
| 1.1 | General condition — | | | ✗ | | | | ✗ | | | | | | | |
| 1.2 | Additional information | | | | | | | | | | | | | | |

o *Brick shed with corr. iron sheeting to curved roof = severe cracking and partial collapse of S/W corner. Datestone dtd 1880.*
o *Brick shed with corr. iron sheeting to curved roof = used by marshman.*
o *Brick chimney stack with lean to south = now capped.*
o *Brick shed with corr. iron sheeting to curved roof = used by farmer.*

| | | C1 | C2 | C3 | C4 | | P1 | P2 | P3 | | N/A | | F/I | | A/I |
|---|---|---|---|---|---|---|---|---|---|---|---|---|---|---|---|
| 2.0 | BOUNDARY WALLS/FENCES | | | | | | | | | | | | | | |
| 2.1 | General condition | | | | | | | | | | ✗ | | | | |
| 2.2 | Additional information | | | | | | | | | | | | | | |

| | | C1 | C2 | C3 | C4 | | P1 | P2 | P3 | | N/A | | F/I | | A/I |
|---|---|---|---|---|---|---|---|---|---|---|---|---|---|---|---|
| 3.0 | GRASSED AND PLANTED AREAS | | | | | | | | | | | | | | |
| 3.1 | General condition — | ✗ | | | | | ✗ | | | | | | | | |
| 3.2 | Additional information | | | | | | | | | | | | | | |

| | | C1 | C2 | C3 | C4 | | P1 | P2 | P3 | | N/A | | F/I | | A/I |
|---|---|---|---|---|---|---|---|---|---|---|---|---|---|---|---|
| 4.0 | TREES/SHRUBS | | | | | | | | | | | | | | |
| 4.1 | Threat to building stability— | | ✗ | | | | | ✗ | | | | | | | |
| 4.2 | General condition | | ✗ | | | | | ✗ | | | | | | | |
| 4.3 | Additional information | | | | | | | | | | | | | | |

*Site heavily overgrown especially to channels. Access clear across marsh from Wickhampton Church. Need consent from marshman. Root damage to channels.*

| | | C1 | C2 | C3 | C4 | | P1 | P2 | P3 | | N/A | | F/I | | A/I |
|---|---|---|---|---|---|---|---|---|---|---|---|---|---|---|---|
| 5.0 | STEPS/RAMPS/PATHS/PAVED AREAS | | | | | | | | | | | | | | |
| 5.1 | General condition | | | | | | | | | | ✗ | | | | |
| 5.2 | Additional information | | | | | | | | | | | | | | |

| | | C1 | C2 | C3 | C4 | | P1 | P2 | P3 | | N/A | | F/I | | A/I |
|---|---|---|---|---|---|---|---|---|---|---|---|---|---|---|---|
| 6.0 | PEDESTRIAN/VEHICULAR ACCESS | | | | | | | | | | | | | | |
| 6.1 | Car parking | | | | | | | | | | ✗ | | | | |
| 6.2 | Signage | | | | | | | | | | ✗ | | | | |
| 6.3 | General condition | | | | | | | | | | ✗ | | | | |
| 6.4 | Additional information | | | | | | | | | | | | | | |

| | | C1 | C2 | C3 | C4 | | P1 | P2 | P3 | | N/A | | F/I | | A/I |
|---|---|---|---|---|---|---|---|---|---|---|---|---|---|---|---|
| 7.0 | GENERAL ENVIRONMENT | | | | | | | | | | | | | | |
| 7.1 | Rubbish disposal | | | | | | | | | | ✗ | | | | |
| 7.2 | Vandalism/theft/graffiti | | | | | | | | | | ✗ | | | | |
| 7.3 | Landscape setting | | ✗ | | | | | ✗ | | | | | | | |
| 7.4 | General condition | | ✗ | | | | | ✗ | | | | | | | |
| 7.5 | Additional information | | | | | | | | | | | | | | |

# APPENDIX C
# HAZARD IDENTIFICATION CHECKLIST

## CHECKLIST

## IDENTIFYING PARTICULAR HAZARDS

Representatives of all the RICS Divisions have contributed to the following checklist. Individual members will recognise the hazards they encounter regularly, and most will benefit from the advice given when working in unfamiliar surroundings. It is the nature of safety matters that no checklist like this can be entirely comprehensive.

## The following items may create danger:
## WHEN SURVEYING BUILDINGS

### Structures

The chance of partial or total collapse of:
- Chimney stacks, gable walls or parapets
- Leaning, bulged and unrestrained walls (including boundary walls)
- Rotten or corroded beams and columns
- Roofs and floors

### Timbers

- Rotten and broken floors and staircases. Flimsy cellar flaps and broken pavement lights
- Floorboards, joists and buried timbers weakened by age, decay or attack
- Projecting nails and screws. Broken glass
- Glazing in windows and partitions may be loose, hinges and sashcords weak or broken. Glass panels in doors and winglights may be painted over

### Roofs

- Fragile asbestos cement and plastic coverings
- Fragile rooflights (often obscured by dirt or temporary coverings)
- Low parapets or unguarded roof edges. Loose copings
- Rusted, rotten or moss covered fire escapes, access ladders and guard rails
- Rotten roof decking and joists
- Slippery roof coverings (slates, moss or algae covered slopes)
- Broken access hatches
- Mineral wool dust, mortar droppings and birds' nesting material and excrement in roof voids. Cornered birds and vermin
- Insects, bugs and lice. Bee and wasp colonies
- Water cooling plant may harbour legionella
- Unguarded flat roofs
- Broken, loose, rotten and slippery crawling boards and escape ladders
- Weak flat roofs and dust covered rooflights
- Slippery roof surfaces
- High winds during roof inspection
- Ill-secured or flimsy, collapsible, sectional or fixed loft ladders
- Concealed ceiling joists and low purlins
- Ill-lit roof voids

### Unsafe atmospheres

- Confined spaces with insufficient oxygen including manholes, roof voids, cellars, vaults, ducts and sealed rooms
- Rotting vegetation which may consume oxygen and give off poisonous fumes
- Accumulation of poisonous or flammable gases in buildings on contaminated land
- Stores containing flammable materials such as paint, adhesives, fuel and cleaning fluids
- Hazardous substances, including toxic insecticides and fungicides
- Gas build-up in subfloor voids

### Danger from live and unsecured services

- Electricity, gas, water and steam supplies
- Awkward entrances into sub-stations and fuel stores
- Temporary lighting installations: mains connections and generators
- Buried cables and pipes

### Hidden traps, ducts and openings

- Lift and services shafts, stairwells and other unguarded openings
- Manholes, including those obscured by flimsy coverings. Cesspools, wells and septic tanks

### Intruders and others

- Physical dangers from squatters and vagrants. Guard dogs
- Health risks (including AIDS) from discarded syringes and condoms
- Structures weakened by vandalism or arson
- Aggressive tenants and property owners

### Contamination

- Asbestos, lead and other substances hazardous to health
- PCB and PCN chemicals in electrical transformers and capacitors in fluorescent lighting fittings
- Overhead electrical cables
- Contaminated water supplies
- Contaminated air conditioning systems (legionella)

### Vermin and birds

- Rats and mice: Weil's and other diseases
- Bird droppings
- Lice may be present in bedding, soft furniture and carpets

## TRAVELLING TO AND FROM SITES

- Driving too fast, too long or when tired
- Use of hand-held car telephones on the move

## WHEN VISITING BUILDING SITES

- Slips, trips and falls
- Unsafe scaffolding and ladders
- Deep unsafe or unsupported excavations
- Cranes and overhead hazards
- Uneven ground
- Discarded materials, especially those with projecting nails
- Electricity
- Unsighted and reversing vehicles
- Inspecting highways or vehicle access points without illuminated clothing and hazard signs
- Hot bitumen and asphalt
- Wet surfaces

## ON MINING AND SIMILAR SITES

### Land and property damaged by mining subsidence

- Uneven ground surface and paved areas
- Loose or structurally unsound walls, floors, roofs, fixtures and fittings
- Gas leaks
- Fissuring

### Mine Shafts and Adits and Shallow Mine Workings

- Unstable ground around the shaft/adit
- Possible existence of nearby shafts with disturbed cappings and filling which may have a potential for collapse
- Toxic and explosive gases emanating from the shaft or adit
- Pitfalls and crown holes associated with old shallow underground mining activities
- Danger from the mining operation and machinery

### Quarries

- Pitfalls and shallow mining
- Steep and/or unstable quarry faces and benches
- Unstable ground at the top of quarry faces or benches
- Danger of loose material falling from above
- Moving parts of machinery
- Unguarded electrical and compressed air equipment
- Blasting
- Mobile excavations and large earth transporters
- Elevated walkways, stagings, platforms and ladders
- Hot surfaces at coating plants, etc
- Slurry ponds, lagoons, tanks and other filled areas
- Noisy and dusty conditions
- Railways and internal haul roads
- Danger from the quarrying operation and mobile plant

### Tips and Land Reclamation Sites

- Unstable slopes and ground
- Water lagoons, ponds and other water filled areas
- Slurry and quicksand areas
- Burning areas where tips are heating or on fire
- Hazardous or harmful chemicals, liquid matters and wastes, contaminated land
- Explosive and toxic gases and vapours

### Gas and Oil Wells

- Pipes and other ground level hazards
- Flare stacks
- Separating lagoons
- Explosive atmospheres
- Danger from the drilling operations

### Exploration, Drilling and Gantry Sites

- Hot muds
- Flying rock, dust and debris
- Water hazards
- Unsafe plant

## ON FARMS

### Farm buildings and land

- Grain storage and handling installations, particularly moving augers and conveyors
- Underground slurry stores, slurry lagoons, drains, deep ditches, wells, tower silos, sewage tanks and silage clamps (note: risk of toxic gases)
- Dust hazards in grain, mill and mix and intensive livestock buildings
- Overgrown areas: concealed manholes
- Poorly maintained buildings — especially loft floors — and fittings
- High voltage electric fencing
- Stored hazardous chemicals
- Rivers, lakes, reservoirs, dangerous bridges, bogs, quick-sands, unstable cliff edges and the sea
- Chemicals, poisons

### Farm machinery

- Packing and grading machines
- Stones and debris thrown from swipes and hedgecutters
- Cranes and the lifting equipment

### Livestock

- Any entire male animal: bulls, boars and rams
- Any female animal with young — calf proud cows and farrowing sows
- Game parks and wild animals
- Horses
- Dogs

### Diseases and pests

- Tetanus, Brucellosis
- Weils Disease (from stagnant water and ponds, hay stores etc)

### Sporting

- Firearms (must be licensed and properly stored and used)

## IN FORESTS

- Tree felling work either in thinning or clear felling operations
- Tree surgery work
- Dangerous and damaged trees, especially if liable to shed limbs
- Any work in woodlands in high winds
- Hand tools, axes and swipes
- Chain saws
- Saw milling and cutting equipment in saw mills and wood yards
- Timber handling equipment e.g. overhead extraction lines
- Fork lift vehicles and cranes

## OFFSHORE

- Moving and often slippery decks of ships and oil rigs
- Poorly secured equipment, including coffee cups and tools near sensitive machinery
- Fire hazards and flammable materials
- The hostile deck environment
- High pressure air gases and gas storage cylinders
- Hydraulic oil leakage

## APPENDIX D
## NORWICH CITY COUNCIL EXTENSIVE SURVEY FORM

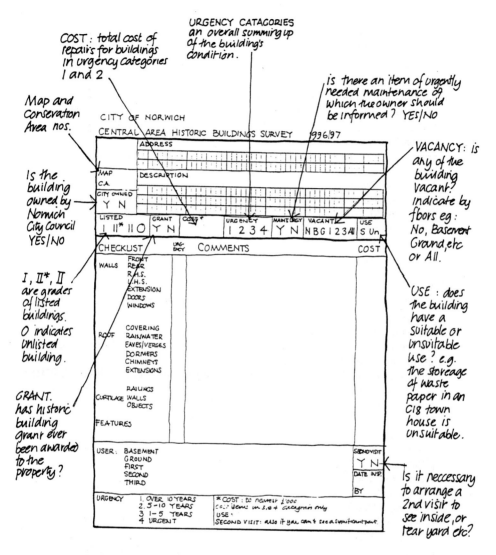

COST: total cost of repairs for buildings in urgency categories 1 and 2

URGENCY CATAGORIES an overall summing up of the building's condition.

Map and Conservation Area nos.

Is there an item of urgently needed maintenance of which the owner should be informed? YES/NO

Is the building owned by Norwich City Council YES/NO

VACANCY: is any of the building vacant? Indicate by floors eg: No, Basement Ground, etc or All.

I, II*, II are grades of listed buildings. O indicates Unlisted building.

USE: does the building have a suitable or unsuitable use? e.g. the storeage of waste paper in an C18 town house is unsuitable.

GRANT. has historic building grant ever been awarded to the property?

Is it neccessary to arrange a 2nd visit to see inside, or rear yard etc?

THE SURVEY FORM
All the information on the upper box indicated thus was put onto computor.

APPENDIX E
USEFUL CONTACTS

The following entries are for those societies, groups and other organizations, concerned directly or indirectly with historic buildings, that are able to offer advice or a professional service.

**Ancient Monuments Board for Wales**
Brunel House, 2 Fitzalan Road, Cardiff, Wales, CF2 1UY. Telephone 01222 465111

**Ancient Monuments Society**
St Ann's Vestry, 2 Church Entry, London, EC4V 5HB. Telephone 0171 236 3934

**Archetype Books**
(Conservation of Antiquities, Archaeology and Museum Studies)
31–34 Gordon Square, London WC1H 0PY. Telephone 0171 388 0283

**Architectural Association**
34–36 Bedford Square, London, WC1B 3ES. Telephone 0171 636 0974

**Architectural Heritage Fund**
27 John Adam Street, London, WC2N 6HZ. Telephone 0171 925 0199

**Architectural Salvage Index**
c/o Hutton + Rostron, Netley House, Gomshall, Surrey, GU5 9QA. Telephone 01483 203221

**Association for Industrial Archaeology (AIA)**
c/o Ironbridge Gorge Museum, The Wharfage, Ironbridge, Telford, Shropshire, TF8 7AW. Telephone 01952 432751

**Association for Studies in the Conservation of Historic Buildings (ASCHB)**
c/o Institute of Archaeology, 31–34 Gordon Square, London, WC1H 0PY

**Association of Conservation Officers (ACO)**
24 Middle Street, Stroud, Gloucestershire, GL5 1DZ. Telephone 01453 753949

**Attic Books**
The Folly, Rhosgoch, Painscastle, Builth Wells, Powys, Wales, LD2 3JY. Telephone 01497 851205

**Avoncroft Museum of Building**
Stoke Heath, Bromsgrove, Worcestershire, B60 4JR. Telephone 01527 31886

**Avongard Crack Monitoring Equipment**
61 Down Road, Portishead, Bristol, BS20 8RB. Telephone 0117 9–849782

**Bat Conservation Trust**
c/o The Conservation Foundation, 1 Kensington Gore, London, SW7 2AR. Telephone 0171 823 8842

**Beacon Books**
Alan Hardiman, 3 Mount Beacon, Bath, BA1 5QP. Telephone 01225 424647

**British Institute of Non-destructive Testing**
1 Spencer Parade, Northampton, NN1 5AA. Telephone 01604 30124

**British Standards Institute**
2 Park Street, London, W1A 2BS. Telephone 0171 629 9000

**Brooking Collection**
University of Greenwich, Oakfield Lane, Dartford, Kent, DA1 2SZ. Telephone 0181 316 9897

**Building Crafts and Conservation Trust**
King's Gate, Dover Castle, Dover, Kent, CT16 1HU. Telephone 01304 225066
**Building Limes Forum (BLF)**
c/o Institute of Advanced Architectural Studies, University of York, King's Manor, York, YO1 2EP. Telephone 01904 433987
**Building of Bath Museum**
The Countess of Huntingdon's Chapel, The Vineyards, The Paragon, Bath, BA1 5NA. Telephone 01225 333895
**Building Research Establishment (BRE)**
Bucknalls Lane, Garston, Watford, WD2 7JR. Telephone 01923 664850
**Buildings of England, Ireland, Scotland and Wales Trust**
27 Wright's Lane, London, W8 5TZ. Telephone 0171 416 3000
**Butterworth-Heinneman Ltd**
Linacre House, Jordan Hill, Oxford OX2 8DP. Telephone 01865 310366
**Cadw** (Welsh Historic Monuments)
9th Floor, Brunel House, 2 Fitzalan Road, Cardiff, Wales, CF2 1UY. Telephone 01222 465511
**Cambridge University Collection of Aerial Photographs**
Mond Building, Free School Lane, Cambridge, CB2 3RF. Telephone 01223 334575
**Castle Bookshop** (Archaeology, Architecture and Topography)
Castle Street, Holt, Clwyd, Wales, LL13 9YW. Telephone 01829 270382
**Central Council of Church Bell Ringers**
Towers and Belfries Committee, Chairman, Windmill House, Wingrave, Aylesbury, Buckinghamshire, HP22 4PD. Telephone 01296 681244
**Civic Trust**
17 Carlton House Terrace, London, SW1Y 5AW. Telephone 0171 930 0914
**Civic Trust for Wales**
4th Floor, Empire House, Mount Stewart Square, The Docks, Cardiff, Wales, CF1 6DN. Telephone 01222 484606
**College of Estate Management (CEM)**
Whiteknights, Reading, Berkshire, RG6 2AW. Telephone 01734 861101
**Commonwealth Association of Architects (CAA)**
The Building Centre, 26 Store Street, London, WC1E 7BT. Telephone 0171 636 7596
**Conference on Training in Architectural Conservation (COTAC)**
Room 328, Keysign House, 429 Oxford Street, London, W1R 2HD. Telephone 0171 973 3615
**Conservation Information Network**
The Conservation Unit, Museums and Galleries Commission, 16 Queen Anne's Gate, London, SW1H 9AA. Telephone 0171 233 3686
**Conservation Unit**
Museums and Galleries Commission, 16 Queen Anne's Gate, London, SW1H 9AA. Telephone 0171 233 3683
**Construction History Society**
c/o Chartered Institute of Building, Englemere, King's Ride, Ascot, Berkshire, SL5 8BJ. Telephone 01344 23355
**Control Risks Group Limited**
83 Victoria Street, London, SW1H 0HW. Telephone 0171 222 1552
**Copper Development Association (CDA)**
Orchard House, Mutton Lane, Potters Bar, Hertfordshire, EN6 3AP. Telephone 01707 50711

**Council for the Care of Churches (Church of England)**
83 London Wall, London, EC2M 5NA. Telephone 0171 638 0971
**Council for the Prevention of Art Theft (CoPAT)**
17 Whitcomb Street, London WC2H 7PL. Telephone 0171 839 5865
**Databuild Information Systems**
Adelphi Mill, Grimshaw Lane, Bollington, Macclesfield, Cheshire, SK10 5JB.
Telephone 01625 572222
**De Montfort**
Centre for Conservation Studies, 12 Castle View, Leicester, LE1 5WH. Telephone 0116 253 2781
**Department of National Heritage (DNH)**
2–4 Cockspur Street, London, SW1Y 5DH. Telephone 0171 211 6000
**Department of the Environment (DoE)**
2 Marsham Street, London, SW1P 3EB. Telephone 0171 276 0900
**DOCOMOMO-UK** (Documentation and Conservation of the Modern Movement) The Building Centre, 26 Store Street, London, WC1E 7BT. Telephone 0171 637 0276
**Donhead Publishing Ltd**
Lower Coombe, Donhead St Mary, Shaftesbury, Dorset, SP7 9LY. Telephone 01747 828422
**Ecclesiastical Architects' and Surveyors' Association**
Scan House, 29 Radnor Cliff, Folkestone, Kent, CT20 2JJ. Telephone 01227 459401
**Ecology Building Society**
18 Station Road, Cross Hills, Keighley, West Yorkshire, BD20 5DR. Telephone 01535 635933
**Elizabeth Dobson** (Second-hand and Out of Print Books on Architecture and Design)
2 Avondale Place, Halifax, West Yorkshire, HX3 0DY. Telephone 01422 362326
**Empty Homes Agency**
195–197 Victoria Street, London, SW1E 5NE. Telephone 0171 828 6288
**English Heritage**
(Historic Buildings and Monuments Commission of England)
23 Savile Row, London, W1X 1AB. Telephone 0171 973 3000
**English Heritage Publications**
23 Savile Row, London, W1X 1AB. Telephone 0171 973 3000
**Fire Protection Association (FPA)**
Melrose Avenue, Borehamwood, Hertfordshire, WD6 2BJ. Telephone 0181 207 2345
**Folly Fellowship**
Woodstock House, Winterhill Way, Burpham, Surrey GU4 7TX. Telephone 01483 565634
**Fort Brockhurst Building Conservation Training Centre**
c/o English Heritage, Room 528, 429 Oxford Street, London, W1R 2HD. Telephone 0171 973 3000
**Friends of Friendless Churches**
St Ann's Vestry Hall, 2 Church Entry, London EC4V 5HB. Telephone 0171 236 3934
**Garden History Society**
77 Cowcross street, London EC1M 6BP. Telephone 0171 608 2409
**Georgian Group**
6 Fitzroy Square, London, W1P 6DX. Telephone 0171 387 1720

**Heritage Support Service**
Building Research Establishment, Bucknalls Lane, Garston, Watford, WD2 7JR. Telephone 01923 894040
**Heriot-Watt University**
Edinburgh College of Art, Lauriston Place, Edinburgh, Scotland, EH3 9DH. Telephone 0131 229 9311
**Historic Farm Buildings Group**
c/o Museum of English Rural Life, University of Reading, Whiteknights, Reading, Berkshire, RG6 2AG. Telephone 01734 318663
**Historic Houses Association (HHA)**
2 Chester Street, London, SW1X 7BB. Telephone 0171 259 5688
**Historic Scotland**
20 Brandon Street, Edinburgh, Scotland, EH3 5RA. Telephone 0131 556 8400
**Hutton+Rostron Environmental Investigations Ltd**
Netley House, Gomshall, Guildford, Surrey, GU5 9QA. Telephone 01486 413221
**Incorporated Society of Valuers and Auctioneers (ISVA)**
3 Cadogan Gate, London, SW1X 0AS. Telephone 0171 235 2282
**Independent Thatch Consultants Ltd**
Wood End Cottage, Wood End, Wootton, Bedford, MK43 9AJ. Telephone 01234 843243
**Industrial Buildings Preservation Trust (IBPT)**
330 St James Road, Bermonsey, London, SE1 5JX. Telephone 0171 237 9016
**Institute of Advanced Architectural Studies (IoAAS)**
University of York, King's Manor, York, YO1 2EP. Telephone 01904 24919
**Institute of Field Archaeologists (IFA)**
Buildings Special Interest Group, Department of Archaeology, University of Liverpool, 12 Abercromby Square, Liverpool, L69 3BX. Telephone 0151 794 2578
**International Institute for Conservation of Historic and Artistic Works (IIC)**
6 Buckingham Street, London, WC2N 6BA. Telephone 0171 839 5975
**Landmark Trust**
Shottesbrooke, Maidenhead, Berkshire, SL6 3SW. Telephone 01628 825925
**Landmark Information Group Ltd**
704 The Chandlery, 50 Westminster Bridge Road, London, SE1 7QY. Telephone 0171 721 7695
**Lead Development Association (LDA)**
34 Berkeley Square, London, W1X 6AJ. Telephone 0171 499 8422
**Lime Centre**
Long Barn, Morestead, Winchester, Hampshire, SO21 1LZ. Telephone 01962 713636
**Loss Prevention Council (LPA)**
Melrose Avenue, Borehamwood, Hertfordshire, WD6 2BJ. Telephone 0181 207 2345
**Mostly Books**
(Second-hand and Out of Print Books including Architecture, Building and Heavy Crafts)
Harvey Leeson, 247 Rawlinson Street, Barrow-in-Furness, Cumbria, LA14 1DW. Telephone 01229 836808
**Museums and Galleries Commission**
16 Queen Anne's Gate, London, SW1H 9AA. Telephone 0171 233 3683

**National Approval Council for Security Systems (NACOSS)**
Queensgate House, 14 Cookham Road, Maidenhead, Berkshire, SL6 8AJ. Telephone 01628 37512

**National Archaeological Record (NAR)**
RCHME, Kemble Drive, Swindon, Wiltshire, SN2 2GZ. Telephone 01793 414600

**National Buildings Record (NBR)**
RCHME, Kemble Drive, Swindon, Wiltshire, SN2 2GZ. Telephone 01793 414600

**National Library of Air Photographs (NLAP)**
RCHME, Kemble Drive, Swindon, Wiltshire, SN2 2GZ. Telephone 01793 414600

**National Monuments Record Centre**
RCHME, Kemble Drive, Swindon, Wiltshire, SN2 2GZ. Telephone 01793 414600

**National Monuments Record for Wales**
Crown Buildings, Plas Crug, Aberystwyth, Dyfed, Wales, SY23 1NJ. Telephone 01970 624381

**National Monuments Record of Scotland**
John Sinclair House, 16 Bernard Terrace, Edinburgh, Scotland, EH8 9NX. Telephone 0131 662 1456

**National Trust**
36 Queen Anne's Gate, London, SW1H 9AS. Telephone 0171 222 9251

**National Trust for Scotland**
5 Charlotte Square, Edinburgh, Scotland, EH2 4DU. Telephone 0131 226 5922

**Nicholas Merchant**
(Reference books on all aspects of the fine and decorative arts)
3 Promenade Court, Promenade Square, Harrogate, North Yorkshire, HG1 2PJ. Telephone 01423 505370

**Protimeter Plc**
Meter House, Marlow, Buckinghamshire, SL7 1LX. Telephone 01628 472722

**Royal Commission on the Ancient and Historical Monuments of Scotland**
John Sinclair House, 16 Bernard Terrace, Edinburgh, Scotland, EH8 9NX. Telephone 0131 662 1456

**Royal Commission on the Ancient and Historical Monuments of Wales**
Crown Buildings, Plas Crug, Aberystwyth, Dyfed, Wales, SY23 1NJ. Telephone 01970 624381

**Royal Commission on the Historical Monuments of England (RCHME)**
23 Savile Row, London, W1X 1AB. Telephone 0171 973 3000

**Royal Institute of British Architects (RIBA)**
66 Portland Place, London, W1N 4AD. Telephone 0171 580 5533

**Royal Institution of Chartered Surveyors (RICS)**
Building Conservation Group, 12 Great George Street, London, SW1P 3AD. Telephone 0171 222 7000

**Royal Town Planning Institute (RTPI)**
26 Portland Place, London, W1N 4BE. Telephone 0171 636 9107

**Salvo**
P. O. Box 1295, Bath, BA1 3TJ. Telephone 01225 445387

**Save Britain's Heritage**
68 Battersea High Street, London, SW11 3HX. Telephone 0171 228 3336

**Scottish Civic Trust**
24 George Square, Glasgow, Scotland, G2 1EF. Telephone 0141 221 1466

**Scottish Conservation Bureau**
Historic Scotland, 3 Stenhouse Mill Lane, Edinburgh, Scotland, EH11 3LR.
Telephone 0131 443 1666
**Shire Publications Ltd**
Cromwell House, Church Street, Princes Risborough, Buckinghamshire, HP27
9AJ. Telephone 01844 44301
**Society for the Protection of Ancient Buildings (SPAB)**
37 Spital Square, London, E1 6DY. Telephone 0171 377 1644
**Stately Homes Hotline**
Ripley Castle, Ripley, Harrogate, North Yorkshire, HG3 3AY. Telephone
01423 770152
**Stone Federation Great Britain**
82 New Cavendish Street, London, W1M 8AD. Telephone 0171 580 5588
**Structural Studies, Repairs and Maintenance of Historic Buildings
(STREMA)**
Computational Mechanics Institute, Wessex Institute of Technology, Ashurst
Lodge, Ashurst, Southampton, SO4 2AA. Telephone 01703 293223
**Textile Conservation Centre**
Apartment 22, Hampton Court Palace, East Molesey, Surrey, KT8 9AU. Tele-
phone 0181 977 4943
**Thatching Advisory Service Ltd**
Rose Tree Farm, 29 Nine Mile Ride, Finchampstead, Wokingham, Berkshire,
RG11 4QD. Telephone 01734 734203
**Theatres Trust**
22 Charing Cross Road, London WC2H 0HR. Telephone 0171 836 8591
**Thesaurus Group Ltd**
Mill Court, Furrlongs, Newport, Isle of Wight, PO30 2AA. Telephone 01983
826000
**Trace Publications Ltd**
38 New Street, Barbican, Plymouth, Devon, PL1 2NA. Telephone 01752 228727
**Traditional Paint Forum**
c/o Honorary Secretary, 179 Canongate, Edinburgh, EH8 8BN
**Twentieth Century Society**
70 Cowcross Street, London, EC1M 6BP. Telephone 0171 250 3857
**United Kingdom Institute for Conservation (UKIC)**
37 Upper Addison Gardens, Holland Park, London, W14 8AJ. Telephone
0171 603 5643
**Upkeep**
(The Trust for Training and Education in Building Maintenance)
Apartment 39, Hampton Court Palace, East Molesey, Surrey, KT8 9BS. Tele-
phone 0181 943 2277
**Vernacular Architecture Group (VAG)**
Membership Secretary, Brick Field, 20 Kiln Lane, Betchworth, Surrey, RH3
7LX. Telephone 01737 843342
**Victorian Society**
1 Priory Gardens, Bedford Park, London, W4 1TT. Telephone 0181 994 1019
**Vincent Wildlife Trust**
10 Lovat Lane, London, EC3R 8DT. Telephone 0171 283 2089
**Vivat Trust**
61 Pall Mall, London, SW1Y 5JA. Telephone 0171 930 2212
**Weald and Downland Open Air Museum**
Singleton, Chichester, West Sussex, PO18 0EU. Telephone 01243 811348

# References and notes

## Chapter One: Surveying buildings

1. Nelson, T. (ed.) (1994) *The Surveyor's Factbook*, London: Gee Publications p. 1/1.
2. Hollis, M. (1991) *Surveying Buildings*, 3rd edn, London: Surveyors Publications.
3. International Council of Monuments and Sites (1964), *Venice Charter for the Conservation and Restoration of Monuments and Sites*, Article 5, Venice: ICOMOS.
4. FEILDEN, B. (1994) *Conservation of Historic Buildings*, 2nd edn, London: Butterworth-Heinemann, p. 3.
5. British Standards Institution (1993) *Glossary of Terms used in Terotechnology* 4th edn, BS 3811:1993, London: BSI.
6. Baines, F. (1923) 'Preservation of Ancient Monuments and Historic Buildings', *RIBA Journal*, **XXXI (4)**, 22 December, 104–6.
7. British Standards Institution (1991) *Guide to the Care of Historic Buildings*, Draft British Standard, Paragraph 6. 4. 9, London: BSI.

## Chapter Two: Forms of building survey

1. Conservation Unit (1992) *Historic Buildings Conservation Guide for Government Departments*, Section 207, London: Department of the Environment Conservation Unit.
2. *Care of Churches and Ecclesiastical Jurisdiction Measure 1991*, Schedule 3, paragraph 2 (a).
3. Royal Institute of British Architects (1990) *Architect's Appointment – Historic Buildings: Repairs and Conservation Work*, London: RIBA Publications Ltd.
4. Royal Institute of British Architects (1992) *Alternative Schedule of Services: Historic Building Repairs and Conservation Work*, London: RIBA Publications Ltd.
5. Royal Institution of Chartered Surveyors (1994) *Conditions of Engagement for Building Surveying Services for Historic Buildings*, Draft copy, London: RICS.
6. Council for the Care of Churches (1995) *A Guide to Church Inspection and Repair*, London: Church House Publishing.
7. Conservation Unit (1992) *Historic Buildings Conservation Guide for Government Departments*, London: Department of the Environment Conservation Unit.
8. National Trust (1993) *Quinquennial Surveys on Buildings Held for Preservation*, Manual of Building: Instruction 9/93, London: National Trust.
9. Woodcock, S. (1992) 'Letter from America II', *Context*, **36**, 7.
10. American Society for Testing and Materials (n.d.) *Guide to Preparation and Use of Historic Structure Reports*, Due for publication by ASTM in 1997.

11. Slaton, D. (1993) *What is an Historic Structure Report?* Draft report, August 1993, Chicago: Task Group on Historic Structure Reports.
12. English Heritage (1992) *Buildings at Risk: A Sample Survey*, London: English Heritage.
13. Royal Institution of Chartered Surveyors (1993) *Home Buyers' Survey and Valuation Standard Conditions of Engagement*, London: RICS/ISVA.
14. Joint Working Party (1994) *Definitions of Inspections and Surveys of Buildings*, Draft document, 14 April, London: ISVA.
15. Royal Institution of Chartered Surveyors/Incorporated Society of Valuers and Auctioneers (1995) *Specification for Residential Mortgage Valuation*, Clause 3. 10, London: RICS/ISVA.
16. Royal Institution of Chartered Surveyors (1995) *RICS Appraisal and Valuation Manual*, Guidance Note 3 (GN 3. 4 and Guidance Notes Appendix 2), London: RICS.

## Chapter Three: Historic buildings

1. Royal Institute of British Architects (1990) *Architect's Appointment – Historic Buildings: Repairs and Conservation Work*, London: RIBA Publications Ltd.
2. Department of the Environment/Department of National Heritage (1994) *Planning Policy Guidance: Planning and the Historic Environment*, PPG 15, September 1994, London: HMSO.
3. Department of the Environment (1987) *Historic Buildings and Conservation Areas – Policy and Procedures*, Circular 8/87, March 1987, London: HMSO.
4. Department of the Environment (1990) *Planning Policy Guidance: Archaeology and Planning*, PPG 16, November 1990, London: HMSO.
5. English Heritage (1992) *Buildings at Risk: A Sample Survey*, London: English Heritage.
6. Department of the Environment (1993) English House Condition Survey 1991, London: HMSO.
7. Sadler, R. and Ward, K. (1992) *Owner Occupiers' Attitudes to House Repairs and Maintenance*, Research Study for the Building Conservation Trust, February 1992.
8. Norfolk County Council (1987) *Historic Buildings in Norfolk: Problems and Opportunities*, Monitoring Report, Consultative Draft, 23 April 1987.
9. Clifton-Taylor, A. (1987) *The Pattern of English Building*, 4th edn, London: Faber and Faber.
10. Brunskill, R. W. (1978) *Illustrated Handbook of Vernacular Architecture*, 2nd edn, London: Faber and Faber.
11. Torraca, G. (1988) *Porous Building Materials: Materials Science for Architectural Conservation*, 3rd edn, Rome: ICCROM.
12. Rodwell, W. (1986) 'Anglo-Saxon Church Building: Aspects of Design and Construction'. In: Butler, L. A. S. and Morris, R. K. (eds), *The Anglo-Saxon Church: Papers on History, Architecture and Archaeology in Honour of Dr H. M. Taylor*, Research Report 60, London: Council for British Archaeology.
13. Thorne, R. (1993) 'The Right Conservation Policy for Post-War Buildings', *The Architects' Journal*, 13 October, 21.
14. English Heritage (1994) *The Investment Performance of Listed Buildings*, London: English Heritage/RICS.
15. Royal Institution of Chartered Surveyors (1994) *The Listing of Buildings: The Effect on Value*, London: RICS.

## Chapter Four: Building surveys I: Basis of inspection

1. Construction Industry Council (1992) *The Procurement of Professional Services: Guidelines for the Application of Competitive Tendering*, London: Thomas Telford Services Ltd.

2. Bourne v. McEvoy Timber Preservations Limited (1975) 237 EG 496.
   Yianni v. Edwin Evans and Sons (1981) 3 All ER 592; (1981) 3 WLR 843; (1982) QB 438.
3. Coulton v. Pickles (1995) *Property Week*, 23 November 1995, 26–7.
4. Institution of Structural Engineers (1991) *Guide to Surveys and Inspections of Buildings and Similar Structures*, Amended May 1992, London: Institution of Structural Engineers.
5. Swindells, D. J. and Hutchings, M. (1993) *A Checklist for the Structural Survey of Period Timber Framed Buildings*, RICS Building Conservation Group, London: Surveyors Holdings Ltd.
6. Royal Institution of Chartered Surveyors (n. d.) *HBSV Report Writer Manual*, Draft document, Expected date of publication 1996, London: RICS Business Services.
7. Dallas, R. W. A. (1980) 'Surveying with a Camera: Rectified Photography', *Architects' Journal* **171(8)**, 195–9.
8. Swallow, P., Watt, D. and Ashton, R. (1993) *Measurement and Recording of Historic Buildings*, London: Donhead Publishing.
9. AutoSurvey software, developed by DataBuild Information Systems, provides an open format which can be modified to the needs of a particular user.

## Chapter Five: Building surveys II: The inspection

1. Fidler, J. (1980) 'Non-Destructive Surveying Techniques for the Analysis of Historic Buildings', *Transactions of the Association for Studies in the Conservation of Historic Buildings*, **5**, 3–10.
2. Hollis, M. (1991) *Surveying Buildings*, 3rd edn, London: Surveyors Publications.
3. Brooke, C. (1989) Ground-Based Remote Sensing, *Institute of Field Archaeologists Technical Paper No. 7*.
4. Building Research Establishment (1989) *Simple Measurement and Monitoring of Movement in Low-Rise Buildings – Part 1: Cracks*, BRE Digest 343, April 1989, Garston: BRE.
5. Building Research Establishment (1989) *Simple Measurement and Monitoring of Movement in Low-Rise Buildings – Part 2: Settlement, Heave and Out-of-Plumb*, BRE Digest 344, May 1989, Garston: BRE.
6. Building Research Establishment (1993) *Monitoring Building and Ground Movement by Precise Levelling*, BRE Digest 386, August 1993, Garston: BRE.
7. Uren, J., Studer, T. R. and Wren, J. C. (1985) 'Monitoring Crack Propagation Using Close-Range Photogrammetry', *Structural Survey*, **4(2)**, 130–3.
8. Uren, J. and Robertson, G. C. (1987) 'Mapping Cracks Photographically', *Structural Survey*, **5(4)**, 340–4.
9. Hume, I. (1994) *Monitoring Structural and Ground Movements*, Internal English Heritage document.
10. Details provided by Mr J. Harrison, School of Construction, Chesterfield College, Derbyshire.
11. British Standards Institution (1992) *Code of Practice for Use of Masonry – Part 1: Structural Use of Unreinforced Masonry*, BS 5628: Part 1: 1992, London: BSI.
12. British Standards Institution (1970) Structural Recommendations for Loadbearing Walls, CP111: Part 2: 1970, London: BSI.
13. Hutton, G. (1995) 'Building Maintenance: The H & R "Curator" and Building Monitoring Systems', *Museum Management and Curatorship*, **14 (1)**, 92–110.

## Chapter Six: Building surveys III: Assessment and report

1. Norwich City Council (1988) *Survey of Historic Buildings 1986/7*, Norwich: Planning Department.

2. Ryder, P. F. (1990) *Bastles and Towers in the Northumberland National Park*, Report on Defensible Farmhouses and Fortified towers, August 1990, Morpeth: Northumberland County Council.
3. Conservation Unit (1992) *Historic Buildings Conservation Guide for Government Departments*, London: Department of the Environment Conservation Unit.
4. Smith v. Bush (1989) 2 WLR 790; (1988) QB 743; (1987) 3 WLR 889; (1987) 3 All ER 179.
5. Harris v. Wyre Forest District Council (1988) 1 All ER 691; (1988) 2 WLR 1173; (1987) QB 835.
6. Henley v. Cloke and Sons (1991) 2 EGLR 141; (1991) 37 EG 145.
7. Council for the Care of Churches (1995) *A Guide to Church Inspection and Repair*, 2nd edn, London: Church House Publishing.
8. Conservation Unit (1992) *Historic Buildings Conservation Guide for Government Departments*, London: Department of the Environment Conservation Unit.
9. National Trust (1993) *Quinquennial Surveys on Buildings Held for Preservation. Manual of Building*, Instruction 9/93, London: National Trust.
10. Donoghue v. Stevenson (1932) AC 562.
11. Buckland v. Watts (1970) 1 QB 27; (1969) 2 All ER 985; (1969) 3 WLR 92.
12. Daisley v. B. S. Hall and Co. (1972) 225 EG 1553.
    Cross v. Martin and Mortimer (1989) 10 EG 110.
    Beaton v. Nationwide Building Society (1991) 2 EGLR 145; (1991) 38 EG 218.
    Lloyd v. Butler (1990) 47 EG 56.
    Syrett v. Carr and Neave (1990) 2 EGLR 161; (1990) 54 BLR 121; (1990) 48 EG 118.
    Hacker v. Thomas Deal and Co. (1991) 2 EGLR 161; (1991) 44 EG 173.
13. Philips v. Ward (1956) 1 All ER 874; (1956) 1 WLR 471.
    Stewart v. H. A. Brechin and Co. (1959) SC 306.
    Drinnan v. C. W. Ingram and Sons (1967) SLT 205.
    Marder v. Sautelle and Hicks (1988) 41 EG 87.
    Heatley v. William H. Brown (1992) 1 EGLR 289.
14. Fryer v. Bunney (1982) 263 EG 158.
    Whalley v. Roberts (1990) 6 EG 104.
15. Fryer v. Bunney (1982) 263 EG 158.
    Bere and Parchment v. Slades (1989) EG 100.
16. Strover v. Harrington (1988) 9 EG 61.
17. Hood v. Shaw (1960) 176 EG 1291.
    Hardy v. Wamsley-Lewis (1967) 203 EG 1039.
    Daisley v. B. S. Hall and Co. (1972) 225 EG 1553.
    Roberts v. Hampson and Co. (1988) 20 HLR 615; (1988) 37 EG 110.
    Allen v. Ellis and Co. (1990) 11 EG 78.
    Henley v. Cloke and Sons (1991) 2 EGLR 141; (1991) 37 EG 145.
    Watts v. Morrow (1991) 1 WLR 1421; (1991) 4 All ER 937; (1991) 23 HLR 608; (1991) EGLR 152; (1991) 43 EG 121.
18. D. and F. Estates Ltd v. Church Commissioners for England (1988) 3 WLR 368; (1988) 2 All ER 992; (1989) AC 177.
19. Dodd Properties (Kent) Ltd v. Canterbury City Council (1980) 1 All ER 928; (1980) 1 WLR 433.
20. Philips v. Ward (1956) 1 All ER 874; (1956) 1 WLR 471.
    Perry v. Sidney Phillips and Son (1982) 3 All ER 705; (1982) 1 WLR 1297.
    Watts v. Morrow (1991) 1 WLR 1421; (1991) 4 All ER 937; (1991) 23 HLR 608; (1991) EGLR 152; (1991) 43 EG 121.
21. Steward v. Rapley (1989) 2 All ER 815; (1989) 1 EGLR 159; (1989) 15 EG 198.
22. Miliangos v. George Frank (Textiles) Ltd. (1975) 3 All ER 801; (1975) 3 WLR 758; (1976) AC 443.
23. Candler v. Crane, Christmas and Co. (1951) 2 KB 164; (1951) 1 All ER 426.
    Hedley Byrne and Co Ltd v. Heller and Partners Ltd (1963) 3 WLR 101; (1963) 2 All ER 575; (1964) AC 465.

Yianni v. Edwin Evans and Sons (1981) 3 All ER 592; (1981) 3 WLR 843; (1982) QB 438.

Harris v. Wyre Forest District Council (1988) 1 All ER 691; (1988) 2 WLR 1173; (1987) QB 835.

Smith v. Bush (1989) 2 WLR 790; (1988) QB 743; (1987) 3 WLR 889; (1987) 3 All ER 179.

Allen v. Ellis and Co. (1990) 11 EG 78.

Lloyd v. Butler (1990) 47 EG 56.

Beaumont v. Humberts (1990) 49 EG 46.

Henley v. Cloke and Sons Ltd (1991) 2 EGLR 141; (1991) 37 EG 145.

24. Horbury v. Craig Hall and Rutley (1991) EGCS 81.
25. Sheldon v. R M H Outhwaite (Underwriting Agencies) Ltd. (1994) 3 WLR 999; (1994) 4 All ER 481.
26. Conway v. Crowe Kelsey and Partners (1994) *Construction Industry Law Letter*, March, 927–8.
27. Summers v. Congreve Horner and Co. (1992) 40 EG 144; (1991) 2 EGLR 139; (1991) 36 EG 160.
28. Royal Institution of Chartered Surveyors (1994) *Review of the Constitution: Methods of Investigating Inadequate Professional Services*, Green paper, April 1994, London: RICS.
29. Hobbs, C. (1994) *Quality Managment for Surveyors: A Step by Step Guide to BS 5750/ISO 9000*, London: Pitman Publishing.

## Chapter Seven: Causes of deterioration and decay

1. Bravery, A. F., Berry, R. W., Carey, J. K. and Cooper, D. E. (1992) *Recognising Wood Rot and Insect Damage in Buildings*, 2nd edn, Building Research Establishment Report, Aylesbury: Building Research Establishment.
2. Torraca, G. (1988) *Porous Building Materials: Materials Science for Architectural Conservation*, 3rd edn, Rome: ICCROM.
3. McArthur, H. (n. d.) *Materials Science – Part 1*. Unpublished notes, School of Land and Building Studies, Leicester Polytechnic.
4. Richardson, B. A. (1991) *Defects and Deterioration in Buildings*, London: E. & F. N. Spon.

## Chapter Nine: Building element II: Walls and structural frames

1. British Standards Institution (1992) *Code of Practice for Use of Masonry – Part 1: Structural Use of Unreinforced Masonry*, BS 5628: Part 1:1992, London: BSI.
2. Teutonico, J. M., McCaig, I., Burns, C. and Ashurst, J. (1994) *The Smeaton Project: Factors Affecting the Properties of Lime-based Mortars for Use in the Repair and Conservation of Historic Buildings (Research Project AC1: Phase 1 Report)*, London: English Heritage.
3. Maxwell, I. (1994) 'The Interaction of Lime Mortar and Scottish Sandstone', *SPAB News*, **15(4)**, 16–18.

## Chapter Ten: Building element III: Ceilings, partitions and floors

1. National Trust (1990) *Erddig*, London: National Trust.
2. Calvocoressi, P. (1991) 'An Early Form of Patent Lathing', *Transactions of the Association for Studies in the Conservation of Historic Buildings*, **16**, 24.

## Chapter Eleven: Building element IV: Doors, windows and stairs

1. Hume, I. (n. d.) *Cantilever or Hanging Stone Stairs*, Internal English Heritage document.

## Chapter Twelve: Building element V: Finishes, fixtures and fittings

1. Brommelle, N. S., Thomson, G. and Smith, P. (eds) (1980) *Conservation within Historic Buildings*, Preprints of contributions to the Vienna Congress, 7–13 September 1980, London: International Institute for Conservation of Historic and Artistic Works.
2. Roy, A. and Smith, P. (eds) (1994) *Preventive Conservation: Practice, Theory and Research*, Preprints of contributions to the Ottowa Congress, 12–16 September 1994, London: International Institute for Conservation of Historic and Artistic Works.
3. Butcher, R. (1993) 'A Case for Traditional and Natural Paints and Coatings', *SPAB News*, **14(2)**, 14–17.

## Chapter Thirteen: Building element VI: Services

1. Information provided by Fischer's Hotel and Restaurant, Baslow Hall, Derbyshire.
2. Girouard, M. (1976) *Hardwick Hall*, London: National Trust.
3. Information provided by Mr N. Peake, Scientific Anglian Bookshop, Norwich.
4. Griffiths, R. (1992) 'Early Heating and Ventilating Systems 1790–1850', *Transactions of the Association for Studies in the Conservation of Historic Buildings*, **17**, 30–50.
5. White, G. (1977) *The Natural History of Selborne*, Harmondsworth: Penguin Books.

## Chapter Fifteen: Industrial monuments and sites

1. Oldham, A. (n. d.). *Norfolk Windmills*, Unpublished study. Norwich Local Studies Library.
2. Jarvis, P. (1994) 'Millwrights' Meeting', *SPAB Wind and Watermill Section Newsletter*, January 1994, **58**, 5–6.

## Chapter Sixteen: Standing ruins

1. Lancaster, O. (1976) 'What should we preserve?' In: Fawcett, J. (ed.), *The Future of the Past: Attitudes to Conservation, 1147–1974*, London: Thames and Hudson, 65–73.
2. Wimble, A. and Thompson, J. (1993) 'Natural Wall Cappings', English Heritage Scientific and Technical Review, *Supplement to Conservation Bulletin 20*, **2**, July 1993, 11–12.

## Chapter Seventeen: A look to the future

1. Sell, J. (1993) 'Excellent Dutch System An Example We Should Follow', *SPAB News*, **14(4)**, 3.

2. Binst, S. (1995) 'Monument Watch in Flanders and the Netherlands'. In Burman, P., Pickard, R. and Taylor, S. (eds), *The Economics of Architectural Conservation*, York: Institute of Advanced Architectural Studies.
3. Osborn, M. J. (1994) 'Lead in Buildings and Surveyors' Responsibilities', *Structural Survey*, **12(2)**, 15–17.
4. Cope, B., Garrington, N., Matthews, A. and Watt, D. (1995), 'Biocide residues as a Hazard in Historic Buildings: Pentachlorophenol at Melton Constable Hall', *Journal of Architectural Conservation*, **1(2)**, 36–44.
5. Foster, L. (1995) 'Access to Historic Properties: A Look Forward', Journal of Architectural Conservation, **1(3)**, 55–69.
6. English Heritage (1995) *Easy Access to Historic Properties*, London: English Heritage
7. Foster, L. (1996) *Access to the Historic Environment: Meeting the Needs of Disabled People*, London: Donhead Publishing.
8. Health and Safety Executive 'six-pack' comprises:
   *Management of Health and Safety at Work Regulations 1992*
   *Provision and Use of Work Equipment Regulations 1992*
   *Health and Safety (Display Screen Equipment) Regulations 1992*
   *Workplace (Health, Safety and Welfare) Regulations 1992*
   *Personal Protective Equipment at Work Regulations 1992*
   *Manual Handling Operations Regulations 1992*
9. Department of the Environment (1990) *Planning Policy Guidance: Archaeology and Planning. PPG 16*, November 1990, London: HMSO.
10. Department of the Environment/Department of National Heritage (1994) *Planning Policy Guidance: Planning and the Historic Environment. PPG 15*, September 1994, London: HMSO.
11. EEC (1992) *Conservation of Natural Habitats and of Wild Fauna and Flora*, Council Directive 92/43/EEC.
12. The Conservation (Natural Habitats etc.) Regulation 1994.
13. Department of the Environment (1994) *Planning Policy Guidance: Nature Conservation PPG 9*, October 1994, London: HMSO.
14. Joint Working Party (1992) 'Atmospheric Pollution and Stone Decay: Summary Report', *Transactions of the Association for Studies in the Conservation of Historic Buildings*, **17**, 26–9.
15. Kay, T. (1993) 'Architectural Salvage: Dealers Keen to Introduce Ethics Code', *Trace*, **58**, 4–7.
16. The conference entitled Modern Matters – Principles and Practice in Conserving Recent Architecture was held on 31 October – 1 November 1995. The proceedings will be published by Donhead Publishing during 1996.
17. Macdonald, S. (1996) 'Reconciling Authenticity and Repair in the Conservation of Modern Architecture, *Journal of Architectural Conservation*, **2(1)**, 36–54.
18. Swanston, R. (1994) *The Nation and its Buildings: Closing the Output Gap*, Inaugural Address by RICS President, Tuesday, 12 July 1994, London: RICS.

# Bibliography

## General background reading

A number of the books in the following general section were published during the 1930s, '40s and '50s at a time when there was a growing interest and awareness in our historic surroundings. Although now out of print, many provide a useful account of building styles and fashions, and can often be found at book fairs and in second-hand bookshops.

Anderson, M. D. (1951) *Looking for History in British Churches*, London: John Murray.
Artley, A. (ed.) (1988) *Putting Back the Style*, London: Swallow Publishing Ltd.
Barley, M. W. (1976) *The English Farmhouse and Cottage*, London: Routledge and Keegan Paul.
Baun, H. (1936) *The English Castle*, London: B. T. Batsford Ltd.
Baun, H. (1956), *A Short History of English Architecture*, London: Faber and Faber Ltd.
Binney, M. and Pearce, D. (eds) (1979) *Railway Architecture*, London: Bloomsbury Books.
Bottomly, F. (1984) *The Explorer's Guide to the Abbeys, Monasteries and Churches of Great Britain*, 2nd edn, New York: Avenel Books.
Brand, S. (1994) *How Buildings Learn: What Happens After they are Built*, Harmondsworth: Penguin Books.
Brown, R. J. (1979) *The English Country Cottage*, London: Arrow Books Limited.
Brunskill, R. W. (1978) *Illustrated Handbook of Vernacular Architecture*, 2nd edn, London: Faber and Faber.
Burke, G. (1976) *Townscapes*, Harmondsworth: Penguin Books Ltd.
Calloway, S. (ed.) (1991) *The Elements of Style: An Encyclopaedia of Domestic Architectural Details*, London: Mitchell Beazley.
Cambridgeshire Historic Churches Trust (1985) *The Cambridgeshire Handbook of Church Fabric*, Cambridge: Cambridgeshire Historic Churches Trust.
Caroe, A. D. R. (1949) *Old Churches and Modern Craftsmanship*, London: Oxford University Press.
Cave, L. F. (1981) *The Smaller English House*, London: Robert Hale.
Chamberlain, R. (1983) *The National Trust Book of the English Country Town*, London: Grafton Books.
Chatterton, F. (1924) *English Architecture at a Glance*, London: Architectural Press.
Clifton-Taylor, A. (1967) *The Cathedrals of England*, London: Book Club Associates.
Clifton-Taylor, A. (1987) *The Pattern of English Building*, 4th edn, London: Faber and Faber.
Clifton-Taylor, A. (1989) *English Parish Churches as Works of Art*, Oxford: Oxford University Press.

Clowney, P. and T. (1986) *Exploring Churches: A Guide to Churches, Cathedrals and Abbeys*, Tring: Lion Publishing plc.

Collinson, H. (1975) *Country Monuments: Their Families and Houses*, Newton Abbot: David and Charles.

Colvin, H. (1995) *A Biographical Dictionary of British Architects 1600–1840*, 3rd edn, London: John Murray.

Cook, O. (1968) *The English House through Seven Centuries*, Weybridge: Whittet Books Ltd.

Crossley, F. H. (1941) *English Church Craftsmanship*, London: B. T. Batsford Ltd.

Cruickshank, D. (1985) *A Guide to the Georgian Buildings of Britain and Ireland*, London: George Weidenfeld and Nicolson Ltd.

Cullen, G. (1971) *The Concise Townscape*, 2nd edn, London: Architectural Press Ltd.

Cunnington, P. (1980) *How Old is Your House?* Sherborne: Alphabooks.

Cunnington, P. (1991) *Care for Old Houses*, 2nd edn, London: A & C Black Ltd.

Cunnington, P. (1993) *How Old is That Church*, 2nd edn, Yeovil: Marston House.

Curl, J. S. (1990) *Victorian Architecture*, Newton Abbot: David and Charles.

Curl, J. S. (1992) *Classical Architecture*, London: B. T. Batsford Ltd.

Curl, J. S. (1993) *Encyclopaedia of Architectural Terms*, London: Donhead Publishing.

Doran, D. K. (1992) *Construction Materials Reference Book*, London: Butterworth-Heinemann Ltd.

Durrant, D. N. (1988) *Living in the Past: An Insider's Social History of Historic Houses*, London: Aurum Press Ltd.

Dutton, R. (1935) *The English Country House*, London: B. T. Batsford Ltd.

Finn, R. W. (1948) *The English Heritage*, 2nd edn, London: MacDonald and Co (Publishers) Ltd.

Foster, M. (ed.) (1983) *The Principles of Architecture, Style, Structure and Design*, Oxford: Phaidon Press Ltd.

Gardner, A. H. (1945) *Outline of English Architecture*, London: B. T. Batsford Ltd.

Geeson, A. G. (1952) *Building Science for Students of Architecture and Building – Volume I; Materials – Volume II; Structures – Volume III*, London: English University Press Ltd.

Georgian Group (n. d.) *The Georgian Townhouse Form and Function*, Georgian Group Guide No 15, London: Georgian Group.

Gimpel, J. (1983) *The Cathedral Builders*, London: The Cresset Press.

Girouard, M. (1978) *Life in the English Country House*, Harmondsworth: Penguin Books Ltd.

Girouard, M. (1987) *A Country House Companion*, London: Century Hutchinson Ltd.

Girouard, M. (1990) *The English Town*, London: Yale University Press.

Gloag, J. (1944) *The Englishman's Castle*, London: Eyre and Spottiswoode.

Godfrey, W. H. (1944) *Our Building Inheritance: Are We to Use or Lose It?* London: Faber and Faber Ltd.

Gotch, J. A. (1985) *The History of the English House*, London: Bracken Books.

Gray, E. (1994) *The British House: A Concise Architectural History*, London: Barrie and Jenkins.

Harris, J. and Lever, J. (1966) *Illustrated Glossary of Architecture 850–1830*, London: Faber and Faber Ltd.

Harvey, J. (1971) *The Master Builders: Architecture in the Middle Ages*, London: Thames and Hudson.

Harvey, J. (1987) *English Mediaeval Architects: A Biographical Dictionary down to 1550*, Gloucester: Alan Sutton Publishing.

Hersey, G. (1988) *The Lost Meaning of Classical Architecture*, London: The MIT Press.

Hewett, C. (1980) *English Historic Carpentry*, London: Phillimore and Company Ltd.

Hole, C. (1947) *English Home-Life 1500 to 1800*, London: B. T. Batsford Ltd.

Hoskins, W. G. (1955) *The Making of the English Landscape*, Harmondsworth: Penguin Books Ltd.

Lake, J. (1989) *Historic Farm Buildings*, London: Blandford Press.

Lewis, P. and Darley, G. (1986) *Dictionary of Ornament*, London: MacMillan London Ltd.

Lucas, E. (1944) *Building Repairs and Maintenance*, London: George Newnes Ltd.

Lutyens, R. and Greenwood, H. (1948) *An Understanding of Architecture*, London: People's Universities Press.

Matulionis, R. C. and Freitag, J. C. (eds) (1991) *Preventive Maintenance of Building*, London: Chapman and Hall.

McKay, J. K. (1967) *Building Construction, Volumes 1–4*, 2nd edn, London: Longman Green and Co. Ltd.

Mercer, E. (1975) *English Vernacular Houses: A Study of Traditional Farmhouses and Cottages*, RCHME. London: HMSO.

Munro, B. (1979) *English Houses: Notes and Pictures for Auctioneers, Estate Agents, Surveyors, Owners and Others*, London: Estates Gazette Ltd.

Muthesius, S. (1982) *The English Terraced House*, London: Yale University Press.

Parissien, S. (1995) *The Georgian Group Book of the Georgian House*, London: Aurum Press.

Platt, C. (1981) *The Parish Churches of Medieval England*, London: Secker and Warburg.

Priestley, H. E. (1970) *The English Home*, London: Frederick Muller.

Quiney, A. (1990) *The Traditional Buildings of England*, London: Thames and Hudson Ltd.

Raeburn, M. (1980) *Architecture of the Western World*, London: Orbis Publishing.

Riden, P. (1983) *Local History: A Handbook for Beginners*, London: B. T. Batsford Ltd.

Risebero, B. (1985) *The Story of Western Architecture*, London: Herbert Press Ltd.

Rodwell, W. (1989) *Church Archaeology*, London: B. T. Batsford Ltd / English Heritage.

Roth, L. M. (1993) *Understanding Architecture: Its Elements History and Meaning*, London: Herbert Press.

Sancha, S. (1979) *The Castle Story*, London: William Collins Sons and Co Ltd.

Sayer, M. (1993) *The Disintegration of a Heritage: Country Houses and their Collections 1979–1992*, Norwich: Michael Russell Publishing.

Seeley, I. (1993) *Building Technology*, 4th edn, London: Macmillan Press Ltd.

Shillito, G. H. (1959) *How to Explore a Village*, 2nd edn, London: Educational Supply Association Ltd.

Singer, C., Holmyard, E. J., Hall, A. R. and Williams, T. I. (eds) (1957) *History of Technology*, Oxford: Clarendon Press.

Smith, J. T. and Yates, E. M. (1987) *Dating of English Houses from External Evidence*, Williton: Field Studies Council.

Stratton, A. (1987) *Elements of Form and Design in Classical Architecture*, London: Bestseller Publications Ltd (Studio Editions).

Summerson, J. (1980) *The Classical Language of Architecture*, London: Thames and Hudson Ltd.

Tabraham, C. (1986) *Scottish Castles and Fortifications*, Edinburgh: HMSO.

Vale, E. (1940) *How to Look at Old Buildings*, London: B. T. Batsford Ltd.

Valentine, D. (ed.) (1994) *Historic Houses, Castles and Gardens in Great Britain and Ireland*, London: Reed Telepublishing Ltd.

Vince, J. (1991) *The Country House: How it Worked*, London: John Murray Ltd.

Wade Martins, S. (1991) *Historic Farm Buildings*, London: B. T. Batsford Ltd.

Wood, M. (1983), *The English Mediaeval House*, London: Harper Colophon Books.

Woodforde, J. (1983) *Farm Buildings in England and Wales*, London: Routledge and Kegan Paul.

Yarwood, D. (1976) *The Architecture of Britain*, London: B. T. Batsford Ltd.

For general reference to buildings, monuments and structures of specific counties, refer to the works of Nikolaus Pevsner, originally published by Penguin Books and now by the newly formed Buildings of England, Ireland, Scotland and Wales Trust. In addition, useful material may be obtained from the volumes of the Victoria County History.

For general reference to publications on vernacular architecture, refer to *Bibliography of Vernacular Architecture*, produced by the Vernacular Architecture Group.

For general introductions to buildings, materials and craft techniques, refer to the Shire Publications Ltd stock-list.

For more detailed coverage of conservation issues, refer to the *Conservation Bulletin*, published by English Heritage, and *The Building Conservation Directory*, together with its special report magazines covering ecclesiastical buildings, historic garden landscapes and financial matters, published by Cathedral Communications Ltd.

## General conservation reading

Alcock, N., Barley, M., Dixon, P. and Meeson, R. (1989) *Recording Timber-framed Buildings: An Illustrated Glossary*, Practical Handbook in Archaeology No. 5, London: Council for British Archaeology.

Ashurst, J. and Ashurst, N. (1988) *Practical Building Conservation: Volume 5 – Wood, Glass and Resins*, Chapter 4: Select Technical Bibliography. English Heritage Technical Handbook. Aldershot: Gower Technical Press.

Bowyer, J. (1981) *Handbook of Building Crafts in Conservation*, London: Hutchinson Ltd.

Brereton, C. (1991) *The Repair of Historic Buildings: Advice on Principles and Methods*, Aspects of Conservation No. 3, London: English Heritage.

Burman, P. (ed.) (1994) *Treasures on Earth: A Good Housekeeping Guide to Churches and their Contents*, London: Donhead Publishing.

British Standards Institution (n. d.) *Guide to the Care of Historic Buildings*, Draft British Standard, London: BSI.

Cathedral Communications Ltd (1996) *The Building Conservation Directory*, 4th edn, London: Cathedral Communications Ltd.

Catt, R. (1983) 'The Surveyor in Conservation: 1 – Conservation Philosophy and Research', *Structural Survey*, **2(2)**: 141–7.

Catt, R. (1983) 'The Surveyor in Conservation: 2 – Sources of Materials for Conservation Works', *Structural Survey*, **2(3)**: 216–23.

Catt, R. (1984) 'The Surveyor in Conservation: 3 – Surveying Churches', *Structural Survey*, **2(4)**: 326–34.

Cocke, T., Findlay, D., Halsey, R. and Williamson, E. (1984) *Recording a Church: An Illustrated Glossary*, 2nd edn, London: Council for British Archaeology.

Cormier, J. M. (1995) *Living With a Listed Building*, Oxford: Courtland Books.

Conservation Unit (1991) *Conservation Sourcebook*, London: HMSO.

Conservation Unit (1992) *Historic Buildings Conservation Guide for Government Departments*, London: Department of the Environment Conservation Unit.

Council for the Care of Churches (1991) *How to Look After Your Church*, 3rd edn, London: Church House Publishing.

Davey, A., Heath, B., Hodges, D., Ketchin, M. and Milne, R. (1995) *The Care and Conservation of Georgian Houses: A Manual for Edinburgh New Town*, Oxford: Butterworth Architecture.

Davey, K. (1991) *Building Conservation Contracts and Grant Aid: A Practical Guide*, London: E. & F. N. Spon.

Earl, J. (1996) *Philosophy of Building Conservation*, Reading: College of Estate Mangement.

English Heritage (1990) *Directory of Public Sources of Grants for the Repair and Conversion of Historic Buildings*, London: HBMCE.

English Heritage/Royal Institution of Chartered Surveyors (1994) *Insuring your Historic Building: Houses and Commercial Buildings*, London: English Heritage.

English Heritage/Royal Institution of Chartered Surveyors (1994) *Insuring your Historic Building: Churches and Chapels*, London: English Heritage.

Erder, C. (1986) *Our Architectural Heritage: From Consciousness to Conservation*, UNESCO Museums and Monuments XX, Paris: UNESCO.

Fawcett, J. (ed.) (1976) *The Future of the Past: Attitudes to Conservation 1147–1974*, London: Thames and Hudson.

Feilden, B. M. (1994) *Conservation of Historic Buildings*, 2nd edn, London: Butterworth-Heinemann Ltd.

Hutton, B. (1986) *Recording Standing Buildings*, Sheffield: University of Sheffield (Department of Archaeology and Prehistory) and RESCUE (British Archaeological Trust).

Insall, D. W. (1972) *The Care of Old Buildings Today: A Practical Guide*, London: Architectural Press.

Jackson, M. (ed.) (1993) *Engineering a Cathedral*, London: Thomas Telford Services Ltd.

Jones, J. (1984) *How to Record Graveyards*, 3rd edn, London: Council for British Archaeology and RESCUE (The Trust for British Archaeology).

Lander, H. (1979) *A Guide to the Do's and Dont's of House and Cottage Conversion*, Redruth: Acanthus Books.

Lander, H. (1982) *A Guide to the Do's and Dont's of House and Cottage Interiors*, Redruth: Acanthus Books.

Lander, H. (1992) *The House Restorer's Guide*, 2nd edn, Newton Abbot: David and Charles.

McDowall, R. W. (1980) *Recording Old Houses: A Guide*, London: Council for British Archaeology.

Mills, E. D. (ed) (1994) *Building Maintenance and Preservation*: 2nd edn, London: Butterworth-Heinemann.

Newsom, G. H. and Newsom, G. L. (1993) *Faculty Jurisdiction of the Church of England: The Care of Churches and Churchyards*, 2nd edn, London: Sweet and Maxwell.

Parsons, D. (1989) *Churches and Chapels: Investigating Places of Worship*, Practical Handbook in Archaeology No. 8, London: Council for British Archaeology.

Powys, A. R. (1995) *Repair of Ancient Buildings*, Re-printed with additional notes, London: SPAB

Riyat, R. (1995) *Conservation and Preservation: A Definitive Statement*, Blackburn: R & J Services.

Sell, J. (1989) *First Aid Repair to Traditional Farm Buildings*, SPAB Information Sheet 7, London: SPAB.

Smith, J. T. (1992) *English Houses 1200–1800: The Hertfordshire Evidence*, London: HMSO.

Swallow, P., Watt, D. and Ashton, R. (1993) *Measurement and Recording of Historic Buildings*, London: Donhead Publishing.

Weaver, M. E. (1993) *Conserving Buildings: A Guide to Techniques and Materials*, New York: John Wiley and Sons.

Wood, J. (ed) (1994) *Buildings Archaeology: Applications in Practice*, Oxford: Oxbow Books.

Wright, A. (1991) *Craft Techniques for Traditional Buildings*, London: B. T. Batsford Ltd.

## Chapter Two: Forms of building survey

English Heritage (1992) *Buildings at Risk: A Sample Survey*, London: English Heritage.

Royal Institution of Chartered Surveyors (1991) *Structural Surveys of Residential Property: A Guidance Note*, 2nd edn, London: RICS Building Surveyors Division.

Royal Institution of Chartered Surveyors (1983) *Guidance Note on Structural Surveys of Commercial and Industrial Property*, London: Surveyors Publications.

Royal Institution of Chartered Surveyors (1993) *Home Buyers' Survey and Valuation*, London: RICS.

Royal Institution of Chartered Surveyors and Incorporated Society of Valuers and Auctioneers (1995) *Specification for Residential Mortgage Valuation*, London: RICS/ISVA.

Royal Institution of Chartered Surveyors and Incorporated Society of Valuers and Auctioneers (1995) *Homebuyers' Survey and Valuation*, Owlion Audio Programme: RICS.

Royal Institution of Chartered Surveyors (1995) *RICS Appraisal and Valuation Manual*, London: RICS.

## Chapter Three: Historic buildings

Brunskill, R. W. (1978) *Illustrated Handbook of Vernacular Architecture*, 2nd edn, London: Faber and Faber.

Burman, P., Pickard, R., and Taylor, S., (eds) (1995) *The Economics of Architectural Conservation*, York: Institute of Advanced Architectural Studies.

Catt, R. (1983) 'The Surveyor in Conservation: 2 – Sources of Materials for Conservation Works', *Structural Survey*, **2(3)**, 216–23.

Clifton-Taylor, A. (1987) *The Pattern of English Building*, 4th edn, London: Faber and Faber.

Cooling, P., Shacklock, V. and Scarrett, D. (1993) *Legislation for the Built Environment: A Concise Guide*, London: Donhead Publishing.

Department of the Environment (1987) *Historic Buildings and Conservation Areas – Policy and Procedures*, Circular 8/87, March 1987, London: HMSO.

Department of the Environment (1990) *Planning Policy Guidance: Archaeology and Planning*, PPG 16, November 1990, London: HMSO.

Department of the Environment/Department of National Heritage (1994) *Planning Policy Guidance: Planning and the Historic Environment*, PPG 15, September 1994, London: HMSO.

Foster, M. (ed.) (1983) *The Principles of Architecture, Style, Structure and Design*, Oxford: Phaidon Press Ltd.

Mynors, C. (1995) *Listed Buildings and Conservation Areas*, 2nd edn, London: FT Law and Tax.

Ross, M. (1995) *Planning and the Heritage: Policy and Procedures*, 2nd edn, London: E. and F. N. Spon.

Sadler, R. and Ward, K. (1992) *Owner Occupiers' Attitudes to House Repairs and Maintenance*, Research Study for the Building Conservation Trust, February 1992.

Strike, J. (1991) *Construction in Design: The Influence of New Methods of Construction on Architectural Design 1690–1990*, London: Butterworth-Heinemann Ltd.

Suddards, R. W. (1988) *Listed Buildings: The Law and Practice of Historic Buildings, Ancient Monuments and Conservation Areas*, London: Sweet and Maxwell.

Wright, A. (1991) *Craft Techniques for Traditional Buildings*, London: B. T. Batsford Ltd.

Yeomans D. (1991) '18C Timber Construction: 1 – Trade and Materials', *Architects' Journal*, **194(2)**, 10 July, 51–6.


## Chapter Four: Building surveys I: Basis of inspection

Bowyer, J. (1979) *Guide to Domestic Building Surveys*, 3rd edn, London: Architectural Press.

Building Research Establishment (1974) *Building Defects and Maintenance*, Lancaster: MTP Construction.

Catt, R. (1984) 'The Surveyor in Conservation: 3 – Surveying Churches', *Structural Survey*, **2(4)**, 326–34.

Central Council of Church Bell Ringers (1979) *Practical Bell Maintenance: A Pocket-Book for Steeple-Keepers*, Morpeth: Central Council Publications.

Chapman, K. and Edwards, V. (1992) 'Structural Surveys of Public Houses', *Structural Survey*, **11(3)**, 227–33.

Conservation Unit (1992) *Historic Buildings Conservation Guide for Government Departments*, London: Department of the Environment Conservation Unit.

Construction Industry Research and Information Association (1986) *Structural Renovation of Traditional Buildings*, CIRIA Report 111, London: CIRIA.

Cook, G. K. and Hinks, A. J. (1992) *Appraising Building Defects*, Harlow: Longman Scientific and Technical.

Council for the Care of Churches (1995) *A Guide to Church Inspection and Repair*, 2nd edn, London: Church House Publishing.

Davidson, M., (1995) 'The English House Condition Survey: Past, Present and Future', *Structural Survey*, **13(4)**, 28–9.

Feilden, B. M. (1994) *Conservation of Historic Buildings*, 2nd edn, London: Butterworth-Heinemann Ltd.

Freeman, T. J., Littlejohn, G. S. and Driscoll, R. M. C. (1994) *Has Your House Got Cracks: A Guide to Subsidence and Heave of Buildings on Clay*, London: Thomas Telford Services Ltd.

Holland, R., Montgomery-Smith, B. E. and Moore, J. F. A. (eds) (1992) *Appraisal and Repair of Building Structures*, London: Thomas Telford Services Ltd.

Hollis, M. (1991) *Surveying Buildings*, 3rd edn, London: Surveyors Publications.

Hoxley, M. (1995) 'How Do Clients Select a Surveyor?', *Structural Survey*, **13(2)**, 6–12.

Institution of Structural Engineers (1980) *Appraisal of Existing Structures*, London: Institution of Structural Engineers.

Institution of Structural Engineers (1991) *Guide to Surveys and Inspections of Buildings and Similar Structures*, Amended May 1992, London: Institution of Structural Engineers.

Kinnear, R. G. (1985) 'Investigation of Fire Damaged Buildings', *Structural Survey*, **4(1)**, 31–4.

Melville, I. A. and Gordon, I. A. (1973) *The Repair and Maintenance of Houses*, London: Estates Gazette Ltd.

Ministry of Defence (1994) *MOD Conservation Manual for Listed Buildings and Scheduled Monuments*, London: HMSO.

Melville, I. A., Gordon, I. A. and Murrells, P. G. (1992) *Structural Surveys of Dwelling Houses*, 3rd edn, London: Estates Gazette Ltd.

Morris, I. (1989) *Bazaar Property Doctor*, London: BBC Books.

National Trust (1993) *Quinquennial Surveys on Buildings Held for Preservation*, Manual of Building: Instruction 9/93, London: National Trust.

Noy, E. A. (1995) *Building Surveys and Reports*, 2nd edn, Oxford: Blackwell Scientific Publications.

Oliver, G. (1989) *Photographs and Local History*, London: B. T. Batsford Ltd.

O'Malley, K. (1992) 'House Inspection in the USA and Canada', *Structural Survey*, **11(3)**, 252–7.

Richardson, R. and Thorne. R. (1994) *The Builder Illustrations Index 1843–1883*, Gomshall: Builder Group plc and Hutton + Roston.

Robson, P. (1991) *Structural Appraisal of Traditional Buildings*, Aldershot: Gower Technical.

Royal Commission on the Historic Monuments of England (1991) *The National Monument Record – A Guide to the Archive Revision of 1991: 50 Years of the National Building Record 1911–1991*, London: RCHME.

Royal Institution of Chartered Surveyors (1986) *A Guide to Fee Tendering for Building Surveying Services*, London: Surveyors Publications.

Royal Institution of Chartered Surveyors (1988) *Conditions of Engagement for Building Surveying Services*, London: Surveyors Publications.

Royal Institution of Chartered Surveyors (1991) *Surveying Safely: A Personal Commitment*, London: RICS.

Seeley, I. H. (1985) *Building Surveys, Reports and Dilapidations*, Basingstoke: Macmillan Publishers Ltd.

Seeley, I. H. (1987) *Building Maintenance*, 2nd edn, Basingstoke: Macmillan Publishers Ltd.

Seeley, I. H. (1995) *Building Technology*, 5th edn, Basingstoke: Macmillan Publishers Ltd.

Son, L. H. and Yuen, G. C. S. (1993) *Building Maintenance Technology*, Basingstoke: Macmillan Press Ltd.

Smith, L. (1985) *Investigating Old Buildings*, London: Batsford Academic and Educational.

Staveley, H. S. (1981) *Structural Surveys*, CIOB Maintenance Information Service No. 15. Ascot: Chartered Institute of Building.

Swindells, D. J. and Hutchings, M. (1993) *A Checklist for the Structural Survey of Period Timber Framed Buildings*, RICS Building Conservation Group, London: Surveyors Holdings Ltd.

Vegoda, V. (1993) *A Practical Guide to Residential Surveys*, Video and accompanying reference book. No. 2 in Need to Know series, London: Lark Productions Ltd.

Walker, R. (1995) *The Cambridgeshire Guide to Historic Buildings Law*, 8th edn, Cambridge: Cambridgeshire County Council.

Weatherhead, M. (1989) 'Structural Surveys in Europe', *Structural Survey*, **8(1)**, 5–8.

## Chapter Five: Building surveys II: The inspection

Addleson, L. (1982) *Building Failures: A Guide to Diagnosis, Remedy and Prevention*, London: Architectural Press.

Ashurst, N. (1990) 'Understanding Dampness in Historic Buildings', *Structural Survey*, **8(3)**, 268–77.

Bowles, R. (1986) 'Techniques for Structural Surveys', *Building*, 17 January, 38–40.

Bravery, A. F., Berry, R. W., Carey, J. K. and Cooper, D. E. (1992) *Recognising Wood Rot and Insect Damage in Buildings*, 2nd edn, Building Research Establishment Report, Aylesbury: Building Research Establishment.

Briggs, J. R. (1980) 'Environmental Control for Old Buildings: Two Case Studies.' In: Brommelle, N. S., Thomson, G. and Smith, P. (eds), *Conservation Within Historic Buildings*, London: International Institute for Conservation of Historic and Artistic Works.

Brooke, C. J. (1986) 'Ground-Based Remote Sensing for the Archaeological Study of Churches'. In: Butler, L. A. S. and Morris, R. K. (eds), *The Anglo-Saxon Church: Papers on History, Architecture and Archaeology in Honour of Dr H. M. Taylor*, Research Report 60, London: Council for British Archaeology.

Brooke, C. J. (1987) 'Ground-Based Remote Sensing for Archaeological Information Recovery in Historic Buildings', *International Journal of Remote Sensing*, **8(7)**, 1039–48.

Brooke, C. J. (1989) *Ground-Based Remote Sensing*, Institute of Field Archaeologists Technical Paper No. 7.

Building Research Establishment (1981) *Rising Damp in Walls: Diagnosis and Treatment*, BRE Digest 245, January 1981, Garston: BRE.

Building Research Establishment (1981) *Assessment of Damage in Low-Rise Buildings*, BRE Digest 251, July 1981, Garston: BRE.

Building Research Establishment (1982) *Common Defects in Low-Rise Traditional Housing*, BRE Digest 268, December 1982, Garston: BRE.

Building Research Establishment (1985) *Surface Condensation and Mould Growth in Traditionally-Built Dwellings*, BRE Digest 297, May 1985, Garston: BRE.

Curwell, S. and March, C. G. (1986) *Hazardous Building Materials: A Guide to the Selection of Alternatives*, London: E. & F. N. Spon.

Demaus, R. (1992) 'Good Vibrations' (Ultrasonic Testing of Structural Timber), *Context*, **35**, 28.

Demaus, R. (1993) 'Good Vibrations II' (Microdrilling of Structural Timber), *Context*, **39**, 25.

Douglas, J. (1995) 'Basic Diagnostic Chemical Tests for Building Surveyors', *Structural Survey*, **13(3)**, 22–7.

Eldridge, H. J. (1976) *Common Defects in Buildings*, London: HMSO.

Feilden, B. M. (1980) 'Architectural Factors Affecting the Internal Environment of Historic Buildings.' In: Brommelle, N. S., Thomson, G. and Smith. P. (eds), *Conservation Within Historic Buildings*, London: International Institute for Conservation of Historic and Artistic Work.

Feilden, B. M. (1994) *Conservation of Historic Buildings*, 2nd edn, London: Butterworth-Heinemann Ltd.

Fidler, J. (1980) 'Non-Destructive Surveying Techniques for the Analysis of Historic Buildings', *Transactions of the Association for Studies in the Conservation of Historic Buildings*, **5**, 3–10.

Fire Protection Association (1995) *Heritage Under Fire*, 2nd edn, London: Fire Protection Association.

Fire Protection Association (1992) *Fire Protection in Old Buildings and Historic Town Centres*, London: Fire Protection Association.

Gauld, B. J. B. (1988) *Structures for Architects*, 2nd edn, Harlow: Longman Scientific and Technical.

Gratwick, R. T. (1974) *Dampness in Buildings*, 2nd edn, London: Granada Publications Limited.

Historic Houses Association (1988) *Conserving the Contents of an Historic House*, Conference proceedings. London: HHA.

Hollis, M. (1989) 'The Push Button Surveyor – Instruments Used to Detect Problem Areas within Buildings', *Structural Survey*, **7(4)**, 461–5.

Hume, I. (n. d.) *Structural Engineering for Conservation*, Internal English Heritage document.

Hume, I. (n. d.) *Scaffolding, Temporary Works and Historic Buildings*, Internal English Heritage document.

Hume, I. (n. d.) *Monitoring of Cracks in Structures*, Internal English Heritage document.

Hume, I. (n. d.) *Structural First Aid after a Disaster*, Internal English Heritage document.

Hume, I. (1989) *Load Testing and Historic Structures*, Internal English Heritage document.

Hume, I. (1994) *Monitoring Structural and Ground Movements*, Internal English Heritage document.

Hum-Hartley, S. C. (1978) 'Non-Destructive Testing for Heritage Structures', *Association for Preservation Technology Bulletin*, **X(3)**, 4–20.

Hutton, T. C. (1991) 'Non-Destructive Testing', *Building Research and Information*, **19(3)**, 138–40.

Institution of Structural Engineers (1994) *Subsidence of Low Rise Buildings*, London: Institution of Structural Engineers.

Locke, P. (1986). *Timber Treatment: A Warning about the Defrassing of Timber*, SPAB Information Sheet 2, London: SPAB.

Lowndes, M. (1991) 'Collapses of Historic Buildings', *Structural Survey*, **10(2)**, 158–62.

Melville, I. A. and Gordon, I. A. (1973) *The Repair and Maintenance of Houses*, London: Estates Gazette Ltd.

Mills, R. (1990) 'Structural Failure and Repair'. In: Ashurst, J. and Dimes, F. G. (eds), *Conservation of Building and Decorative Stone (Vol 2)*, London: Butterworth-Heinemann, 55–70.

Moore, J. F. A. (1992) *Monitoring Building Structures*, Glasgow: Blackie Academic and Professional.

Parnell, A. and Ashford, D. H. (n. d.) *Fire Safety in Historic Buildings – Part 1: Fire Dangers and Fire Precautions*, SPAB Technical Pamphlet 6 (no longer available), London: SPAB.

Pryke, J. (1993) 'Subsidence: The Time is Ripe for Change', *Structural Survey*, **11(4)**, 357–65.

Radevsky, R. (1993) 'Why Do Structural Surveyors and Valuers Go Wrong with Subsidence?', *Structural Survey*, **11(4)**, 354–6.

Richardson, C. (1985) 'Structural Surveys – 1: Technique and Report Writing', *Architects' Journal*, 26 June, 56–65.

Richardson, C. (1985) 'Structural Surveys – 2: General Problems', *Architects' Journal*, 3 July, 63–71.

Richardson, C. (1985) 'Structural Surveys – 3: The Industrial Revolution', *Architects' Journal*, 10 July, 45–52.

Richardson, C. (1985) 'Structural Surveys – 4: Common Problems 1850–1939', *Architects' Journal*, 17 July, 63–9.

Richardson, C. (1985) 'Structural Surveys – 5: The Post-War Building Boom', *Architects' Journal*, 24 July, 63–70.

Seeley, I. (1987) *Building Maintenance*, 2nd edn, London: Macmillan Press Ltd.

Skingley, B. (1994) 'Understanding and Managing the Environment of Historic Buildings', *English Heritage Science and Technology Supplement*, Supplement to *Conservation Bulletin 24*, Issue 3, November 1994, p. 13.

Son, L. H. and Yuen, G. C. S. (1993) *Building Maintenance Technology*, Basingstoke: Macmillan Press Ltd.

Sterry, N. (1994) *Dampness in Old Buildings is Not a Straightforward Issue*, SPAB Notes, London: SPAB.

Thomson. G. (1980) 'Some Hints on Measurement and Control of Climate in Historic Houses.' In: Brommelle, N. S., Thomson, G. and Smith, P. (eds) *Conservation Within Historic Houses*, London: International Institute for Conservation of Historic and Artistic Works.

Uren, J., Studer, T. R. and Wren, J. C. (1985) 'Monitoring Crack Propagation Using Close-Range Photogrammetry', *Structural Survey*, **4(2)**, 130–3.

Uren, J. and Robertson, G. C. (1987) 'Mapping Cracks Photographically', *Structural Survey*, **5(4)**, 340–4.

## Chapter Six: Building surveys III: Assessment and report

Hodgson, J. (1992) 'The Dual Nature of Professional Liability', *Structural Survey*, **11(2)**, 195–9.

Lavers, A. P. (1989) 'Interpretation of Findings by Surveyors in Reporting to Clients', *Structural Survey*, **8(2)**, 126–9.

Murdock, J. and Murrells, P. (1995) *Law of Surveys and Valuations*, London: Estates Gazette Ltd.

Murrells, P. (1995) ' "Jerry Building" – Surveyors Liability Arising out of Mortgage Valuations', *Structural Survey*, **13(1)**, 25–8.

Noy, E. A. (1995) *Building Surveys and Reports*, 2nd edn, Oxford: Blackwell Scientific Publications.

Richardson C. (1985) 'Structural Surveys – 1: Technique and Report Writing', *Architects' Journal*, 26 June, 56–65.

Seeley, I. H. (1985) *Building Surveys, Reports and Dilapidations*, Basingstoke: Macmillan Publishers Ltd.

Urbanowicz, C. (1985) 'Weaponry in Structural Surveys – Part 1: Effective Diagnosis of Material Problems and Defects in Building and Construction', *Structural Survey*, **4(1)**, 42–6.

Urbanowicz, C. (1986) 'Weaponry in Structural Surveys – Part 2: Common Building Defects and their Diagnosis', *Structural Survey*, **5(2)**, 109–20.

Vegoda, V. H. (1992) *A Concise Summary of Some Seminal Cases on Surveyor's Negligence*, London: Vegoda and Co.

## Chapter Seven: Causes of deterioration and decay

Beckman, P. (1994) *Structural Aspects of Building Conservation*, London: McGraw-Hill.

Building Research Establishment (1981) *Rising Damp in Walls: Diagnosis and Treatment*, BRE Digest 245, January 1981, Garston: BRE.

Building Research Establishment (1985) *Surface Condensation and Mould Growth in Traditionally-Built Dwellings*, BRE Digest 297, May 1985, Garston: BRE.

Building Research Establishment (1985) *Dry Rot: Its Recognition and Control*, BRE Digest 299, July 1985, Garston: BRE.

Building Research Establishment (1985) *Preventing Decay in External Joinery*, BRE Digest 304, December 1985, Garston: BRE.

Building Research Establishment (1986) *Identifying Damage by Wood-Boring Insects*, BRE Digest 307, March 1986, Garston: BRE.

Conservation Unit (1992) *Science for Conservators: Volume 1 – An Introduction to Materials*, Conservation Science Teaching Series, London: Routledge.

Conservation Unit (1992) *Science for Conservators: Volume 2 – Cleaning*, Conservation Science Teaching Series, London: Routledge.

Conservation Unit (1992) *Science for Conservators: Volume 3 – Adhesives and Coatings*, Conservation Science Teaching Series, London: Routledge.

Feilden, B. M. (1994) *Conservation of Historic Buildings*, 2nd edn, London: Butterworth-Heinemann Ltd.

Gordon, J. E. (1976) *The New Science of Strong Materials or Why You Don't Fall Through the Floor*, 2nd edn, London: Penguin Books.

Gordon, J. E. (1978) *Structures or Why Things Don't Fall Down*, London: Penguin Books.

Historic Houses Association (1988) *Conserving the Contents of an Historic House*, Conference proceedings, London: HHA.

Hughes, P. (1987) *The Need for Old Buildings to 'Breathe'*, SPAB Information Sheet 4, London: SPAB.

Hutton, T. C., Lloyd, H. and Singh, J. (1991) 'The Environmental Control of Timber Decay', *Structural Survey*, **10(1)**, 5–20.

Property Services Agency (1989) *Defects in Buildings*, London: HMSO.

Richardson, B. A. (1991) *Defects and Deterioration in Buildings*, London: E. & F. N. Spon.

Ridout, B. V. (1992) 'Fungal Decay in Oak Building Timbers', *Structural Survey*, **10(4)**, 339–43.

Ridout, B. V. (1992) *An Introduction to Timber Decay and Its Treatment*, Scientific and Educational Services Ltd: Romsley.

Price, C. and Brimblecombe, P. (1994) 'Preventing Salt Damage in Porous Materials.' In: Roy, A. and Smith, P. (eds), *Preventive Conservation*, London: International Institute for Conservation of Historic and Artistic Works.

Singh, J. (1991) 'Preventing Decay after the Fire,' *Fire Prevention*, **244**, 26–9.

Singh, J. (ed.) (1994) *Building Mycology: Management of Decay and Health in Buildings*, London: E. & F. N. Spon.

Skingley, B. (1994) 'Understanding and Managing the Environment of Historic Buildings', *English Heritage Scientific and Technical Supplement*, Supplement to *Conservation Bulletin* 24, Issue 3, November 1994, p. 13.

Teutonico, J. M. (1995) *Current Building Materials Research*, Supplement to *Conservation Bulletin* **25**, March 1995, London: English Heritage.

Thomas, A. A. (n. d.) *Treatment of Damp in Old Buildings*, SPAB Technical Pamphlet 8, London: SPAB.

Torraca, G. (1988) *Porous Building Materials*, Materials Science for Architectural Conservation, 3rd edn, Rome: ICCROM.

Weaver, M. E. (1993) *Conserving Buildings: A Guide to Techniques and Materials*, New York: John Wiley and Sons.

Wild, R. (1991) 'Dry Rot in the Refurbished Building', *Structural Survey*, **10(2)**, 131–6.

## Chapter Eight: Building element I: Roofs

Alcock, N., Barley, M., Dixon, P. and Meeson, R. (1989) *Recording Timber-framed Buildings: An Illustrated Glossary*, Practical Handbook in Archaeology No. 5, London: Council for British Archaeology.

Ashurst, J. and Ashurst, N. (1988) *Practical Building Conservation: Volume 4 – Metals*, English Heritage Technical Handbook, Aldershot: Gower Technical Press.

Ashurst, J. and Ashurst, N. (1988) *Practical Building Conservation: Volume 5 – Wood, Glass and Resins*, English Heritage Technical Handbook, Aldershot: Gower Technical Press.

Boutwood, J. (1993) *The Repair of Timber Frames and Roofs*, SPAB Technical Pamphlet 12, London: SPAB.

Boniface, S. (1995) 'The Future of Thatch', *RICS Building Conservation Newsletter*, **12**, 9–12.

Briffett, C. (1984) 'Roof Space Surveying', *Structural Survey*, **3(2)**, 110–14.

Brockett, P. and Wright, A. (1986) *The Care and Repair of Thatched Roofs*, SPAB Technical Pamphlet 10, London: SPAB.

Clifton-Taylor, A. and Ireson, A. S. (1994) *English Stone Buildings*, 2nd edn, London: Victor Gollancz Ltd.

Darby, K. (1988) *Church Roofing*, London: Church House Publishing.

Dodson, J. (1990) 'Thatch Surveys', *Structural Survey*, **9(3)**, 243–50.

Georgian Group (n. d.) *Roofs*, Georgian Group Guide No 10, London: Georgian Group.

Hollis, M. (1987) 'Georgian Roofs', *Structural Survey*, **5(3)**, 218–25.

Norfolk Reed Growers' Association (1972) *The Reed ('Norfolk Reed')*, 2nd edn, Norwich: Norfolk Reed Growers' Association.

Poole, A. L. (1991) 'Roof Slates and Tiles – The Cheaper Alternatives to the "Real Thing"', *Structural Survey*, **10(2)**, 123–6.

Watkin, E. (1993) 'Shingles in Britain: A Disease or a Roof Covering?', *Context*, **40**, 29–31.

West, A. (1995) 'Fire Retardancy and Fire Barriers for Thatched Roofs', *Structural Survey*, **13(3)**, 9–10.

West, R. C. (1987) *Thatch: A Manual for Owners, Surveyors, Architects and Builders*, Newton Abbot: David and Charles.

Yeomans, D. (1991) '18C Timber Construction: 3 – Roof Structures', *Architects' Journal*, **194(4/5)**, 24 and 31 July, 45–50.

Yeomans, D. (1992) *The Trussed Roof: Its History and Development*, Aldershot: Scolar Press.

## Chapter Nine: Building element II: Walls and structural frames

Alcock, N., Barley, M., Dixon, P. and Meeson, R. (1989) *Recording Timber-framed Buildings: An Illustrated Glossary*, Practical Handbook in Archaeology No. 5, London: Council for British Archaeology.

Andrew, C. (1994) *Stone Cleaning: A Guide for Practitioners*, Edinburgh: Historic Scotland and Robert Gordon University.

Ashurst, J. (1983) *Mortars, Plasters and Renders in Conservation*, London: Ecclesiastical Architects' and Surveyors' Association.

Ashurst, J. (1985) *Cleaning Stone and Brick*, SPAB Technical Pamphlet 4, London: SPAB.

Ashurst, N. (1994) *Cleaning Historic Buildings: Vol 1 – Substrates, Soiling and Investigation*, London: Donhead Publishing.

Ashurst, N. (1994) *Cleaning Historic Buildings: Vol 2 – Cleaning Materials and Processes*, London: Donhead Publishing.

Ashurst, J. and Ashurst, N. (1988) *Practical Building Conservation: Volume 1 – Stone Masonry*, English Heritage Technical Handbook, Aldershot: Gower Technical Press.

Ashurst, J. and Ashurst, N. (1988) *Practical Building Conservation: Volume 2 – Brick, Terracotta and Earth*, English Heritage Technical Handbook, Aldershot: Gower Technical Press.

Ashurst, J. and Ashurst, N. (1988) *Practical Building Conservation: Volume 3 – Mortars, Plasters and Renders*, English Heritage Technical Handbook, Aldershot: Gower Technical Press.

Ashurst, J. and Ashurst, N. (1991) *Cleaning Stone and Brick*, SPAB Technical Pamphlet 4, 3rd edn, London: SPAB.

Ashurst, J. and Dimes, F. G. (eds) (1990) *Conservation of Building and Decorative Stone*, 2 vols, London: Butterworth-Heinemann.

Boutwood, J. (1993), *The Repair of Timber Frames and Roofs*, SPAB Technical Pamphlet 12, London: SPAB.

British Standards Institution (1970) *Code of Practice 111: Structural Recommendations for Loadbearing Walls*, London: BSI.

British Standards Institution (1992) *Code of Practice for Use of Masonry: Part 1. Structural Use of Unreinforced Masonry*, BS 5628:Part 1:1992, London: BSI.

Brunskill, R. W. (1990) *Brick Building in Britain*, London: Victor Gollancz Ltd.

Brunskill, R. W. (1994) *Timber Building in Britain*, 2nd edn, London: Victor Gollancz Ltd.

Building Research Establishment (1977) *Repairing Brickwork*, BRE Digest 200, April 1977, Garston: BRE.

Building Research Establishment (1982) *Damage Caused by Masonry or Mortar Bees*, Building Research Advisory Service Technical Information 64, August 1982, Garston: BRE.

Building Research Establishment (1990) *Assessment of Damage in Low-Rise Buildings with Particular Reference to Progressive Foundation Movement*, BRE Digest 251, Revised August 1990, Garston: BRE.

Building Research Establishment (1991) *Why do Buildings Crack?* BRE Digest 361, May 1991, Garston: BRE.

Building Research Establishment (1991) *Building Mortar*, BRE Digest 362, June 1991, Garston: BRE.

Carey, J. (n. d.) *Tuck Pointing in Practice*, SPAB Information Sheet 8, London: SPAB.

Carrington, D. and Swallow, P. G. (1996) 'Lime and Lime Mortars – Part Two,' *Journal of Architectural Conservation*, **2(1)**, 7–22.

Caroe, A. and Caroe, M. (1984) *Stonework: Maintenance and Surface Repair*, London: CIO Publishing.

Charles, F. W. B. and Charles, M. (1995) *Conservation of Timber Buildings*, London: Donhead Publishing.

Clifton-Taylor, A. and Ireson, A. S. (1993) *English Stone Buildings*, 2nd edn, London: Victor Gollancz Ltd.

Cooke, R. U. and Gibbs, G. B. (1993) *Crumbling Heritage? Studies of Stone Weathering in Polluted Atmospheres*, Wetherby: National Power plc and PowerGen plc.

De Vekey, R. C. (1988) *Ties for Cavity Walls: New Developments*, BRE Information Paper IP16/88, December 1988, Garston: BRE.

Devon Earth Building Association (1993) *Appropriate Plasters, Renders and Finishes for Cob and Random Stone walls in Devon*, Exeter: DEBA.

Georgian Group (n. d.) *Georgian Brickwork*, Georgian Group Guide No. 2, London: Georgian Group.

Georgian Group (n. d.) *Render, Stucco and Plaster*, Georgian Group Guide No. 5, London: Georgian Group.

Georgian Group (n. d.) *Stonework*, Georgian Group Guide No. 12, London: Georgian Group.

Harris, R. (1979) *Discovering Timber-Framed Buildings*, 2nd edn, No. 242 in Discovering series, Princes Risborough: Shire Publications Ltd.

Hill, P. R. and David, J. C. E. (1995), *Practical Stone Masonry*, London: Donhead Publishing.

Historic Scotland (1995) *Preparation and Use of Lime Mortars*, Technical Advice Note 1, Edinburgh: Historic Scotland.

Induni, B. and Induni, L. (n. d.) *Using Lime*, Lydeard St Lawrence: Induni.

Ireson, A. (1987) *Masonry Conservation and Restoration*, Rhosgoch: Attic Books.

Johnston, J. S. (1992) 'Bonding Timbers in Old Brickwork', *Structural Survey*, **10(4)**, 355–62.

Ley, T. (1995) 'Traditional Crafts Updated', *Structural Survey*, **13(4)**, 4–12.

Locke, P. (1986) *The Surface Treatment of Timber-Framed Houses*, SPAB Information Sheet 3, London: SPAB.

Lynch, G. (1990) *Gauged Brickwork: A Technical Handbook*, London: Gower.

Lynch, G. (1993/94) 'Historical Brickwork: Parts I and II', *Structural Survey*, **11(4)** and **12(1)**, 388–95 and 17–20.

Lynch, G. (1994) *Brickwork: History, Technology and Practice – Volumes 1 and 2*, London: Donhead Publishing.

Macgregor, J. E. M. (1985) *Outward Leaning Walls*, SPAB Technical Pamphlet 1, London: SPAB.

Mason, H. J. (1978) *Flint: The Versatile Stone*, Ely: Providence Press.

Nash, W. G. (1986) *Brickwork Repair and Restoration*, Eastbourne: Attic Books.

Oates, D. W. (1984) *Epoxy Resins in the Repair of Timber Structures*, CIOB Technical Information Service No. 43, Ascot: CIOB.

Parsons, D. (ed.) (1990) *Stone: Quarrying and Building in England AD 43–1525*, London: Phillimore.

Pearson, G. T. (1992) *Conservation of Clay and Chalk Buildings*, London: Donhead Publishing.

Pickering, J. (1992). 'Assessing Ancient Mortars', *Context*, **34**, 23–4.

Reid, K. (1989) *Panel Infilling to Timber-Framed Buildings*, SPAB Technical Pamphlet 11, London: SPAB.

Schofield, J. (1995) *Lime in Building: A Practical Guide*, 2nd edn, Crediton: Black Dog Press.

Schofield, J. (1995) 'An Introduction to Lime', *Structural Survey*, **13(2)**, 4–5.

Sowden, A. M. (1990) *The Maintenance of Brick and Stone Masonry Structures*, London: E. & F. N. Spon.

Stagg, W. D. and Masters, R. (1983) *Decorative Plasterwork: Its Repair and Restoration*, Eastbourne: Orion Books.

Stratton, M. J. (1993) *The Terracotta Revival*, London: Victor Gollancz Ltd.

Swallow, P. G. (1994) 'Our Architectural Ceramic Heritage', *Structural Survey*, **12(2)**, 20–3.

Swallow, P. G. and Carrington, D. (1995) 'Lime and Lime Mortars – Part One,' *Journal of Architectural Conservation*, **1(3)**, 7–25.

Swindells, D. J. (1987) *Restoring Timber-Framed Houses*, Newton Abbot: David and Charles.

Swindells, D. J. and Hutchings, M. (1993) *A Checklist for the Structural Survey of Period Timber Framed Buildings*, RICS Building Conservation Group, London: Surveyors Holdings Ltd.

Teutonico, J. M., McCaig, I., Burns, C. and Ashurst, J. (1994) *The Smeaton Project: Factors Affecting the Properties of Lime-based Mortars for Use in the Repair and Conservation of Historic Buildings (Research Project AC1: Phase 1 Report)*, London: English Heritage.

Townsend, A. (1989) *Rough-Cast for Historic Buildings*, SPAB Information Sheet 11, London: SPAB.

Urquart, D. C. M., Young, M. E., Wakefield, R. D., Tonge, K. and Nicholas, K. (1996) 'A Field Investigation of Algal Growths and Biocide Efficacy on Sandstone Buildings and Monuments', *Journal of Architectural Conservation*, **2(1)**, 55–73.

Webster, R. G. M. (ed.) (1992) *Stone Cleaning and the Nature, Soiling and Decay Mechanisms of Stone*, London: Donhead Publishing.

Williams, G. B. A. (1991) *Pointing Stone and Brick Walling*, SPAB Technical Pamphlet 5, London: SPAB.

Williams-Ellis, C. (1919) *Cottage Building in Cob, Pisé, Chalk and Clay: A Renaissance*, London: Country Life.

Wingate, M. (n. d.) *An Introduction to Building Limes*, SPAB Information Sheet 9, London: SPAB.

Wright, J. A. (1949) 'Repair and Preservation of Masonry', *RIBA Journal*, January, 121–5.

Yeomans D. and Cleminson, A. (1991) '18C Timber Construction: 4 – Walls and Partitions', *Architects' Journal*, **194(6)**, 7 August, 43–6.

## Chapter Ten: Building element III: Ceilings, partitions and floors

Bowley, B. (1994) 'Historic Ceilings', *Structural Survey*, **12(2)**, 24–6.

English Heritage (1994) *Office Floor Loading in Historic Buildings*, London: English Heritage.

Georgian Group (n. d.) *Floors*, Georgian Group Guide No. 11, London: Georgian Group.

Fowler, D. (1992) *Church Floors and Floor Coverings*, London: Church House Publishing.

Hayward, C. H. (1925) *English Rooms and their Decoration at a Glance – Volume I: 1066–1620*, London: Architectural Press.

Hayward, C. H. (1925) *English Rooms and their Decoration at a Glance – Volume II: 1620–1800*, London: Architectural Press.

Hughes, P. (1988) *Patching Old Floorboards*, SPAB Information Sheet 10, London: SPAB.

Hume, I. (1992) 'Floor Loadings and Historic Buildings', *English Heritage Conservation Bulletin*, **18**, October 1992, 1–2.

Macgregor, J. E. M. (1985) *Strengthening Timber Floors*, SPAB Technical Pamphlet 2, London: SPAB.

Schofield, J. (1991) 'Early Ornamental Plasterwork: Part 1', *Structural Survey*, **10(3)**, 232–6.

Schofield, J. (1992) 'Early Ornamental Plasterwork: Part 2', *Structural Survey*, **10(4)**, 320–5.

Stagg, W. D. and Masters, R. (1983) *Decorative Plasterwork: Its Repair and Restoration*, Eastbourne: Orion Books.

Stainton, S. (1980) 'The Care of Floors and Floor Coverings.' In: Bromelle, N. S., Thomson, G. and Smith, P. (eds), *Conservation Within Historic Buildings*, London: International Institute for Conservation of Historic and Artistic Works.

Yeomans D. (1991) '18C Timber Construction: 2 – Floor Structures, *Architects' Journal*, **194(3)**, 17 July, 46–51.

Yeomans D. and Cleminson, A. (1991) '18C Timber Construction: 4 – Walls and Partitions', *Architects' Journal*, **194(6)**, 7 August, 43–6.


# Chapter Eleven: Building element IV: Doors, windows and stairs

Ashurst, J. and Ashurst, N. (1988) *Practical Building Conservation: Volume 5 – Wood, Glass and Resins*, English Heritage Technical Handbook, Aldershot: Gower Technical Press.

Bacher, E. (1980) 'The Decay of Mediaeval Stained Glass: Climatic and Environmental Influences.' In: Bromelle, N. S., Thomson, G. and Smith, P. (eds), *Conservation Within Historic Buildings*, London: International Institute for Conservation of Historic and Artistic Works.

Crewe, S. (1987) *Stained Glass in England c. 1180–c. 1540*, London: HMSO.

Fisher, A. (1995) 'Period Window Glass: The Glazier's Role', *Context*. **48**, 9–11.

Georgian Group (n. d.) *Windows*, Georgian Group Guide No. 1, London: Georgian Group.

Georgian Group (n. d.) *Georgian Doors*, Georgian Group Guide No. 3, London: Georgian Group.

Gray, A. S. and Sambrook, J. (1990) *Fanlights*, London: A. & C. Black.

Hayward, C. H. (1925) *English Rooms and their Decoration at a Glance – Volume I: 1066–1620*, London: Architectural Press.

Hayward, C. H. (1925) *English Rooms and their Decoration at a Glance – Volume II: 1620–1800*, London: Architectural Press.

Historic Scotland (1994) *Performance Standards for Timber Sash and Case Windows*, Technical Advice Note 3, Edinburgh: Historic Scotland.

Hume, I. (n. d.) *Cantilever or Hanging Stone Stairs*, Internal English Heritage document.

Kerr, J. (1991) *The Repair and Maintenance of Glass in Churches*, London: Church House Publishing.

Rickards, L. C. and Rush, S. J. (1995) 'Period Window Glass: The Colouring of Glass', *Context*, **48**, 13–15.

Munn, H. (1983) *Joinery for Repair and Restoration Contracts*, Eastbourne: Orion Books.

Salmond, C. (1995) 'Period Window Glass: A Brief History of Glass', *Context*, **48**, 6–8.

Townsend, A. and Clarke, M. (1993) *The Repair of Wood Windows*, SPAB Technical Pamphlet 13, London: SPAB.

Victorian Society (1992) *Doors*, Victorian Society Guide No. 1, London: Victorian Society.

Yeomans D. (1991) '18C Timber Construction: 6 – Stair Building', *Architects' Journal*, **194(8/9)**, 21 and 28 August, 43–7.

## Chapter Twelve: Building element V: Finishes, fixtures and fittings

Alcock, N. W. and Hall, L. (1994) *Fixtures and Fittings in Dated Houses 1567–1763*, Practical Handbook in Archaeology No. 11, York: Council for Archaeology.

Allsop, B. (1952) *Decoration and Furniture: The English Tradition*, London: Sir Isaac Pitman and Sons Ltd.

Ashurst, J. (1983) *Mortars, Plasters and Renders in Conservation*, London: Ecclesiastical Architects' and Surveyors' Association.

Ashurst, J. and Ashurst, N. (1988) *Practical Building Conservation: Volume 3 – Mortars, Plasters and Renders*, English Heritage Technical Handbook, Aldershot: Gower Technical Press.

Ashurst, J. and Ashurst, N. (1988) *Practical Building Conservation: Volume 5 – Wood, Glass and Resins*, English Heritage Technical Handbook, Aldershot: Gower Technical Press.

Beard, G. (1990) *The National Trust Book of the English House Interior*, London: Penguin Group.

Bristow, I. (1986) *Redecorating Your Church*, London: Church House Publishing.

Brun, R. (1989) Church Security: A Simple Guide, London: Church House Publishing.

Burman, P. (ed.) (1994) *Treasures on Earth: A Good Housekeeping Guide to Churches and their Contents*, London: Donhead Publishing.

Burnham-Stähli, E. (1980) 'Textile Problems in Historic Houses and Buildings.' In: Bromelle, N. S., Thomson, G. and Smith, P. (eds.), *Conservation Within Historic Buildings*, London: International Institute for Conservation of Historic and Artistic Works.

Butcher, R. (1991) 'Varnish', *Structural Survey*, **10(2)**, 137–43.

Butcher, R. (1993) 'A Case for Traditional and Natural Paints and Coatings', *SPAB News*, **14(2)**, 14–17.

Charles, F. W. B. (1991) 'Vernacular Colour', *Transactions of the Association for Studies in the Conservation of Historic Buildings*, **16**, 63–4.

Drury, P. (1991) '18C Timber Construction: 5 – Joinery', *Architects' Journal*, **194(7)**, 14 August, 36–41.

Georgian Group (n. d.) *Paint Colour*, Georgian Group Guide No. 4, London: Georgian Group.

Georgian Group (n. d.) *Render, Stucco and Plaster*, Georgian Group Guide No. 5, London: Georgian Group.

Georgian Group (n. d.) *Wallpaper*, Georgian Group Guide No. 6, London: Georgian Group.

Georgian Group (n. d.) *Mouldings*, Georgian Group Guide No. 7, London: Georgian Group.

Georgian Group (n. d.) *Lighting*, Georgian Group Guide No. 13, London: Georgian Group.

Georgian Group (n. d.) *Curtains and Blinds*, Georgian Group Guide No. 14, London: Georgian Group.

Hamm, J. and Hamm, P. D. (1980) 'Historic Wallpaper in the Historic Structure: Factors Influencing Degradation and Stability.' In: Bromelle, N. S., Thomson, G. and Smith, P. (eds), *Conservation Within Historic Buildings*, London: International Institute for Conservation of Historic and Artistic Works.

Hayward, C. H. (1982) *English Period Furniture*, London: Van Nostrand Reinhold Company.

Historic Scotland (1994) *The Conservation of Plasterwork*, Technical Advice Note 2, Edinburgh: Historic Scotland.

Hoskins, L. (ed.) (1994) *The Papered Wall: The History, Patterns and Techniques of Wallpaper*, London: Thomas and Hudson.

Kerr, J. (1993) 'Fixtures and Fittings', *English Heritage Conservation Bulletin*, **21**, November 1993, 6–8.

Landi, S. and Marko, K. (1980) 'The Maintenance In Situ of Architecturally Related Textiles.' In: Bromelle, N. S., Thomson, G. and Smith, P. (eds), *Conservation Within Historic Buildings*, London: International Institute for Conservation of Historic and Artistic Works.

Munn, H. (1983) *Joinery for Repair and Restoration Contracts*, Eastbourne: Orion Books.

National Association of Decorative and Fine Arts Associations (1993) *Inside Churches: A Guide to Church Furnishings*, London: Capability Publishing/NADFAS.

Rouse, E. C. (1980) *Discovering Wall Paintings*, 3rd edn, No. 22 in Discovering series.,Princes Risborough: Shire Publications Ltd.

Sandwich, H. and Stainton, S. (1991) *The National Trust Manual of Housekeeping*, 2nd edn, London: Penguin Books Ltd.

Schofield, J. (1985) *Basic Limewash*, SPAB Information Sheet 1, London: SPAB.

Stagg, W. D. and Masters, R. (1983) *Decorative Plasterwork: Its Repair and Restoration*, Eastbourne: Orion Books.

Simpson and Brown, Architects (1994) *Conservation of Plasterwork: A Guide to the Principles of Conserving and Repairing Historic Plasterwork*, Edinburgh: Crambeth Allen.

Taverne, E. and Wagenaar, C. (1992) *The Colour of the City*, Netherlands: V+K Publishing.

Victorian Society (1992) *Decorative Tiles*, Victorian Society Guide No. 2, London: Victorian Society.

Victorian Society (1993) *Coming Unstuck: The Removal of Fixtures from Listed Buildings*, London: Victorian Society.

Victorian Society (1993) *Interior Mouldings*, Victorian Society Guide No. 4, London: Victorian Society.

Victorian Society (1993) *Wallcoverings*, Victorian Society Guide No. 5, London: Victorian Society.

Wright, A. (1989) *Removing Paint from Old Buildings*, 2nd edn, SPAB Information Sheet 5, London: SPAB.

## Chapter Thirteen: Building element VI: Services

Bordass, W. T. (1984) *Heating Your Church*, London: Church House Publishing.

Council for the Care of Churches (n. d.) *The Protection of Churches against Lightning*, London: CCC.

Council for the Care of Churches (1981) *Insurance, Security, Theft: It Won't Happen to Us*, London: CCC.

Council for the Care of Churches (1988) *Lighting and Wiring of Churches*, 4th edn, London: Church House Publishing.

Council for the Care of Churches (1989) *Security: A Simple Guide*, London: CCC.

Fire Protection Association (1995) *Heritage Under Fire*, 2nd edn, London: Fire Protection Association.

Georgian Group (n. d.) *Fireplaces*, Georgian Group Guide No. 9, London: Georgian Group.

Georgian Group (n. d.) *Lighting*, Georgian Group Guide No. 13, London: Georgian Group.

Griffiths, R. (1992) 'Early Heating and Ventilating Systems 1790–1850', *Transactions of the Association for Studies in the Conservation of Historic Buildings*, **17**, 30–50.

Hall, F. (1995) *Building Services and Equipment – Volumes 1, 2 and 3*, London: Longman Scientific and Technical Publications.

Hunt, A. (1985) *Electrical Installations in Old Buildings*, SPAB Technical Pamphlet 9, London: SPAB.

Lampton, L. (1978) *Temples of Convenience*, London: Gordon Fraser.

Loss Prevention Council (1995) *Code of Practice for the Protection of Unoccupied Buildings*, Borehamwood: LPC.

Lingel, M. (1992) 'The Survey and Repair of Flues and Chimneys', *Structural Survey*, **11(2)**, 129–34.

Pickard, R. (1994) 'Fire Safety and Protection in Historic Buildings in England and Ireland – Parts I and II', *Structural Survey*, **12(2)** and **12(3)**, 27–31 and 8–10.

Rosier, C. (1994) 'Architectural Theft: Some New Initiatives', *Context*, **43**, 23–5.

Shacklock, V. and Copping, A. (1993/4) 'The Protection of Anglican Cathedrals from Damage by Fire: A Review Based on Insurance Data', *Structural Survey*, **12(5)**, 4–10.

Tucker, D. M. and Read, R. E. H. (1982) 'Assessing Fire Damaged Structures', *Structural Survey*, **1(1)**, 32–6.
Victorian Society (1993) *Fireplaces*, Victorian Society Guide No. 3, London: Victorian Society.
West, T. (1976) *The Fireplace in the Home*, Newton Abbot: David and Charles.
Weston, K. (1993) 'Fire Damage: When the Fire is Over', *Context*, **38**, 9–11.
Williams, G. B. A. (1985) *Chimneys in Old Buildings*, SPAB Technical Pamphlet 3, London: SPAB.
Wright, L. (1960) *Clean and Decent, the Fascinating History of the Bathroom and WC*, London: Routledge and Kegan Paul.
Wright, L. (1964) *Home Fires Burning, the History of Domestic Heating and Cooking*, London: Routledge and Kegan Paul.

## Chapter Fourteen: Site and environment

Ashurst, J. and Ashurst, N. (1988) *Practical Building Conservation: Volume 4 – Metals*, English Heritage Technical Handbook, Aldershot: Gower Technical Press.
Blake, L. W. and Adams, P. F. (1992) 'Domestic Radon: The Legal Implications for Surveyors', *Structural Survey*, **11(1)**, 15–24.
Building Research Establishment (1989) *Freestanding Masonry Boundary Walls: Stability and Movement*, Defect Action Sheet 129, Garston: BRE.
Building Research Establishment (1989) *Freestanding Masonry Boundary Walls: Materials and Construction*, Defect Action Sheet 130, Garston: BRE.
Building Research Establishment (1989) *Site Investigation for Low-Rise Building: the Walk-Over Survey*, BRE Digest 348, Garston: BRE.
Carver, M. (1987) *Underneath English Towns: Interpreting Urban Archaeology*, London: B. T. Batsford Ltd.
Catt, R. (1993) 'Trees and Historic Buildings: Part I', *Structural Survey*, **11(4)**, 366–74.
Catt, R. (1994) 'Trees and Historic Buildings: Part II', *Structural Survey*, **12(1)**, 11–16.
Catt, R. (1995) 'Small Urban Spaces', *Structural Survey*, **13(2)**, 21–5.
Catt, R. (1995) 'Railings', *Structural Survey*, **13(3)**, 21–5.
Cutler, D. F. and Richardson, J. B. K. (1989) *Tree Roots and Buildings*, Harlow: Longman Scientific and Technical.
Dutton, R. (1937) *The English Garden*, London: B. T. Batsford Ltd.
Georgian Group (n. d.) *Ironwork*, Georgian Group Guide No. 8, London: Georgian Group.
Green, N. (1994) 'Protecting the Street Scene: Traditional Paving', *Context*, **41**, 7–8.
Goulty, S. M. (1992) *Heritage Gardens: Care, Conservation and Management*, London: Routledge.
Hume, I. (1995) 'The Effects of Road Traffic Vibration on Historic Buildings', *Context*, **47**, 28.
Hutton, T. C. and Dobson, J. (1992) 'The Control of Feral Pigeons: An Independent Approach', *Structural Survey*, **11(2)**, 159–67.
Jacques, D. (1991) 'Garden Archaeology and Restoration', *Transactions of the Association for Studies in the Conservation of Historic Buildings*, **16**, 13–23.
Jacques, D. (1995) 'The Treatment of Historic Parks and Gardens,' *Journal of Architectural Conservation*, **1(2)**, 21–35.
Rackham, O. (1986) *The History of the Countryside*, London: J. M. Dent and Sons Ltd.
Smith, J. (1994) 'Stealing a Look Round Gardens', *Country Life*, CLXXXVIII(5), 3 February, 28–31.
Smith, J. (1994) 'Alarm But No Despondency', *Country Life*, CLXXXVIII(7), 17 February, 49–51.
Tait, J., Lane, A. and Carr, S. (1988) *Practical Conservation: Site Assessment and Management Planning*, London: Open University / Nature Conservancy Council.
Traditional Homes (n. d.) *Ironwork Gates and Railings*, Traditional Homes Technical Information Leaflet No. 2, London: Traditional Homes.
Victorian Society (1994) *Cast Iron*, Victorian Society Guide No. 6, London: Victorian Society.

## Chapter Fifteen: Industrial monuments and sites

Alderton, D. (n. d.) *Industrial Archaeology In and Around Norfolk*, Telford: Association for Industrial Archaeology/Norfolk Industrial Archaeology Society.

Association for Industrial Archaeology (1991) *Industrial Archaeology: Working for the Future*, Telford: Association for Industrial Archaeology.

Bodey, H. and Hallas, M. (1978) *Elementary Surveying for Industrial Archaeologists*, Princes Risborough: Shire Publications Ltd.

Cossons, N. (1993) *The BP Book of Industrial Archaeology*, 3rd edn, Newton Abbot: David and Charles.

English Heritage (1995) *Industrial Archaeology: A Policy Statement*, London: English Heritage.

Major, J. K. (1975) *Fieldwork in Industrial Archaeology*, London: B. T. Batsford.

Palmer, M. and Neaverson, P. (1994) *Industry in the Landscape 1700–1900*, London: Routledge.

Palmer, M. and Neaverson, P. (1992) *Industrial Landscapes of the East Midlands*, Chichester: Phillimore & Co. Ltd.

Seago, R. M. (1992) *Appraisal of Timber and Steel Stocks*, Unpublished report prepared for Norfolk Windmills Trust (Norfolk County Council), November 1992.

## Chapter Sixteen: Standing ruins

Baines, F. (1923) 'Preservation of Ancient Monuments and Historic Buildings', *RIBA Journal*, **XXXI(4)**, 22 December, 104–6.

Baines, F. (1924) 'Preservation of Ancient Monuments and Historic Buildings-Part II', *RIBA Journal*, **XXXI(6)**, 26 January, 165–74.

Chitty, J. (1987) 'A Prospect of Ruins', *Transactions of the Association for Studies in the Conservation of Historic Buildings*, **12**, 43–60.

Hume, I. (n. d.) *Fabric Consolidation of Ancient Monuments*, Internal English Heritage document.

Lancaster, O. (1976) 'What should we Preserve?' In: Fawcett, J. (ed.), *The Future of the Past: Attitudes to Conservation, 1147–1974*, 65–73, London: Thames and Hudson.

Thompson, M. W. (1981) *Ruins: Their Preservation and Display*, London: British Museum Publications Ltd.

Wimble, A. and Thompson, J. (1993) 'Natural Wall Cappings', *English Heritage Scientific and Technical Review*, Supplement to *Conservation Bulletin 20*, **2**, July 1993, 11–12.

## Chapter Seventeen: A look to the future

Douglas, J. (1993/4) 'Developments in Appraising the Total Performance of Buildings', *Structural Survey*, **12(6)**, 10–15.

Hutton, T. and Lloyd, H. (1993) 'Mothballing Buildings: Proactive Maintenance and Conservation on a Reduced Budget', *Structural Survey*, **11(4)**, 335–42.

Kendler, B. S. (1994) 'Environmental Lead Contamination: A Metaphor for Destructive Industrial Practices; Lead Abatement: A Model for Ineffective Societal Responses', *Structural Survey*, **12(3)**, 13–23.

Mika, S. L. J. (1991) 'Improving Surveying Skills with Computer-Aided Learning Tools – Part 2', *Structural Survey*, **10(2)**, 150–7.

Osborn, M. J. (1994) 'Lead in Buildings and Surveyors' Responsibilities', *Structural Survey*, **12(2)**, 15–17.

Rooley, R. (1995) 'Sick Building Syndrome – the Real Facts: What is Known, What can be Done', *Structural Survey*, **13(3)**, 5–8.

Royal Institution of Chartered Surveyors (1993) *Energy Appraisal of Existing Buildings: A Handbook for Surveyors*, London: Surveyors Holdings Ltd.

Weaver, M. (1995) 'Forensic Conservation and other Developments on the Conservation of Heritage Resources and the Built Environment', *Journal of Architectural Conservation*, **1(3)**, 26–41.

# Index